George Doud Freeman

Midnight and Noonday

Or, The incidental History of southern Kansas and the Indian Territory

George Doud Freeman

Midnight and Noonday
Or, The Incidental History of southern Kansas and the Indian Territory

ISBN/EAN: 9783337142254

Printed in Europe, USA, Canada, Australia, Japan

Cover: Foto ©ninafisch / pixelio.de

More available books at **www.hansebooks.com**

MIDNIGHT AND NOONDAY

OR

THE INCIDENTAL HISTORY OF SOUTHERN KANSAS AND THE INDIAN TERRITORY,

GIVING TWENTY YEARS EXPERIENCE ON THE FRONTIER; ALSO
THE MURDER OF PAT. HENNESEY, AND THE HANGING
OF TOM. SMITH, AT RYLAND'S FORD, AND
FACTS CONCERNING THE

TALBOT RAID ON CALDWELL.

ALSO THE

DEATH DEALING CAREER OF McCARTY

AND

INCIDENTS HAPPENING IN AND AROUND CALDWELL, KANSAS,
FROM 1871 UNTIL 1890.

BY
G. D. FREEMAN, CALDWELL, KANSAS,
1892.

ENTERED ACCORDING TO AN ACT OF CONGRESS, IN THE OFFICE OF
THE LIBRARIAN AT WASHINGTON, BY G. D. FREEMAN, 1890.

THE AUTHOR'S PREFACE.

FROM time immemorial it has been the custom of the writers of books to give to the reading public the reasons for so doing. In accordance with this old time custom I will say to the reader that the notoriety obtained by Caldwell, "Queen of the Border," not only at home, but far away in Eastern States, is such that the public, seeing in newspapers deeds of daring and bloodshed, are led to wonder if such things are merely fiction and "nothing more."

The inquisitive mind will naturally want to learn the particulars, thinking thereby to discover the true from the false, or the straight veracity from the fictitious. Many of the events herein chronicled have been done so for the first time, while several have been imperfectly published in the newspapers of the land. It has been my utmost endeavor in this book to ascertain the real facts and particulars of events before publishing the same. Realizing the fact that "truth is stranger than fiction," and that the historical student is after only that kind of history, the title of my book, "Midnight and Noonday," is in itself suggestive of a conclusion. There is presumed to be no darker time than midnight or no brighter time than noonday. The early history of all countries seems to be fraught with peril, daring and bloodshed. And especially is this true of border towns. The desperado is social in his nature, courts danger and strives to conquer. The town affords him an opportunity to gratify all of his attributes; the saloon in which to be social, the drunken brawl in which he finds danger, and the civil law and her officers to conquer.

I give the reader deeds of crime and dark deeds of horror as "Midnight," and the beautiful country of the plains and the grand "Queen of the Border," as they are seen to-day, as "Noonday."

    Respectfully,

      G. D. FREEMAN, Caldwell, Kan.

Index to Chapters.

CHAPTER I.
Trip to Caldwell, · · · · · · 9

CHAPTER II.
View of Caldwell, · · · · · 21

CHAPTER III.
Shooting of Fred Crats, · · · · - 28

CHAPTER IV.
Adventure with a Mountain Lion, · · · 39

CHAPTER V.
The Killing of George Peas, · · · · 43

CHAPTER VI.
Organization of the County, · · · · 51

CHAPTER VII.
The Killing of Wm. Manning, · · · - 56

CHAPTER VIII.
Buffalo Hunting, · · · · · · 63

CHAPTER IX.
The Lost Men on their way Home, · · · - 76

CHAPTER X.
Murder of Dave Fielder, · · · · 88

CHAPTER XI.
The Killing of Doc Anderson, - - - - 95

CHAPTER XII.
The Shooting of McCarty, - - - - 103

CHAPTER XIII.
Busey Nicholson Arrested, - - - - - 118

CHAPTER XIV.
The Unseen Midnight Duel - - - - 125

CHAPTER XV.
Killing of Oliver's herder, - - - - - 131

CHAPTER XVI.
Stealing of My Team and Wagon, - - - 138

CHAPTER XVII.
In Pursuit of the Thieves, - - - - - 145

CHAPTER XVIII.
Arrest of Tom Smith, - - - - - 157

CHAPTER XIX.
Hanging of Tom Smith, - - - - - 171

CHAPTER XX.
The "Last Chance" Ranch, - - - - 184

CHAPTER XXI.
The Grass Hopper Raid, - - - - - 194

CHAPTER XXII.
Fight with Indians, - - - - - 202
Indian Raid on Kiowa, - - - - 204

CHAPTER XXIII.
In Pursuit of the Indians, - - - - - 210

CHAPTER XXIV.
A Laughable Episode, - - - - - 218

CHAPTER XXV.
Indians on the War Path, - - - - - 226

CHAPTER XXVI.
Horse Stealing, - - - - - - 238

CHAPTER XXVII.
Lynch Law, - - - - - - - 253

CHAPTER XXVIII.
Lynching of Oliver, - - - - - 260

CHAPTER XXIX.
First Election at Caldwell, - - - - - 265

CHAPTER XXX.
Cowboys on the Rampage, - - - - 275

CHAPTER XXXI.
Killing of George Flat, - - - - - 284

CHAPTER XXXII.
Frank Hunt Slain, - - - - - - 294

CHAPTER XXXIII.
Murder of George Brown, - - - - - 299

CHAPTER XXXIV.
New Marshals Appointed, - - - - 304

CHAPTER XXXV.
Murder of Bank Officers, ... 312

CHAPTER XXXVI.
Hanging the Robbers, ... 320

CHAPTER XXXVII.
Arrest of a Thief, ... 325

CHAPTER XXXVIII.
Killing an Indian, ... 330

CHAPTER XXXIX.
A Court Room Scene, ... 338

CHAPTER XL.
Escape of a Horse Thief, ... 351

CHAPTER XLI.
Citizens Battle with Talbot's Desperadoes, . . 361

CHAPTER XLII.
Pursuing Talbot's Party, ... 373

CHAPTER XLIII.
Hanging of Frank Noyes, ... 381

CHAPTER XLIV.
Murder of Bob Sharp, ... 386

CHAPTER XLV.
Conclusion 393

CHAPTER I.

Trip to Caldwell—Geographical Description of the Country—Attempted Horse Race on the Ninnescah—Our Fellow Travelers—A Race with a Horse Thief—Arrival at Caldwell.

In the early part of the spring of 1871, I conceived the idea of profiting by the advice of a wise statesman, "Go West young man and grow up with the Country." Having lived in a civilized portion of Kansas for a number of years, I considered myself able and competent to battle with the roughs and privations of an early pioneer settler. But little did I dream of the insurmountable hardships of a frontier settlement. Neither did I in my most wandering imagination, conceive to what extent ruffianism, theft, murder and crimes of various sorts are carried when beyond the pale of civil law.

In this book, I shall attempt to narrate truthfully, incidents as they occured under my own observation or near at hand, without being ornamented by fiction or embellished by romance. And as I necessarily shall be compelled to refer to my personal experiences I hope the reader will not criticize me as an egotist.

In the late winter and early spring of the year above referred to, it was currently reported, that Sumner County was the one offering the greatest inducements of any frontier county to the immigrant seeking a home. This county is located on the South line of Kansas, bordering on the Indian Territory, and about the center of the state, East and West. Many towns were rapidly springing up in the county, each striving for a supremacy. Some were vying with each other as to which of them should be the county seat; while others were content to rely on local and transient trade for support, and look to natural advantages, fine climate and future greatness, etc. Among the latter class and the most noted of them was Caldwell, located on the southern border of the county, and about two and one-half miles from the Indian Territory and at a point where the great thoroughfare, known as the Chisholm Cattle Trail, enters the state. This trail was laid out and cattle driven over it first in 1868, by a Texas cattle man by the name of Chisholm, and hence the name. The State of Texas in its early history was a vast unfenced scope of pasture land. In time, cattle men, owners of ranches and large herds of cattle began to seek a market for their herds. Markets were far distant. The nearest shipping point by railroad for Western Texas cattle was Abiline, a town on the Kansas Pacific, about 100 miles north of the south line of Kansas. As the Texas cattle were originally from the old spanish stock, introduced into Old Mexico and Southern Texas by the

OR, DARK DEEDS UNRAVELED.

Spaniards, in a very early day. They are of lean and lank build and well able to travel thousands of miles to a shipping point or to a market if necessary. During the summer of 1868 the trail reaching from Central Texas to Abilene, Kansas, was started and quite a number of herds were driven over the trail to the shipping point that season. During the summer season of 1869, the number of cattle driven over the trail was increased by many thousands, and for several succeeding years, the drive showed a still greater increase.

I have thus given the reader a partial geographical description of the country and the location of Caldwell, that he may more fully understand the thrilling events which I am about to record in these pages, after receiving many flattering reports of the country around Caldwell, and of the probability of that town being the great metroplis of the new Southwest, I reasoned after this fashion : I, at that time, had a wife and three children; we all stood greatly in need of a home to call our own; Uncle Sam, at that time, had plenty of land around Caldwell, out of which to make homes for the homeless; I thought that the transient trade, afforded by the travel over the trail by Texas men with herds from Texas, could not fail to make a red hot town. Yes indeed a red hot town it did become; for many a time did the wild and wooly cow-boy "paint the town red."

On a bright, balmy and breezy morning on the twenty-second of May 1871, I concluded to go and visit Caldwell and vicinity, that I might see for myself if newspaper reports were fully verified by actual facts. So, I hitched my team to the wagon and in company with W. B. King, afterwards known as Buffalo King, to use western slang we "lit out" for the famous border town. After leaving Augusta, we traveled all day without incident worthy of mention, and at night arrived at Wichita and camped there for the night. The next morning, leaving Wichita at our backs, and looking to the right and to the left, in front as far as the eye could reach, there was presented to view a grand panorama of nothingness. Save an occasional herd of cattle, there was nothing to be seen that bore the slightest impress of civilization. Whether or not the grand march of American Civilization would ever reach, and beautify this immense expanse of apparently waste land, once known as "The Great American Desert," time alone could tell. For hundreds of years, the Indian and the Buffalo had held full dominion and had truthfully been "monarchs of all they surveyed." But now, the signs of the times, point to a change. The great struggle for the Union has long since passed away. The smoke of battle, where first it raised its curling head is now settled in slumber. Peace and good will now reigns supreme in Kansas, where was the first battle ground of the great struggle. The Star of Empire points Westward. Millions of American people are without homes of their own and it only remained to be seen whether or not this immense tract of prairie land could be so utilized, as to make profitable homes for the poverty stricken homeless.

After traveling till nearly night, we reached Cowskin Creek. This creek after winding itself like a serpent through the prairie for about fifty miles, enters the Arkansas River. On the bank of this stream, where the trail crossed and as we were traveling on the trail, where we also crossed the creek, there was a trader's ranch. Now, for the benefit of the eastern reader, I will say that this word *Ranch*, is borrowed from the Mexican word *Ranchero*, and has a double meaning, as used in the southwest. A trader's ranch is a house of some description in which is kept for sale, such articles as the traveler or drover usually needs. These ranches in those days were never considered as having a complete stock, unless they kept a barrel or two of the poorest kind of whiskey. The cattle drover himself is usually a man of temperate habits. But his employees or cow-boys as they are called, are many times addicted to the use of strong drink. The second use of the word *Ranch*, as used in the southwest, is in connection with the raising and keeping of live stock. The stock ranch is the general headquarters for the men who are in charge of the stock. Here they meet to take their meals and at night to take their rest. The herders are sometimes supplied by the owner of the herd, with a cheaply provised cabin, but more frequently they have to be content with a tent or a common dugout, as a place to call their home. As I digress so frequently from my description of my trip to Caldwell, I hope the reader will bear with me, if I should fail at any time to gracefully "ketch on" where I left off.

We passed the ranch that night, about a mile and went into camp. After supper was over, as the shades of night began to chase the shadows away, I began to feel the loneliness of the situation. My partner, sitting by the embers of the smouldering camp-fire, was soon fast asleep. And, by the way, my partner was a most noted sleeper. If the thunder roared and the lightning flashed, he was sure to be asleep. If he was set to making a fire and getting dinner, he would go to sleep before it was done. If he were placed on guard, to keep theives from stealing our horses, he was sure to go to sleep. Or if his meal was cooked, and coffee boiled and his tin cup filled for him, he was liable to go to sleep, and spill his coffee while the tin was being carried to his mouth. Yes, indeed he was a number one on the sleep. I sometimes used to think he would take a nap while riding a fast horse on a race course. Well, I guess I had not better go back on my partner in this way; I will just say the cause of his being so sleepy was said to be a disease called Somnia.

As I said, I began to feel lonesome. My partner asleep, I felt as much alone as if I had been a thousand miles from anybody. On different sides around me, I could hear the night herder's lullaby to his cattle. This however, only added to my far away off and lonesome feeling. For, every man we had seen that day, seemed to me as if he bore marked resemblance to the noted Claude Duval, or some other fictitious outlaw. I presume that most of the men we had seen that day were cattle drovers and cow-boys, and that they were not near as bad looking as they seemed to me. In that day it seemed to be a part of the cow-boys business to carry two heavy revolvers and sometimes a large knife, in his belt. I was what, in the West has been styled a "tenderfoot," and such moving arsenals did not exactly meet my notions of propriety. But I soon learned by future experience that a tenderfoot, in the West, was quite sure to have his feet hardened so that he would soon pass as an old frontiersman.

The night was spent with very little sleep for me. I was the owner of the team we were driving, and a very good one it was, too, and I thought if anybody's team would be worth stealing it would certainly be mine. These reflections, together with the appearance of the men seen the day before, led me to conclude that I had better keep an eye on my horses, lest they should be stolen. I slept at short intervals during the night and in the morning found my horses all right and my partner, as usual, asleep. After we had got up and had our breakfast we again started on our way to the city (town it was then) on the border. The cattle herds were growing thicker as we go southward. They got so thick on the trail that there was but little room for us to use as a highway. But as we met the herds we drove around and by them the best we could, but made very slow progress on our journey. In the forenoon we passed a stream called the Ninnescah. This stream after running about a hundred miles in a southeasterly course empties its waters into the Arkansas.

On the north bank of the Ninnescah was a trader's ranch with a few little shanties around it, giving a slight evidence of a town in embryo. It was plainly evident that the ranchman here did not fail to keep the one thing needful to the cow-boys' happiness—a little of the ardent. A couple of them undertook to run a horse-race, but neither of them could ride as business had been most too good for the ranchman on that day in that special line of goods.

After leaving the Ninnescah we again began traversing a gently rolling prairie quite similar to the one we had recently passed over, but a little more rolling. After going a short distance we stopped to rest and graze our horses and get some dinner. The great number of cattle that had been grazed along the trail for the past month made picking rather short for our horses, so we remained in camp until 2:30 o'clock when I hitched up my team, awoke my partner and we rolled on. At about 4 o'clock in the afternoon we arrived at a small stream called Slate Creek. This stream, like the others we had crossed, was ornamented by a trader's ranch. As the day was only partly gone we concluded to make a short drive on our road before camping for the night. After we had crossed the creek and while we were looking for wood to camp with, two men on horseback came riding across the creek. In conversation with them I learned that they, also, were on their way to Caldwell. They proposed to ride along with us till camping time and to camp with us, if we did not object. My partner by this time being engaged in taking a nap, I was expected to make the reply. First looking at one, then the other, and as one of them wore a palm-leaf hat, and neither of them either by clothes or appearance, showed any signs that they were either ruffians or thieves, after hesitating a moment, I said, "all right."

The names of these two men were A. M. Colson and J. A. Ryland. Some of the readers of these pages, I have no doubt, know them, as they both became old settlers near Caldwell. During this trip my greatest fears were that some one would steal my horses, and thus I would be left a long ways from home with a wagon to ride in but no team to pull it. And another and stronger reason for not wanting my team taken was, that not being sumptuously supplied with this world's goods I was not able to lose my horses.

We soon secured wood enough for the night's camping, and then with our new found fellow travelers we rolled out. After traveling five or six miles we reached the head-waters of Prairie Creek and camped for the night. It was one of those calm, still nights that make one think of an earthly heaven. The air seemed to come to the nostrils of the weary traveler heavy laden with purity; after supper, the moon in all her resplendent loveliness raised her head above the Eastern horizon; as she sailed forth in the heavens, she shed her radiant light over hill and dale, making it almost as light as day. Although the night was uncommonly bright, I thought it might be safer to bring my team up to the wagon under which I slept. The country furnished such a grand chance for stealing horses, I feared my team might tempt some thief more than he was able to bear. The prairies at that time furnished plenty of grass for stock, so that a thief with a stolen horse and a handful of "grub" could travel to the southwest for hundreds of miles without being seen by anyone. That horse-thieves were abroad in the land no one could doubt, judging by the numerous horses that had "strayed off" from their owners and could never be found.

That night we slept well, but before retiring, I cautioned our new friends not to go near any of our horses during the night, as I should sleep with my Winchester by my side, and, if I should see any one near the horses I might think it a thief and treat them as such. This caution however, was entirely unnecessary, as they, second only to my partner, were excellent sleepers, for the next morning when they awoke the sun was shining in their faces. Soon as we had cooked and eaten our morning meal we again hitched up and pursued our journey. After we had gone perhaps a mile or so there passed us on the trail a man riding a very fine horse. From his general appearance, the quality and speed of the horse he rode, we concluded that he probably was a horse thief and that the horse was stolen property. We noticed that as we drove faster he would also increase his speed, and to put the matter to still further test we selected two of the fastest horses in our outfit and Colson and I pursued him, leaving the remaining two boys to bring the wagon. We had not pursued the chase a very great distance before we were quite well satisfied that he had the fastest horse. He gained on us so rapidly that before we had followed him more than five or six miles he had left us entirely out of sight. Who he was or where he went we never knew, but probably he was a member of a gang of thieves and cut-throats that at that time infested the southwest. The horse was quite likely a race horse stolen from some border settlement.

At about 10 o'clock we crossed the Chikaskia River. On the north bank of this stream there was a ranch kept by Frank Barrington and Dr. Hahn. These were the first ranchmen whom we had seen on our trip that looked as if they had ever lived "back east." After a drive of about eight miles over as fine appearing country as nature ever brought into existence, we arrived at Caldwell about 1:30 o'clock on the 25th of May 1871.

CHAPTER II.

View of Caldwell—Talk with Thomas—Claim Takers—Claim Jumpers—Meeting with Reed—A Bit of Reed's Bitter Experience—Trading For His Claim—Arrival Home.

As it was afternoon and we had not yet had our dinner, we concluded to drive a short distance southeast of town, and camp on the banks of a creek known by the name of Fall Creek. This creek flows to the southeast and surrounds the town on two sides, its course being from the northwest to southeast. The town is located where the creek makes a bend in its course.

Here we found a good supply of wood to use as fuel. After we had eaten our dinner, we turned our horses loose to graze, and leaving my partner as watchman, also to keep the horses from straying far from camp, we started for the town.

We had not proceeded far, when I turned and looking in the direction of camp, saw my partner leaning against the wagon wheel enjoying a good sleep. We did not intend to be gone but a short time and thought the horses would not go very far from camp, so we decided to go on.

Upon arriving at the town, we found two log cabins used as store-rooms. The first building was erected by C. H. Stone, on March 15th, 1871, and used as a grocery store, with liquid groceries predominating.

Time passed on, when Cox & Epperson, inspired by the greed for gold, settled down by him and also sold wet and dry groceries. J. M. Thomas was under their employ as clerk in the establishment.

There was also a building about fourteen by sixteen feet in dimensions, with a roof in shape like a car roof. This building was used as a saloon, and in it was kept some of the cheapest grades of whiskey. The proprietor was a man by the name of John Dickie.

After looking around awhile, we fell in conversation with J. M. Thomas. He gave us considerable information in regard to the country, and in conclusion told us where in all probability, we might secure two good claims near the town.

We returned to camp, waked up our partner who had put in a couple of hours sleeping, hunted our horses, which we experienced no difficulty in finding, and started to look over the country, and to try and secure the claims spoken of by our new found friend.

To say we were pleased with the country would be putting it too mild. We were perfectly delighted with the beautiful and ever changing panorama, which excited our highest admiration. Looking to the North, South and East, we were enabled to scan the country as far as the eye could reach, presenting to us a picture of living verdure.

As we journeyed to the West, after leaving our home in Augusta, we began penetrating the Indian Country, leaving civilization behind us, we no longer enjoyed the sights of forests, for the only trees to be seen were scattered along the banks of the streams.

Upon examining the soil, we found it to be a deep black loam, resting on a lighter colored sub-soil, consisting of a loam, gravel and clay, both soil and sub-soil being so porous that surface water rapidly passes through them.

We came back to town and to our noon camp along near sundown. We had traveled quite a distance up Fall Creek and over to another stream about a mile away called Bluff Creek. It was not difficult to find plenty of excellent claims, but it seemed that all of them that were very desirable had been taken sometime previous to our arrival there. I learned afterwards that many times a half-dozen or more claims were taken by one individual under different names. The taking of a claim simply consisted of placing on said claim in the form of a log house foundation, four logs, and in sticking in the ground a board, upon which was the taker's name. It will readily be seen that the one who sailed under the most aliases, could take the most claims.

The few parties at that time up and down the creeks were single men, and generally lived in a dug-out and "batched it." By taking several claims each, they would be prepared to sell a claim to anyone who came into the country and wanted to secure a home for himself and family. I had come to the country in search of a home, and expected to get one at "Uncle Sam's" price under the exemption laws. Here I found, that for the sake of gain, roving plainsmen had taken and marked all of the choicest claims. Of course a person desiring a claim could have "jumped" one of those already taken, but the character of the ones holding them, would lead one to conclude that it might be a little dangerous. To shoot a man in those days was not considered a very grave offense unless the person doing it should be caught, and the chance to get away was so good, a "claim jumper" might be left dead to hold the claim, while the murderer had gone to (for him) a more healthful clime.

As I said, we arrived at camp where we had stopped for dinner, a little before sundown. Soon after our arrival, and after we had unhitched our team, we began to consider what we had best do. After thinking and talking over the claim matter for a short time, we noticed at about a hundred yards distant on the banks of the creek, was what seemed to be a clay bank or knoll. Soon we saw a man coming up the bank near where the knoll was and start in the direction of our camp; when he arrived, he said that *that* was his claim, and what we had thought to be a clay bank, was his dug out.

From him we learned that his name was Reed, and that he was the oldest settler in this vicinity, having located his claim in 1871. The many privations, he and his family had endured, words will ever fail to express. A few things however in reference to his life, here may be of interest to the reader.

Reed was a Scotchman by birth, and came to America when in his minority. His father rented and farmed land in Illinois for a good many years. Finally young Reed became of age and married a young lady in Illinois. He also engaged in his father's avocation, that of the farmer. After living in Illinois for several years he moved to Missouri; he remained there two years, when the tide of immigration began to flow into Kansas, he with his family—a wife and five children—fell in line in the Westward march.

He, like most immigrants into a new country, would like to be exactly suited with a claim before taking it.

He kept going until he reached the place where we found him. When leaving Missouri, he had a team to haul his effects, and also enough money, with what he could earn teaming, to keep him, until he could get a start on his farm. But how often it is, the brightest hopes are not realized, and grief and sorrow take their places. In this case it was fully verified. He arrived at his destination in the fall of 1871; soon after his arrival his horses took sick and died, thus leaving him without any means of support except his two hands and what little money he had. Labor was quite scarce, except freighting, and as he had no team he could not freight. He had not lived in his new home very long before his family were all sick with chills and fever; as cold weather came on they gradually recovered, all except his wife, who lingered for sometime and finally died. Now he drinks his griefs to the dregs. With five children, some of them small, his wife dead, and provisions fifty miles away, while he had but little money to buy with and no team to go after them! let us draw a curtain over the scene until we tell you that dire necessity drove him to the extremity of carrying his provisions fifty miles on his back to keep his family alive.

Well, Mr. Reed had become dissatisfied with the country, and wanted to sell his claim and leave. After some bartering, I bought his claim, agreeing to give him the horse I was driving and fifty dollars upon my return from a trip after my family. This piece of land afterward became very valuable, it being a part of the town, and the Rock Island and Santa Fe Depots were built upon it.

The next morning, my partner and I awoke early, got our breakfast, hitched up our team and started to Butler County after our families, leaving our friends Colson and Ryland, at Caldwell. We arrived safely at our homes and found all anxiously awaiting our return.

CHAPTER III.

The Return to Caldwell—Reed Backs Out of His Bargain—Takes a Claim—A Fright Caused by Indians—The Shooting of Fred Crats—Building the "Dug-Out"—A Shot at Gray Wolves.

On the 6th day of June we arrived in Caldwell and immediately drove to our claim. We were suprised to find that Reed had regretted his trade with me and had concluded to back out. He did not think he was receiving enough for it, therefore would not trade that way. He finally told me, however, that if I would give him another horse, one that I was driving, he would call it a trade. I told him I would not trade that way, as I, like himself, was getting sick of my bargain, for the place was not a desirable one on which to take my family, as the cattle trail run through the place upon which thousands of cattle were driven. Besides this objection I had another reason for not wanting it. My wife had been living in a good neighborhood with many friends with which to associate, and I realized this fact, that if I lived here she would, more or less, see a rougher class of people than she was accustomed to seeing, and it would naturally have a tendency to make her discontented with her surroundings. She was a very timid woman and of a nervous temperament and it would have been far wiser to have never brought her on the western frontier.

And now here I was with my family and with no place to call my home. I left my family at Reed's while King and myself went to see if we could find us a claim.

We had no trouble in getting each of us a good one. Mine was located one and a half miles West of town, King's claim joining mine on the North. King was not satisfied there, but continued to live there until fall, when he took another claim about six miles farther west. This time he got a choice piece of land on the Bluff Creek bottoms. He continued to live on his farm until a couple of years ago, when he sold it and went to Washington Territory, where he is still living.

When we had found our claims we returned to Reed's after our families, and moved to our new home. We camped under a large cottonwood tree, whose shade made it very pleasant during the day. Near by was a spring which afforded good drinking water; also plenty for cooking purposes.

My partner concluded to camp with us until we could build each of us a house, as the women would get very lonely in our absence from camp. We were very comfortably settled and enjoyed ourselves nicely.

The weather had been delightful during our trip from Augusta. The nights had been equally as beautiful as the days, and the moon was now full and shone so brightly, making it almost as light as day.

Nothing happened to mar our happiness and contentment until the next day about 10 o'clock, when J. M. Thomas, the man I have referred to before as the clerk of Cox & Epperson, came riding up to our camp at full speed, saying the Indians were making trouble in our locality and that they had probably killed a man by the name of Fred Crats. While he was telling us about it, C. H. Stone came up and said he did not think there was any danger of the Indians molesting us, as they were going up Bluff Creek. This creek was about two miles south of our camp.

Upon hearing this startling news my wife became badly frightened and it was some time before we could quiet her fears. I was well aware that when people were frightened they were liable to misrepresent circumstances and make things appear as bad as they possibly can.

I will tell the actual facts relating the shooting of Crats by the Indians, as he afterwards told it.

It seems Crats had a claim on Bluff Creek some five or six miles from Caldwell. At the time the shooting occurred he had been to town and was on his return home. He was riding on a fine, large mule and was about a mile and a half from town when he was overtaken by two Indians. The Indians were riding ponies and one was armed with a gun while the other had a bow and a quiver of arrows.

As they came up to him he saluted them with the usual way of saluting the Indian, by saying, "How." Their responding salutation consisted of low grunts. His fears were aroused by their manner of addressing him, as they commonly address a man with, "How, John."

As they rode up to his side one of them threw up his coat tail, as he supposed, to see if he was armed. In those days if a man had no gun with him he was almost sure to have on a belt containing a couple of revolvers and many times a knife.

Crats had neither a gun, revolver or knife, (excepting a small pocket knife) which they soon found out by raising his coat. Crats said it was the only time he had ever left home without taking his revolvers.

The Indians appeared very brave after they saw they had the advantage of him, and Crats knowing that fact became submissive at once. He was a German and a powerfully built man, and could have whipped them both in a fist-fight, but that was not their mode of fighting just then.

One of the Indians rode in front, took nold of the mule's bridle, while the other pretended to drive it. By their gestures and broken English they told Crats they wanted him to go on a buffalo hunt; which Crats knew meant death for him. He thought they wanted his mule, and to get it they would take him away from the settlement and kill him.

They traveled until they were within a hundred yards or more from a bend in the creek. Then, seeing a chance for life, he quickly jumped from his mule and started on a run for the brush and bluffs.

When he had got a short distance the one with the gun fired at him, but the bullet had nearly spent its force before reaching him. About this time the gun was a new weapon to the Indians, and consequently they were not very well versed in the manner of loading them; many times they would load too heavy and often they would load their guns only putting in powder and paper.

The bullet from the Indian's gun did not have force enough to kill him, for when it struck his back-bone it glanced off and did not enter his body.

The other Indian shot at him with his bow, this shot taking effect. The arrow struck him in the arm, glanced upward, tearing his arm in a frightful manner up to his shoulder.

When they saw he was not yet their game they let the mule loose and started and ran after him. He dodged them and succeeded in crossing the creek. They saw him after he had crossed and started to find a place they could cross with their ponies. Here the creek has bluffs on both sides and it is very difficult to cross only at the fords, which are sometimes many miles apart. Perhaps it would be well enough to say Bluff Creek derived its name from its banks, which are very high and bluffy.

The Indians went down the creek for the purpose of finding a crossing, thinking Crats would hide in the grass and they could easily find him. But instead of going south he again crossed the creek and hid himself in a pile of driftwood, which would merely conceal him from their view should they come that way.

The idea did not strike them that he would return to the north bank, so, after searching among the bluffs and looking through the tall grass without finding him, they rode on up the creek. They also failed to catch the mule again after turning it loose, when they were in pursuit of Crats.

Crats lay for several hours in the drift and was bleeding profusely, weakening him very much. He managed to reach Reed's dug-out where a physician was called to attend him.

His escapade nearly cost him his life, and as it was he was left considerably defective in a physical point of view. It is said Crats presented a claim to the government against the Osage Indian fund for five thousand dollars. Whether his claim was allowed or not I never learned. But I am quite sure his claim for damages was entirely too low, as he, in all probability, will be an invalid and a partial cripple for life; for, the bullet entering his back affected the spine causing a lameness of the back, and the arrow entering his arm making a cut which caused a partial paralysis.

When we had recovered from our Indian scare sufficiently to change the theme of conversation, I told Mr. Thomas we were about to commence building a dug-out to live in. He said he would get some help for us, and went back to town. Soon after several men came, bringing spades, shovels and axes with them. We were soon at work plowing, digging and shoveling dirt.

My dug-out was to be fourteen by twenty-eight feet in dimensions. To make it required three logs twenty-eight feet long; also poles enough to cover the top closely. First we plowed what we could, then took spades and shovels and began spading the earth out in the shape required. After digging, perhaps six or seven feet in the ground, we made a door at the opening, put on a ridge pole in the center, then laid on the

poles we had hauled for that purpose and covered it
with dirt, after first covering the poles with straw, dried
grass or hay.

The dirt is thrown on top until the dug-out resembles an ordinary mound of earth some four or five feet
in height.

We worked far into the night and about 9 o'clock
the finishing strokes were done and we began unloading
the wagons. Our household furniture was very limited.
When we spoke of the cupboard, in reality we meant a
cracker-box with a partition in the center of it, the box
being fastened against the wall. And often when we
spoke of a chair, in reality we would mean a box which
we used in the place of that article.

Our beds many times were made of poles and
corded with a rope, which we used in preference to
making slats of cottonwood poles.

The next in order would be something to eat, which
the women soon prepared. Our friends and co-laborers
ate supper with us and several remained over night at
our dug-out.

The men, or cow-boys, as they were called, worked
manfully. They were very energetic and a nice class
of young men. The reader must not picture the cowboy as a desperado, for many times they are kindhearted and sympathetic. I have known a number of

very fine, cultured young men, who hungered for notoriety, who satisfied this appetite by becoming cow-boys. The majority of the cow-boys are a drinking, carousing set of young men, and are rough when under the influence of liquor, but take them when they are sober and you will not find any one that will help you in time of trouble more than this class of young men.

The cow-boy endures many hardships while attending to his duty; rain or shine, hot or cold, he is always to be found at his post. The more severe the weather the more his services are needed; their life is indeed a hard one to live; quite often they use their saddle for a pillow, the saddle blanket for a coverlet and mother earth as their bed.

They are generally a healthy class of boys when they first begin to "herd," but, a continuation of sleeping on the ground, night herding in the rain or snow storm and the habit of frequently indulging in a social glass of whiskey, soon break them down in constitution and before they have lived to that age in which manhood is supposed to reach its prime, they find themselves to be old men and a wreck, physically speaking.

We were now comfortably fixed and settled down to housekeeping; my wife busied herself with her duties and household cares, while I set myself to work fixing up our new home. Sometimes I would take my gun and dogs, and go hunting. Game was very plentiful, and it was not difficult to go out a short distance from the dug-out and shoot either a plover, prairie chicken or jack rabbit.

Wolves too, abounded here; the few chickens which were brought from the East fared very hard; at night they were shut up in a close coop, to keep the wolves from getting them.

One beautiful moonlight night I heard my dog howling, and seemingly, coming in the direction of the dug-out, every yelp he gave I thought would be his last; I got my gun, a trusty Winchester rifle, and went to the door; I had no sooner opened it, when the dog leaped into the room and seemed to be very much frightened.

I looked out to see what had caused his terrrible fright, and saw four big, gray wolves, within thirty yards of the dug-out.

I shot at them but did not kill any. The next morning I was out in that direction and saw where I had shot my plow; it had been left there on the prairie, where we had been plowing.

We were well pleased, this far, with our late move. The women were lonesome, but they enjoyed themselves in roaming up and down the banks of the little stream, near our claims.

The weather continued to be delightful, the air pure

and fragrant, the climate entrancingly mild; the sky clear and blue, and we thought we had, indeed, found a paradise.

I began plowing and planting corn; I broke the prairie, then planted the corn on the sod; I also planted some late garden seeds, and in a short time we reaped a benefit from both, for the season proved to be a favorable one for us.

CHAPTER IV.

Adventure with a Mountain Lion—The Mountain Lion Seeks Refuge in the Dug-out Window—A Fight in which Both Dogs are Whipped—The Lion Makes J. M. Thomas Leave The Road—Finally Killed by O. G. Wells.

Soon after my arrival in Caldwell in 1871, and while I was living on my claim one and a half miles west of town, I had an adventure with a mountain lion.

One beautiful moonlight night, after we had retired for the night, I had about entered the land of dreams, when I was aroused from my slumbers by the barking of my dog; I hastily left my bed, without taking the necessary time to arrange my toilet, and I just got to the door in time to see an animal jump into the dug-out window with my dog in pursuit, not very far distant, barking furiously.

I concluded to take in the chase, and ran out the door, and up to the window and looked in to see where and what it was.

I saw what I supposed to be a dog, and thinking to start the chase again, I would kick it and thereby cause it to jump out of the window. In this I was mistaken, for, instead of retreating, it manifested a desire to hold the fort; so you may imagine who did the retreating.

By this time my wife appeared on the scene, and asked "what is it?" I made the reply, "we'll soon see what it is," and went out and untied a large dog, which I kept as a watch dog.

I knew the fighting qualities of that dog was hard to beat, as he was sure to be the champion in a dog fight, and I thought he would come out victorious now.

As soon as he knew he was loose, he started for the animal, and I suppose, he "smelt the battle afar," and knew it was better to run like a man than be whipped like a coward. For, notwithstanding my many words of encouragement, and with a promise to help him win the day, he stood as still as a monument.

I finally told my wife to keep the dogs with her and I would reconnoiter a little. I soon had my gun, and entered the dug-out for the purpose of shooting the animal.

In the dug-out I had a portion partitioned off in which I kept my horses at night.

To get in a suitable position for shooting, I had to pass between my horses; when I had arrived at a place in which I could use my gun to an advantage, the animal, like the dog, had "scented the battle afar," and I have no doubt, concluded the reception would be too warm for it.

As it leaped from the window, both dogs were soon

FIRST WHITE CHILD BORN IN CALDWELL.

upon the animal, I ran out to see the fight, thinking the dogs would surely kill it. I soon saw, to my surprise, that the dogs were getting the worst of the fight, as they would give an occasional yelp, which convinced me that they were being badly dealt with.

I could not shoot to advantage for fear of hitting one of the dogs, and I soon saw it was not a dog they were fighting, but a large mountain lion.

These lions are very ferocious when attacked by man. They resemble the African lion in most respects, only in size, the mountain lion being the smaller of the two. Had I known what it was, I certainly should have hesitated before kicking at it.

After fighting the dogs awhile, it started on the run; before I could get ready to shoot, it had bounded away in the darkness.

The next morning J. M. Thomas had an encounter with the lion, near my house. He had been to the ranch of Cox & Epperson and was on his return home. He said he was riding along peacefully, enjoying the morning air, when suddenly his horse shied, and on looking before him saw a mountain lion in the road.

He rode on, thinking every moment to see it bound away and hunt a place of refuge. But to his astonishment, he found it had no idea of leaving just then.

He concluded that "discretion is the better part of

valor" and pulled his horses rein to guide him safely by.

A short time after this happened, O. G. Wells shot and killed a mountain lion. Upon measuring it, it was found to be nine foot two inches long.

The lions are often seen near the cattle ranches, and many times show a disposition to fight, when they are attacked by man. They are frequently to be seen devouring a cow which they have killed and many are the calves which give up their lives to satisfy their appetites.

CHAPTER V.

A Brief History of Caldwell—The Killing of George Peas—The Friends of Peas Act as Watchers—Arrival of the Winfield Sheriff—O'Bannan Skips the Country.

After giving the reader a description of Caldwell as she appeared in her infancy, I will endeavor to give a history of facts and incidents that have actually occured within her borders.

Every name given in this book being real, not fictitious, and many of the people, whom I shall mention before this work is completed, are residents of Caldwell, or are earning their living by honest toil, living on their farms in this vicinity.

On March 1st, 1871, the town of Caldwell was located, and named in honor of United States Senator Caldwell, of Leavenworth, Kansas, by a company consisting of C. H. Stone, J. H. Dagner and G. A. Smith.

The great Chisholm trail entering the State, near this town, gave it the name of a "cattle town." Consequently it had in and about it a class of people who have caused much disorder and bloodshed.

From its location, it was always the favorite resort of the desperadoes and thieves, as it was only a short distance from the Indian Territory, which place afforded them a hiding place after they had indulged in some shooting affray or had been on a thieving expedition. It was also the home of the "cow-boy" upon entering the state, after a long, dusty twelve hundred mile ride. Need we wonder why, in its early day, it was a fast and dangerous town.

The "cow-boy" was not considered a resident, for his was only transient trade. Upon entering the state they would visit the supply stores, lay in a supply of coffee, flour, bacon, and gather in the entire stock of liquids.

As the tide of civilization crowded west, and men of integrity, ability, and of a determined character immigrated to the western towns and became enterprising citizens, the rougher element could not prevail, hence they too must immigrate west to the frontier towns. It has been said that on these conditions, the crowded cities of Emporia, Newton and Wichita gave up their most reckless citizens to make up a band of rustlers, horse thieves and bad characters to populate Caldwell.

It is said by many that Caldwell was started with a population of two, and both of them non-residents.

The railroad terminus was about one hundred and fifty miles distant; consequently all supplies had to be hauled on wagons. Emporia furnished the base of supplies for the groceries and saloon. Articles in the line of provisions were very limited. The grocers stock consisted of flour, bacon, salt, soda, coffee, tobacco and whiskey. Often the "cow-boy" would buy all his groceries; he would then buy another invoice very much like the first, excepting that it was not so large and of a poorer quality.

I will now chronicle the killing of George Peas, which occured on the second day of July, 1871. He was the first victim to fall at the hands of his adversary. In those days strength was not the criterion by which we read the character of the man, relative to his bravery. Strength only consisted in the man who stood the firmest behind the six-shooter, and the six-shooter cut quite a figure in the early part of the history of Caldwell.

This man Peas was a claim taker and was looked upon by the people as a man that would use "stray stock" to his own advantage, and for the good of his pocket-book.

He was a large, well built man, some six feet in height, and probably weighing two hundred pounds. He was a very quarrelsome man when under the influence of whiskey, always boasting of his physical strength. He was rarely engaged in a fight because his arrogant boasts would intimidate his comrades.

He was living on a claim five or six miles East of

Caldwell, near Bluff Creek, and on adjoining claims lived four or five friends of his. They were "batching" and spent the greater part of their time in town.

The man who killed him, O'Bannan by name, was a very different man in disposition and character. O'Bannan was a Canadian by birth, a man small of stature, but very different in character. He bore a favorable reputation, was courageous in movements of peril, was not hasty in disposition and controlled his temper at his bidding.

He, in company with George Mack and H. H. Davidson, was living in a "dug-out" west from Caldwell, about five miles. They were also keeping cattle on the same range together, and the three men "batched" together.

On the day the shooting occured, Peas with his friends were in Caldwell, having a fine time, so to speak. Peas was considerably under the influence of whiskey, and his friends thought he was liable to have trouble and took his revolver from him. O'Bannan happened to be in town the same day, and to all appearances was attending to his own business affairs.

Peas came up to O'Bannan and wanted to fight, O'Bannan knew Peas would be the best man in a fight, and not wanting to have anything to do with him, told him he did not care to fight and left Peas. He turned and went into the store, followed by Peas, who soon began to talk in an insulting manner and all the while trying to get O'Bannan to fight with him. O'Bannan finally told him to let him alone, and if he did not he would certainly wish he had, and went out of the store.

Soon he was followed by Peas, who by this time was determined to pick a quarrel; he walked up to O'Bannan as though he intended to take hold of him. At this O'Bannan pulled his revolver intending to shoot at him. The revolver was on the cap and ball style and would not go off. He then told Peas to let him alone, saying "my revolver failed to fire that time, but perhaps it won't next time."

O'Bannan borrowed a revolver from a friend of his; this one proved to be a good one, as the friends of Peas found out after he had been its target. As soon as Peas saw O'Bannan again, he became abusive as before. By this time, "forbearance had ceased to be a virtue" with O'Bannan, and he was determined he would not be imposed upon by Peas.

As Peas came to him he took his revolver from his belt and taking deliberate aim, seemingly as cool as though he was going to shoot a beef, pulled the trigger and Peas staggered backward and fell, saying as he did so, "God, boys' I'm shot."

O'Bannan seemed wholly unconcerned, but was

satisfied. His aim had been true and his bullet had accomplished its errand, There on the sidewalk in front of him lay Peas breathing his last breath. As soon as the report and the smoke of the revolver had died away, O'Bannan turned on his heel, half-way round, and facing the friends of Peas, said, "gentlemen, I have killed Peas, now if there is any one here that wants to take it up, they have the privilege of doing so, for I am in good shooting order."

The friends of Peas had nothing to say and O'Bannan got on his horse and left town.

It was then late in the afternoon and the friends of Peas took his body to an old vacant building, which I think had been used as a saloon. They intended to act as "watchers" over the dead body of their friend. They were still drinking freely of the vile stuff, known as whiskey.

After they had removed Peas' body, they took turns in drinking and watching. They would get on their horses, ride up and down the street yelling like demons and firing off their revolvers. Then they would return to the house, talk to their dead friend and beg of him to get up and take a drink. This barbarous treatment was kept up during the night, and when the sun rose above the horizon it looked upon a scene which would arouse the sympathy of any kind heart, and put a blush of shame upon the cheek of the drunkard.

O'Bannan went to King's camp, (which was located on my claim in front of my dug-out) after leaving town, and on his way shot and killed a steer belonging to Cox & Epperson. I heard of it and told them about it. O'Banann found out I had reported to Cox & Epperson concerning it, and threatened my life. I did not know but what he would come to my place and make trouble. But if he had any idea of carrying out his threat, he certainly thought it best not to try it, for when we got up next morning we found he had left King's camp.

In the meantime the officers at Winfield had been informed of the shooting affray at Caldwell, and Deputy Sheriff T. H. B. Ross, came over to arrest O'Bannan. O'Bannan had said no live man could arrest him, as he considered he had only defended himself. Ross remained in Caldwell several days thinking O'Bannan would come to town. O'Bannan's friends sent him word that the Deputy Sheriff was in town for him, and after remaining in his dug-out for a few days he left the country.

From Caldwell, he went to Abilene, Kansas, and I heard he said "while he believed he was justified in killing Peas, he did not care to stand trial."

Thus the chapter closes, chronicling the first murder committed in Caldwell.

CHAPTER VI.

Organization of the County—Officers Elected—Towns Contending for the County Seat—Governor Harvey Makes Appointments—Wellington Comes Out Victorious. Arrests made by the Officers—Prisoners cut their way out of the "Cooler"—The Bondsmen Pay the Bond.

Up to this time the county was yet unorganized. The people began to awaken to the fact that county officers were badly needed. For the past two years, the rougher element had full control of the county, but now the people were determined that lawlessness should not prevail at all hazards. The people had organized themselves into committees, by different names, the most conspicuous assuming the name of the Vigilants. The majority of the law-abiding citizens became members of this committee, and concluded to take the law into their hands, for murder, thefts and lawlessness of various kinds must be subdued either by civil law, or justice meted out at the end of a rope, which was tied to the limb of a cotton-wood tree.

The people were becoming aroused by the numerous outrages committed, and deemed it necessary to act immediately upon some measure to quell all disturbances, and have peace and good-will reign supreme.

This county was named in honor of Hon. Charles Sumner, of Massachusetts. Many of the Senator's admirers, opposed the proposition of giving the name of Sumner to this treeless and trackless portion of "The Great American Desert," contending it would be an insult to his greatness.

Sumner County is thirty-three miles wide, North and South, and thirty-six miles wide, East and West, the Indian Territory bordering it on the South its entire length. It contains 760,320 acres of land.

The county was formally organized by the governor's proclamation on February 7th, 1871, and the first county seat election, and election of permanent county officers, was held on September 26th, 1871. The county was divided into three commissioner's districts, and into four voting precincts. The election of the first precinct was held at Belle Plaine; the election of the second precinct was held at the house of Henry Brown, in Greene Township; the third precinct held their election at Wellington; the fourth voting precinct included the southwest quarter of the county; the election was held at Colson and Ryland's Ranch. This territory has since been divided, and now includes the following named townships: Morris, Chikaskia, Downs, Jackson, South Haven. Falls, Caldwell and Bluff.

The first county officers elected were the following

named individuals: County Commissioner, First District, David Richards; Second District, A. D. Rosencrans; Third District, Reuben Riggs; County Clerk, C. S. Broadbent; County Treasurer, R. Freeman; Probate Judge, G. M. Miller; Register of Deeds, J. Romine; Sheriff, J. J. Ferguson; Coroner, Charles D. Brande; County Attorney, George N. Godfrey; Clerk of the District Court, W. A. Thompson; Superintendent of Public Instruction, A. M. Colson; County Surveyor, W. A. Ramsey.

As this book relates largely to the southern part of the county, I will only name the officers elected to office in the Fourth Precinct: C. E. Sullivan, Trustee; M. H. Lester and George Mack, Justices of the Peace; Frank Barrington, Clerk; G. W. Peters, Treasurer; C. P. Epps and John J. Youell, Constables; T. S. Anderson and Noble Jewitt, Road Overseers.
The total number of votes polled in the county was 805.

During this time a great race was being made to determine where the county seat should be located. The towns contesting for the county seat were, Wellington, Sumner City, Meridian and Belle Plaine. Gov. Harvey issued a proclamation on February 7th, 1871, appointing Meridian as the temporary county seat; in accordance with the prayer of a petition from Meridian, also appointed W. J. Ughler, J. S. McMahon and J. J. Abell, Temporary County Commissioners.

As a matter of fact, Meridian was at this time, a purely imaginary town, as its site had not been so much as staked out or stepped off. It was not until July 17, 1871, that the town company was organized. No steps were taken toward providing for the seat of county government at Meridian, and when the commissioners met on June 15, 1871, on the open prairie near the supposed site of the town, they ordered the future business of the county to be transacted at Wellington. After much wrangling between towns, and several elections, Wellington became the permanent county seat.

It was now to be hoped that lawlessness would cease, and that our county would make rapid strides toward civilization, and assume the responsibility placed at her hand, with a determined corps of officers. Arrests were made by the officers; the offender tried, his fine being paid, he was set at liberty. Sometimes the party arrested could not pay his fine, then he was taken to Wellington and put in the "cooler." This was a light, frame building, and was not substantially built, and often the prisoner escaped by cutting his way out with his pocket knife, or used some implement to break the lock on the door.

Sometimes if the prisoner had committed a grave

offense, he was taken to Topeka for safe-keeping, And quite often, the prisoner was arrested, tried and found guilty of the charges set forth in the evidence, some friend or friends of his would give the necessary bond demanded by the court, and the criminal would watch his chances and "skip the country."

Everything would run along smoothly until the time for trial, when to the dismay of the bondsmen, they were called upon to replenish the county treasury by forfeiting the bond. The criminal is probably by this time, enjoying himself in some eastern city, or can be found in some frontier hamlet, and is still engaged in his reckless way of living.

Such is life in the Far West.

CHAPTER VII.

The Killing of Wm. Manning—Epps Surrender and Trial—The Manning Brothers' Threat—Warrant Issued for their Arrest—Deputy Sheriff and Possee make the Arrest—The Prisoners Escape.

After the laspe of almost a year the curtain raises, showing many changes and different scenes. The immigrant still comes from the East to get a home on the frontier of southern Kansas; the character of society is fast changing, and at no distant day the law abiding settler will predominate in the community. The county has been organized and municipal officers have been elected, but justices of the peace and constables seem afraid to do their full duty, but wait a little while and we shall see the law prevail, but not yet; to settle a dispute by murder is still not uncommon.

In February 1872, one of my horses had either strayed or was stolen, and in hunting for it I went to Bluff Creek and there saw a man by the name of Epps. This man had taken a claim about two miles from my place, and had built a dug-out and was living there. I found my horse had not been seen by him and started up the creek to look for it. At this time the settlers had all taken claims near some creek or river; this was done for several reasons, viz: the land bordering the streams was confirmed by many as being the best land, as the richest of the soil was gradually washed to the bottom land, or the land bordering the streams; then again, they wanted this land for its watering facilities and also for the fuel; the only trees seen here were those on the banks of a stream, hence, by getting a claim which was watered by a stream, they would get wood for fuel, and trees for sheltering stock both from the hot sun and from the winter blasts.

After getting about two hundred yards from Epps dug-out, I met a man by the name of William Manning.

This man Manning, in company with three brothers of his was keeping a bunch of cattle near the Bluff Creek country, and had wintered them there during the winter of 1871 and 1872.

As Manning came up to me I spoke to him and I noticed his greeting was not very cordial. I rode on however, and had only gone a short distance when I heard the report of a gun, in the direction of Epps' dug-out.

I turned and rode back to the dug-out, and found Epps standing in the door, and Manning lying on the ground, near the door, dead. Epps had shot him, the charge taking effect in his breast; I found afterwards that the cause of the shooting was occasioned by a dispute or quarrel, which Epps and Manning had in a settlement about some hay, which Epps had cut and stacked for the Manning brothers.

It seems they could not agree on a settlement, each getting angry about it. When they parted it was agreed that they should shoot on sight, and the one getting the lucky shot would be the most fortunate, as far as his life was concerned, at least. Manning was buried two miles south of Caldwell and to-day the place is called Mannings' Peak. Epps went to Sumner city and gave himself up to the officers of the law, had his trial, and was cleared; the jury giving in a verdict to the effect, that he acted in self-defence, for had he not defended himself, in all probability Manning would have killed him.

Soon after this the remaining Manning brothers threatened the life of Epps, consequently Epps went to Wellington, the county seat of Sumner county, and got out a warrant for the arrest of the three Manning brothers; the deputy sheriff came down to make the arrest and deputed about twenty men to help him, myself included in that number.

The Manning brothers had heard of this and left their home, and went to the house of H. H. Davidson and took refuge in his dug-out. A man with his daughter and child were living in the dug-out at the time.

The deputy sheriff and posse arrived at the dug-out at about two o'clock in the morning, and the deputy sheriff demanded their surrender. They would not surrender for reasons of their own, and told the deputy they would never surrender to us. I suppose they presumed we were a mob of reckless characters, and that their surrender would probably, mean death for them.

The deputy told them they would not be hurt, but would be tried and settled with according to law; if that was the cause of their hesitation, he assured them that they should have justice; notwithstanding all this they would not consent to a surrender.

I told the deputy I would arrange to get them out if he was willing to have me try. He consented to my proposal and willingly turned the management into my hands; there was a hay-stack near by, so I said we would smoke them out of the dug-out. A couple of men and myself, went to the stack, and got some hay, and twisted it up in a solid bundle, put it into the chimney and then lit the hay.

We soon heard from them in this manner; they said the woman and child were almost suffocated with the smoke, and asked us to put the fire out; the deputy told them the only way to get rid of the smoke would be to surrender. They replied that they would not surrender.

I told the deputy to tell them that if they did not, in a few minutes we would let the dug-out roof in on them, which he did. Everything was quiet for a few minutes then one of them asked to know who the parties were, that wanted their surrender. He named the parties over to them, and the finally said for one of us to come into the dug-out and they would try and fix up the matter; we thought their reason for wanting one of us in the dug-out was to keep us from caving in the roof on to them.

We finally agreed to their proposition provided they would let the man out again, in case they did not agree to surrender. To this they consented; so one of the men went into the dug-out and they said they would surrender, if we would get C. H. Stone and Mr. Dixon to come to the dug-out.

Rather than give the woman and child further trouble we sent for Mr. Stone and Dixon; these gentlemen were in Caldwell, it was about eight o'clock in the morning when the men arrived on the scene, the Manning brothers gave themselves up to the sheriff's keeping.

He returned to Caldwell, and soon after the sheriff and two men started to take the prisoners to Wellington.

They stopped for the night at Smith's ranch, which was about eight miles north of Caldwell, on the banks of the Chikaskia river. This ranch has two rooms, and in the back-room was a window considerably larger than the other windows. After supper the men engaged themselves at a game of cards, leaving one idle to act as guard over the prisoners.

No sooner had they began playing cards, when they they also began drinking whiskey, the two are usually in company with each other. So it was this time, and the men became very much interested in their game, the drinking was kept up until all, more or less, were intoxicated; and the more intoxicated they became, the more interested they became in their game of cards.

They were having a jolly time, enjoying themselves to their hearts content, drinking and playing, playing and drinking; but the curtain must soon be drawn, the first scene is almost completed; draw the curtain upon this crowd of hilarity and let us see scene the second.

The curtain raises showing the deputy sheriff and his men, but the Manning brothers, oh, where are they? It seemed they were terrible thirsty, and the water was in the back room; the guard by this time become interested, and told them, the prisoners, that they could enter the room and help themselves, which they did; they also took the advantage given them, and opened the window and skipped out. Once more they are free men.

They started for Caldwell and arrived there about two o'clock in the morning; their journey had given each a good appetite; they got something to eat, and left town, never to return.

The deputy sheriff and the men that were with him stayed at the ranch all night, and next morning arrived in Caldwell, after the prisoners had fled.

The reader will readily see the class of people usually found in the western frontier towns; we do not intimate that all the residents are of the desperado style, but we say that the rougher element prevails in these towns. In christianized communities, these towns are called hard "places," and, indeed they are hard places, and many will have to surrender their lives to the grim monster death, before our book is finished.

CHAPTER VIII.

The Buffalo Hunt—Overtaken by a Storm—Taking Shelter in a quickly made Log Cabin—A Woman and Children about to Perish—The Buffalo Range reached and Two of the Party Lost—A Futile Effort in Searching for Them.

In the winter of 1871, I was living in Butler County, Kansas, eleven miles East of Augusta. A party of us conceived the idea of going on a buffalo hunt. As this part of Kansas is nearly all prairie land, the farmer has nothing to busy himself at in the winter months. In the East, the farmer has fences to rebuild, wood to cut and haul, timber land to clear and many other ways of keeping himself busy through the winter.

On the morning of January 20th, the sun shone bright and clear; the day bid fair to be a beautiful one. We had made the necessary arrangements to start on our proposed hunt on that day. So our party, consisting of eight or ten of our friends and neighbors, including father, brother and myself, bid farewell to our friends, homes and familiar scenes, turned our faces westward, and started for the land of the buffalo, fully expecting to reap a rich harvest upon our arrival there.

The first and second days of our trip were beautiful ones, but when we stopped and made arrangements to camp on the evening of the second day, a dark cloud was visible in the North and soon settled back as if "it had not been."

I suggested that we blanket our horses for the night, as there was going to be a storm. The men laughed at my predictions and said "it had been too nice a day to think of a North'er so soon." But as a wise man has said "thou can'st not tell what a day may bring forth," was surely true this time, for about three o'clock in the morning the wind changed its course from the South to the North, the heavens were black with angry looking clouds, the wind began blowing a furious gale which warned us of the approaching storm. For fully ten minutes the wind could be heard roaring in the distance, and almost in an instant the storm was upon us in all its fury. About daylight, snow began to fall, or whirl rather, as the wind seemed to come from all directions, and turn in any position possible, the snow seemed to blow in our faces. As soon as it was sufficiently light enough to see, we hitched our teams to the wagon and started for the Little Arkansas River, knowing there was plenty of timber there for fuel and shelter; also a cattle ranch, at which place we might find food and shelter if necessary.

W. B. KING.   "BUFFALO KING."

Upon our arrival on the Little Arkansas River, we went to work cutting logs, preparing to make us a shelter of some description for ourselves and horses. We succeeded in getting enough logs to make the four sides of a shanty, but what were we to cover it with, was the question. At last some one suggested the wagon sheet. Well, we took the sheet off one of the wagons and tied it over the top of the shanty, thereby sheltering us from snow and wind. We soon had a rousing fire in the center of the shanty, and the boys were singing "I'm always light-hearted and easy, not a care in this world have I."

The weather continued to be cold and disagreeable the rest of the week ; the snow had fallen to about the depth of ten inches ; as we were very comfortable in our new home, we concluded to camp there until the weather was more favorable. We succeeded in passing the time spent in camp very pleasantly. We had now been in camp from Thursday morning until Sunday. On Saturday the weather moderated to such an extent that Sunday morning found us up by daylight, making arrangements to start on our journey.

Once more we are in our wagons wending our way westward, fully determined to push on until our goal is reached. Little did we dream what the future had in store for our little party, and e'er we would turn our faces homeward, the many disappointments and hardships, the suffering and heartaches some of our little party would be subject to.

We traveled a distance of six miles when we came to the Arkansas River; the severe cold weather had frozen it over so we could cross over on the ice. There we would leave the last ranch and would necessarily have to lay in a supply of hay and provisions, realizing if we were far from habitation and should have the misfortune to be in another blizzard, we would need a good supply of the necessaries of life.

We traveled until evening when we came to a small log house in which lived a widow with three children; we found them to be in destitute circumstances. She told us they had nothing to eat; before the storm came she had but very little provision in the house, and that during the storm she would not send her boy from home, for fear he would get lost or frozen. We gave them some bacon, a turkey, a paper of coffee and some flour.

We camped near the house that night, the next morning we started by daylight and traveled three days in a southwest direction.

On the third day, about two o'clock, we reached the land where the buffalo roamed unmolested, save when an occasional hunter or Indian breaks in upon the scene, either for the sport of killing the buffalo, or for the many pounds of delicious meat they get after it is killed.

We selected a good camping place of which I will endeavor to give the reader a brief description. The country here was broken by ravines of greater or less extent, though not perceptible at a glance. These ravines, if followed, would be found to grow deeper and deeper, until, after running their course for an indefinite extent, they would terminate in the valley of some running stream.

The land was ornamented with little knolls and an occasional sand hill. These knolls are frequently found with trees or brush of some description, growing on top of them.

The knoll selected for our camping place was the only one with trees on it, and it could be seen for miles, besides giving us a splendid view of the surrounding country, it also afforded us the satisfaction of knowing we had plenty of good wood at our command, with which we could warm our aching fingers and cook our frugal meal.

After unhitching my horses, watering them and giving them their feed, I took my gun and in company with one of the men, started to hunt for game of some description. We failed to find anything, and started to go back to camp when we met two of the boys, I call them boys, but their ages were seventeen and twenty-two. The people of the West have a habit of saying "boys" when many times they really mean old men. They use it as a familiar term, showing the good will and friendly feeling they have for each other.

The boys, too, had started for the purpose of trying their luck at the sight of game. We wanted them to go back to camp, but they said "supper was not ready and they would hunt awhile."

We told them "not to go far, and to keep in sight of the knoll." They replied, "all right," and went on.

It had been a fine day, clear and warm, but the signs were not favorable for a good day on the morrow. A cloud was rising in the northwest, the wind began blowing and soon the snow began to fall. It was then about 4 o'clock in the afternoon.

After remaining in camp a short time I saw a herd of buffalo coming in the direction of camp. I took my gun and went to a sand-hill about two hundred yards from camp. I stationed myself on the hill and waited until they were within shooting distance. I succeeded in killing one and wounding another. One of the men at camp brought a team and wagon, took the buffalo to camp, while myself, brother and the father of one of the boys that had gone hunting, followed the wounded buffalo in hopes we could get a lucky shot at it and succeed in killing it.

After following it until nearly dark we finally concluded to give up the chase and go back to camp. Not noticing in what direction we had started or the many turns we had made we began to consider in what direction camp would be found.

Neither of us agreed as to the direction we were to go, and I told them if they would remain where they were I would go and hunt for some land-mark by which we might determine where we were and in which direction to take to find our camp. I told them I would fire my revolver off two times in succession in case I concluded we were lost.

After wandering around for some time, not knowing which way to go I concluded we were lost. I took my revolver from my belt, held it in the air and pulled the trigger once,—twice The sound rang out in the cold air, leaving an awful stillness, in which I could almost hear the beatings of my heart.

The silence was broken by an answering shot fired from camp and how gladly we turned our steps in that direction. When I shot my revolver I saw the two boys I have spoken of before, about a mile to the north of where I was standing and I supposed they would arrive at camp about the same time we would. To guide us the boys at camp had taken an old fashioned bake oven, fastened it to the end of a ten-foot pole, then made a fire in the oven and held the pole up, thinking we could see the light and thereby reach camp in safety.

The light in the oven made an excellent guide for us and we arrived safely in camp, but very tired and hungry after our long tramp.

After eating our supper, which consisted of coffee, bacon and bread, we related our adventure to the boys at camp. Then the question was asked, "Where are the remaining boys?" As it was getting late and they had had ample time to reach camp, since they were last seen, we concluded to fire our guns, knowing if they were lost and heard the report of the guns they could follow in the direction of the sound and reach camp, and if they were not lost they would probably think all was not right at camp and reach there as soon as they possibly could.

We kept up the firing all night. We had an old army musket and filled it with sand and fired it off. Our efforts were all in vain.

The father and brothers of the lost boys were nearly wild with grief. Daylight found us prepared to go and hunt for the lost boys. A heavy fog hung like a curtain over the horizon; it was very difficult to see a short distance from camp, but we saddled our horses and were soon on what proved to be a fruitless search for our friends.

We started east and were situated in a line north and south from each other. As I mentioned before, it was dark, foggy and misty, and to keep from getting separated or lost from each other, we were to halloo every few minutes. I was at the north end of the line. I would halloo the next to answer, and so on the entire length of the line of men. The wind was blowing from the north and each could easily hear the halloo above him.

At 12 o'clock I was to fire off my revolver, each of the boys to do the same, but no person to fire two times unless the boys had been found.

After firing our revolvers we started for the same point, and upon arriving there we made a fire, boiled some coffee and ate our dinner.

I have often wished we had fired off our revolvers every few minutes, as the lost boys afterward told me they heard the report of our guns at noon and started in the direction from whence they thought the sound came. After walking a mile or two they listened and could not hear any more shooting, thought perhaps it was imagination, and turned and started back from whence they came.

When our horses were through eating their corn

and we had eaten our dinner, we started on our homeward march after this fashion: The man that was on the south end of the line, as we left camp, was to follow his horse's tracks toward camp and we were to follow him, each keeping within hearing distance of each other.

Great anxiety prevailed throughout the entire party concerning the fate of the lost boys. As the day star sank in the west and the night stars came out one by one, and the shades of night settled around our little camp, it was with many misgivings that we lay down upon our blankets to rest.

I told the father of one of the lost boys that on the morrow I would take one of my horses, some provisions for myself and horse, and a blanket, and see if I could get any trace of the lost boys. In the meantime I told them to kill enough buffalo to load the wagons, which they could easily do, as the range a short distance from camp was alive with them.

The morning dawned finding me fully equipped and ready for my journey. After drinking a refreshing cup of coffee I bade adieu to the little party I was leaving behind and started on my search.

I rode rapidly in a northest direction galloping across ravine and plain. Occasionally, as I dashed across a ravine, I would startle a few buffalos from their slumber and cause them to wonder who was this strange party disturbing their peaceful repose.

After traveling all day without the least sign to urge me on, I concluded about sun-down that I would go into camp. A large cottonwood tree was in sight and I turned my horse's head in that direction intending to stop there for the night.

I found, to my good luck, a large cave in the south side of a large sand-hill near the tree, and thought it would afford me a place of shelter.

I unsaddled my horse and found he was very tired after a day's hard travel. I fed my horse, looked around and found some dry limbs to make a fire, cooked my supper, and will here tell the reader that it was not a feast and far from being a famine. After partaking of my supper I lit my pipe and indulged in my accustomed evening smoke.

Oh, how lonely it seemed to me, with nothing to break the monotony of my loneliness, save an occasional howl of the gray wolf, and their howl only had a tendency to make me melancholy and have a yearning for my home far away.

It was not a very desirable place to be in I assure you. I had seen places where the Indians had camped but a short time before. I knew unless I should be taken unawares or by surprise that I was prepared for a small band, as I was well armed, having with me two good revolvers, a shot gun and a Winchester rifle. My dog was some company for me. I put my saddle under my head for a pillow and prepared for a night's rest.

I was tired and weary after my long ride, as all who have been in the saddle all day know how to appreciate a good place to lie down and sleep when the night begins to draw near.

I could not sleep; my thoughts were on the lost boys' condition. I knew they would suffer with cold, as only one had an overcoat on; also that they would suffer from hunger unless they were fortunate enough to kill something to eat.

Morning dawned finding me in the saddle to again resume my search. I started in a southeast direction, thinking I might find their trail in the snow. I rode until noon, stopped and fed my horse, built a fire out of buffalo chips and made some coffee. I traveled the rest of the day as fast as I deemed best. About dark I heard some one chopping. I rode in the direction from whence the sound came and found it was one of the men chopping wood to make a fire at camp.

I told the boys' father that I had seen nothing of them. He said it was no use to hunt further, for in all probability if the lost boys had not reached a settlement or ranch they were frozen to death.

In my absence the men had killed enough buffalo to load our wagons, so we concluded to start for home on the following morning. In my next chapter I will endeavor to tell the reader more about our trip and the final result of our buffalo hunt.

CHAPTER IX.

A Buffalo Hunt—The Homeward March—A Man's Track Found—Arrival at Wichita—The Lost Boys' on their Journey Homeward—Nearly Famished with Hunger—A Friend in Need is a Friend Indeed—Returned Safely to Home and Friends.

The morning dawned finding us in our wagons before it was sufficiently light enough to view the surrounding country.

As we wended our way towards our homes, I could not help but notice how silently our little party trudged along. The father and brother mourning for the lost ones, and looking, perhaps upon scenes and places for the last time, but, which time could not erase from their memory. Although many years have passed since then, yet when I recall that Buffalo hunt to my mind I am apparently young again, ready for any emergency which may come before me.

We had not proceeded far on our journey, perhaps a mile, when one of the party had the misfortune to lose one of his horses. To all appearances the horse was well when we started, but soon began to reel in walking, and upon investigation it was found to have the blind staggers; it was too sick to travel and rather than leave it there on the prairie one of the boys shot it. The old man came to me and wanted to know if I would haul their bedding and provisions home for them; he said he would burn his wagon rather than leave it there for the Indians. I told him it was useless to burn his wagon as he could have my leaders and take his wagon home with him. He took my front team and hitched to his wagon and we were soon on our road again.

In the afternoon about four o'clock we came to a small creek which we thought we would have difficulty in crossing, one of the boys started up the stream to find a place safe to cross; after finding a fordable place, he, by chance saw a man's track, and hallooed to us "here is a man's track," words would indeed be poor vehicles with which to convey to the mind of the reader how eager we were to see for ourselves, and examine the tracks. Our conclusions were that they were the lost boys tracks and were made the following morning after they had left camp; as the snow was thawing we thought it would be useless to try and follow them.

When the father saw the tracks, he gave way to his grief, the tears trickled down his cheeks as he said "my poor boy is lost, and perhaps dead, Oh! how I wish we could find him."

About dark we stopped for the night, our camping

place was on the bank of a little stream. The weather was very agreeable overhead. The night was a beautiful one, nothing happened to disturb our rest, save an occasional howl of a coyote or the fluttering of a bird which was startled from its perch in the limbs of a tree.

We were up by daylight and soon on our way; after traveling four days we arrived at Wichita. We made inquiry there of the lost boys, but could hear nothing concerning them.

We camped about two miles east of Wichita that night, and were thirty one miles from home.

The following morning was very disagreeable, a misting rain was slightly fal'ing. The weather had moderated to such an extent that the snow had melted making the roads slushy and muddy. We did not make a very big days drive that day, only reaching Augusta at night. Our camping place was on the Big Walnut River. We started for home early the next morning.

After driving six miles we met one of my brothers, and a brother of one of the lost boys. How glad we were to hear all were well at home, and we were almost overjoyed on hearing the lost boys were alive and that they were now on their way after them intending to bring them home.

We arrived home safely, without further adventure

and I will tell you the experience the lost boys had as they related it to me.

"After leaving camp we started north and continued that course for a few hours; after traveling for some time we changed our course thinking we could easily find camp. We had traveled until quite dark before we gave up, realizing we were lost.

"The reader may little imagine, than to have me describe our feelings when the thoughts flew through our minds, with the rapidity of lightning, that we were lost. How our hearts sank within us, when we would picture to our minds eye; our warm fireside, with our father and mother in their easy chair, waiting for our coming. We thought perhaps we would not be found, and we would be left to perish on the western plains. How vividly our past life came back to our memory, what a terrible picture the future presented to us. We prayed that we might escape the hands of the Indians.

"Gradually the actual fact that we were lost and far from habitation, took possession of our senses, and we concluded to act immediately upon that fact.

"We endeavored to press on, hoping to be rescued by our friends, or that we might by chance find a ranch

"We wandered all night, never stopping to rest and did not realize how tired we were. The next morning was damp and foggy, and very difficult to see two hundred yards from us. We knew from the lay of the country that the course of streams here was east, and we thought we would start in that direction.

"We had not proceeded far before we came to a small creek or ravine. We thought that by following it we sooner or later would find where it emptied its waters, knowing if we followed its course we would in time reach the Arkansas river.

"We followed the ravine all day, wandering around with it in its meanderings, through hill and plain. About night we came to the terminus of the ravine, or rather where it entered a stream. On the banks of this stream we saw a herd of Antelope; we tried to shoot one, but fate was against us and soon we were left alone, our four footed friends having left us, giving us the right of way and full possession of the creek.

"We had now given up all hopes of reaching a settlement, and our only source of rescue was to strike a ranch on the banks of the creek, or to follow it until we would reach a settled portion of the state.

"The ground was covered with snow, the wind was blowing a furious gale from the north, chilling our bodies; had we had some matches we could have made a fire and one slept while the other kept up the fire; but all the sleep we had was when we could find the south side of a hill; then, as the snow was on the ground we had to make a bed by pulling up dry grass to lie down on, then one of us would lie down with the overcoat over him and take a sleep, while the other one, like a soldier on his beat, would walk around to keep himself warm. After each of us had taken a little nap, we would start on our travels again. We traveled three days without having anything to eat. Oh! how ravenous our appetites were; on the morning of the fourth day my friend gave up in despair. He said he did not care to go any further; he was so weary both in body and mind and he did not believe we would find a settlement; we were nearly starved for something to eat.

"I told him I would never leave him there to perish on the plains, and rather than leave him there I would kill him. I drew my gun on him and I suppose he thought "as long as there is life there is hopes," and he concluded to try and keep up strength and courage.

"We traveled all day; at night we came to a river, which we afterwards found was the Nennescah. We were then 19 miles west of Wichita, and were within one-half mile of a house. Little did we imagine we were so near help.

"Just at sunrise the next morning we again resumed our journey; upon crossing the river and walking up the bank to our surprise and joy we saw a house; at the sight of the house our strength seemed to leave us, and in order to reach it we were compelled to crawl on our hands and knees.

"When we arrived at the house it was twelve o'clock, and the family were preparing to eat their dinner. Perhaps it would be well enough to say that the ranch was kept by Captain Davis. He and his family moved there in an early day.

"The Captain saw us first, and knew by our emaciated appearances that we were famishing for food.

"He told his wife to clear the table of the provisions; upon hearing this we drew our guns on him and told him we would kill him if he did not let us have something to eat. The Captain told us we could have something to eat, and told his wife to get them some beef soup. He knew we were not in the condition to go to the table, which was well spread with eatables. Mrs. Davis gave each a pint cup half full of soup and a slice of light bread.

"We will never forget the kindness shown us, for they indeed treated us as they would one of their own children.

"Mr. Davis had his team ready to start for Wichita, as soon as he had eaten his dinner, but he postponed his trip and stayed at home to care for us. We thought several times that we would take his life, because he would not let us satisfy our craving appetite.

"The Captain had been a soldier in the Civil War, and by way of interesting us, he would tell us how the soldier's suffered in the Andersonville prison; also related his experience as a soldier, and of the many fights he had witnessed.

"Had we been in a different condition we would have enjoyed his reminiscences very much, but, as we were nearly famishing our only thought was to satisfy our appetites.

"The night drew on and we began to get sleepy. Mrs. Davis made us a bed, the Captain slept near by and all through the night was ready to wait upon us, giving us soup every hour.

"The next day we were allowed to sit at the table, but ate only what the Captain said was best for us. I presume we were not very mannerly at the table. After dinner was over the captain invited us to go with him to see his stock, stable and corral, which was about one hundred yards distant.

"We first went to the corrals to see the cattle. The Captain was the owner of a large herd of cattle, and was a man that took great pride in his home and surroundings. He took us out for the purpose of showing us shi home and possessions.

"After admiring his cattle, we thought we had best go in the house and rest, as we were yet very weak. We rested a couple of hours, had a refreshing sleep and felt very much better. About four o'clock the Captain had us go with him again; we stayed with him until he had done his feeding.

"After supper we, in company with the Captain and his wife, went to spend the evening with a neighbor living near by.

"The captain related the story of our adventure, how we had come to his house nearly starved and how we had suffered from cold as well as hunger. We had the sympathy of the people, and they said we were lucky to find such a man and family to care for us.

"That night we were allowed to sleep without being disturbed, how well we appreciated that bed will never be known as I am unable to fully express myself.

"On the next morning my friends feet were getting very sore, he having had them badly frozen. He could not walk without the crutches which the Captain had been kind enough to make for him.

"We remained with the Captain about ten days, when the boys came for us to go home with them. We were very glad to see them and we had a general hand shaking all round. Nothing would do them but we must tell of the suffering and privations we had experienced since we left home but a short time before, but to us it seemed years since we had started on our buffalo hunt, full of expectations and bright prospects before us.

"Had we known we were to be the victims of such an experience, we would have shuddered at the thoughts of it. But here we are apparently well and happy and have had our share of the sufferings and disappointments of the buffalo hunter.

"Early the next morning we bade the Captain and his family goodby. Thanking them for their heartfelt kindness, telling them they would long be remembered by us, and that we considered it was to them that we owed our lives, for, had they not been so considerate with us, in all probability we would have fared much worse.

Late in the evening we arrived at Augusta and as we were so near home, we wanted the boys to continue our journey; the boys wanted us to stop over night in Augusta, but we were determined to reach home that night.

"I will not attempt to describe our meeting with father and mother, suffice it to say that we were all very thankful that we were restored to our loved ones again."

I will not tire the reader by relating how each reached his home, nor of the happy meeting afterwards, but will add that one of them lost all of his toes off his feet, and the last I heard of him he was living in Indiana. The other was not badly frozen, but the exposure was too great a strain on his constitution and he died the following fall. This ended the buffalo hunt upon which we started, with our hopes bouyant, and our anticipation bright as we pictured to ourselves; the many monarchs of the plains that would give up their lives to satisfy our appetites for the pleasure of killing them.

I have had many a buffalo hunt, and have realized a great deal of enjoyment while chasing them over the plains, and as I recall such scenes to memory, in the language of the poet I feel like saying, "backward, turn backward, oh! time in your flight."

While we were fortunate in having our friends restored to us, yet, how many have wandered from their camp and were never found. Quite likely they either died from starvation or were frozen to death, and perhaps many had the misfortune to fall into the hands of the cunning Indian, and were either burned to the stake or suffered a similar death.

About this time the Indians were to be greatly feared. The tide of civilization had gradually driven them west to the plains. Occasionally the buffalo hunter would wander too far, and be surprised to find himself surrounded by a small band of the Noble Red Men, who, after taking him prisoner, would discuss by what means they would kill or torture him to death, while the poor fellow would pray to God for help, knowing he would have no mercy at their hands.

Thus ends our buffalo hunt, and the readers may decide with themselves whether it was an enjoyable affair for us or not.

CHAPTER X.

M'Carty Pulls Fielder out of Bed—Fielder Resents Such Treatment—Fielder Gives M'Carty a Whipping—M'Carty Gets on a Drunk and Hunts for Fielder—Fielder Goes to Reed's Dug-out—M'Carty Calls for Fielder—M'Carty a Murderer and Flees to the Indian Territory—Public Sentiment Aroused.

Scarcely had one month, one small month passed since the tragedy at Epps dug-out, which resulted in the killing of William Manning, than the people received the startling intelligence, that another had seen the sun set for the last time.

Spring was just making her appearance and was donning her robe of vernal beauty. Little did the victim think that before the bud changed to blossom that he would be sleeping under the grass, with a bullet in his breast.

During the winter of 1871 and 1872, two men, by the name of Dan Fielder, and —— McCarty were batching together in a dug-out, on Bluff Creek, located about two miles from town. Each I believe had taken a claim a short distance from town, and as it would be very lonely living alone, they concluded to batch together and time would not seem so monotonous for either.

Fielder was formerly from Pottowattomie county, this state, and was a man about medium size in height and weight, and bore the marks of a gentleman, save in regard to his dress, which partook of the rowdy element. He was not considered a bad man, was a lover of peace, and still the organizer of discord. He would shrink from courting danger, and yet when it did come he was ready to meet it. He was not the man to be imposed on, and would resent an insult heaped upon him by a friend, in the most quiet and unassumming manner possible.

As McCarty will be presented before the minds of the reader, for a considerable length of time, perhaps it would be well to note his many characteristics. No character in this history presents a more remarkable career than does that of McCarty.

His was a strange character, one which the novelist might gloat over. In person he was about five feet ten inches in height, straight as a warrior, well formed chest and limbs, and a face strikingly handsome. His hair and complexion were those of the perfect brunette; the former laid in ringlets about his head. His costume was that of a dandy, with the taste and style of a frontiersman. He was well educated and in manner resembled a cultured gentleman.

Of his courage there could be no question, as it had

been tested on several occasions. He was formerly from Texas. His use of the revolver was unerring, and his practice at target shooting would make the people shudder at the daring feats he displayed. At times he would show his skill in shooting at the sole of some boot, and again he would point his revolver over the shoulder of some one who was reading a letter and put a bullet hole through the paper. Numerous were his ways of displaying his skill with the revolver.

There had been no law recognized by the frontiersman beyond the fact that might makes right. The quarrel was not from from a word to a blow, but from a word to the revolver, and he who could draw and fire first was the best man.

In the early part of April, 1872, McCarty came in to town and indulged freely in drinking whiskey with some companions of his. He remained in town until late at night when he left town and returned to his dugout. By this time he was considerably under the influence of the whiskey and was in a quarrelsome mood.

After putting his horse away for the night, he went to the dug-out and found that Fielder had gone to bed. McCarty requested Fielder to get up and Fielder replied that he would not. At this McCarty's evil spirits were aroused and he went to Fielder and caught hold of his hair and pulled him out of the bed, onto the floor. Fielder again sought his bed and McCarty, as before, pulled him out by the hair.

This was too much for Fielder to endure and he resented such treatment by giving McCarty a good whipping, which had a tendency to sober him and he soon became quiet and went to bed.

Nothing more was thought or said about the trouble by Fielder, and to all outward appearances McCarty too had laid all predjudices aside and said nothing about it. But there was certainly a feeling of revenge being kindled in his heart, only to break out of its place of bondage at the first opportunity which presented itself.

As we have mentioned before, his manner and style were not of the desperado type, nor had he the look of a murderer upon his features, and yet he proved to be a double murderer and a desperado. Truly, we cannot tell by man's appearance, what lies hidden in the recesses of the heart. And yet, I believe whiskey was the cause of McCarty's downfall, which terminated in his ignomonious death, at the hands of a law-abiding eople.

On the following Sunday, after the trouble, McCarty was again in town and drank until he became very much intoxicated. Fielder heard McCarty was drunk and imagined he would be quarrelsome, so he left their dug-out, and went to Reed's, thinking thereby to escape further trouble with McCarty. Upon going home and not finding Fielder, he went back to town and began making inquiry of Fielder's whereabouts. Some of his friends, not thinking that McCarty held malice against Fielder, told him that Fielder was at Reed's dug-out.

McCarty got his horse and rode in that direction, and it seems, in the still and voiceless night, he wanted to avenge himself of the ill-treatment he had received at the hands of his friend Fielder. He did not stop to consider or realize that it was he who provoked the quarrel which resulted in his supposed ill-treatment.

He took the precaution to roll a blanket about his body in such a condition that it would be difficult for a bullet to penetrate through its thickness and enter his body, this precaution probably saved his life, as will be shown before this chapter closes.

Upon his arrival at Reed's, he called for Fielder and was told by one of the family that he was not there. He got off his horse, holding it by the bridle rein, and called again for Fielder. At this, Fielder said with an oath, "here I am, come in here if you want anything," no sooner had the words left his lips than he was standing, revolver in hand, ready for any emergency.

Fielder was facing the door and in such a position, that as soon as the door was thrown open he had a good view of McCarty. As McCarty opened the door, he also raised the blanket to get his revolver; and as he was in this act, Fielder fired, his shot taking effect within the folds of the blanket around McCarty's body, and glanced off without injury to his person. As quick as lightning, McCarty shot several times in succession at Fielder, one of the bullets taking effect in his lung which caused his immediate death.

McCarty then got on his horse and left town, and was not seen again for several days.

Fielder's body was properly buried by the citizens of town, while tears of sympathy were shed over the newly made grave.

Thus another victim enters that long sleep that knows no waking.

Public sentiment revolted at such acts of lawlessness and bloodshed. The question was asked "can a man commit murder and go free and unpunished?" The public mind was thoroughly aroused, it felt that this state of things was a disgrace to civilization. A change must be made let it cost what it will. It was coming like the rushing of a mighty wind, soon to burst forth in all its fury.

The law-breaker, the murderer and desperado must go, or submit to the inevitable will of the people. Crowds of by-standers were talking in undertones of the terrible state of affairs that were now existing in our little town and its surrounding country. Wait, and time will determine when the tide shall turn and we shall realize this fact, that the " right must prevail."

During the spring of 1872, I was elected constable of Caldwell and vicinity, and soon after I was appointed Deputy United States Marshal, under United States Marshal Place.

The offices I held placed me under obligations to be with the rougher element the greater part of my time, and I experienced the many trials the officer had to endure, whether at home in my native town or on the western plains, in pursuit of the horse-thief or murderer.

Many times have I sat in the saddle, day and night, in search of the fugitive fleeing from justice, and have returned to my home, utterly worn out from exposure and fatigue, after a long, weary, fruitless chase.

In my next chapter I will relate to the reader a second shooting by McCarty, and it is said, completed a record in which he killed his ninth man. Had his been a charmed life? Had fate decreed that he should die a shameful death and be denied a decent burial? Me thinks I hear the faint whisperings of the wind as it mournfully whispers, Yes.

CHAPTER XI.

Killing of Anderson—The Fatal Plug Hat—McCarty's Recklessness—Theories in Regard to the Murder—The "Last Chance"—The Proprietor.

Time flies, oh, how swiftly, and in its flight many are the changes it brings and different are the scenes presented to our view. Man plays many parts on the world's stage. The novelist may fascinate us with his romance of fiction, but the novelist's dreams fade utterly away. When the checkered lives of men pass before us in their different stages of life, filling our minds with their wonderful history of adventure, heroism and bravery.

In the chapter preceding this I mentioned to the reader the killing of Fielder, by McCarty, and now, so soon, I must add another victim to the list of men murdered at his hands. On the following Monday, a week after the Fielding tragedy, McCarty came into town in company with one Webb. This was the first time he had been seen in town since his flight into the Territory, after the murder of Fielder. As was his custom, he again indulged freely in drinking and was soon under the influence of whiskey. He and Webb went into the store formerly occupied by Cox and Epperson, now, of which J. M. Thomas was the proprietor, and loitered around apparently with no aim in view; Thomas was busy looking at some goods which a man by the name of Doc Anderson had for sale.

This man Anderson had been the proprietor of a store in Butler County, and after closing out a greater part of his goods, he brought the balance to Caldwell and was trying to make a sale to Thomas.

On his way to Caldwell he stopped at Wellington over night, and while there, he in company with others bought a plug hat from some party, for the purpose of gambling over a game of cards, the winner to have the hat. Anderson was the lucky man and won the hat; but unfortunately for him that game of cards, together with the hat, sealed his fate. 'Tis strange upon how small a pivot our destiny swings.

As Anderson was showing Thomas the goods, McCarty noticed that he wore a plug hat, (probably this was the first plug hat seen in the town) and remarked to Webb that he would like to shoot a hole through that man's hat. Webb said, "no you won't shoot through a man's hat." "Oh no," said McCarty, "of course I wouldn't unless the man wanted me to," and just then Anderson turned round to get more goods when quick as a flash McCarty shot at him, the ball tearing the top of Anderson's head off; Anderson fell, and died without a struggle at the feet of his assassin. It is said some one remarked "there McCarty you have killed that man," "well," said McCarty, "he is out of luck, that's all."

McCarty then went to his horse and rode south towards the Indian Territory. Whether he shot at Anderson with the intention of killing him remains to be told, or whether he shot at the hat and accidently hit "his man" also remains a mystery. It was currently reported afterwards as a rumor, that Anderson had used his influence against a gang of horse thieves which had infested Butler County, which resulted in the hanging of seven thieves on the Walnut river, in one night, and caused such a cleaning up that many left that country in a short time, whether they were guilty of any crime, and feared they would be used in a like manner, was never known; but the rumor was to the effect that in all probability either McCarty was there at the time and left, or he had friends among the doomed men and swore to avenge their death, by killing any party he might find in his ramblings.

It did not matter whether he shot at the hat to show his skill as a marksman, or if he shot to avenge a friends untimely end, it was enough that he committed murder unprovoked by his victim, and he was looked upon by the people as double murderer.

Had he not "killed his man" such a short time previous to the last murder, probably the public would not have been so thoroughly indignant over the affair, but to have a double murderer in their midst and at large, free to roam at his pleasure, was more than they would submit to, and they were determined that such characters must emigrate to some "healthier clime," or take the consequences which were sure to come, were they to continue in their lawlessness and murderous inclinations.

Upon the killing of Fielder a dark cloud had begun to gather in the horizon of public sentiment. The time is fast approaching when there must be a speedy reckoning for crime. Fielder is dead; public feeling is warm and needs but a spark more to ignite the flame; the last straw is on the camels back. The killing of Fielder appeared to be a free fight, Fielder assuming the role of a duelist, but the killing of Anderson caused the cloud to arise, and with its black wings hovering over our heads, ready to burst at a given signal. Here was a man killed without any provocation and without even the privilege of defending himself, and without a word of warning.

There were several theories concerning the killing of Anderson. One was that McCarty did not intend to kill him, but shot at his hat, as I have before mentioned to show his skill as a marksman, and his aim being too low, shot the man in the head, the bullet entering the top of his head, leaving about two inches intact.

Another theory was, that Anderson had been living in Butler County previous to coming here, and had probably taken a part in ridding the country of supposed horse thieves. Public indignation ran so high that eight men were hung in one night, and many parties, whether they were suspicioned or not, left the country. Whether McCarty was there or was guilty of any crime and left, was not confirmed. Some thought he was avenging the death of some particular friend, and, like the red man of the western plains, killed the first white man he saw.

It was reported that McCarty became conscience stricken and told some parties at a ranch near town, that he had accidently killed a man in town, and that he was very sorry and wished he could recall that shot, also that if money could call back the life he had taken, he would willingly work all his life for one penny per day. He was by nature a kind hearted man and like his relatives in "ould Ireland" was possessed with great "mother wit." But his love for whiskey caused his ruin and death.

Anderson was killed about four o'clock in the evening; I was not in town at that time and knew nothing about it until the following morning. The evening of the shooting, a man came to my house and called for a man who was living with me. I went to the door and asked him what he wanted; he said he was after the man that was living with me, and for me to be prepared to serve a warrant in the morning. The two men got on their horses and rode in the direction of town.

I was very anxious to know what the trouble was and consequently was restless during the night. I knew both men well, and knew they were excited over something unusual.

The night was a very dark one. A party of about fifteen or twenty men went to a ranch, located about one mile South of town, on the cattle trail, and called the "Last Chance;" so called on account of its being the last chance where whiskey could be bought after leaving the state line until the line of Texas is reached. The government laws prohibited the sale of, and also of carrying whiskies into the Indian Territory.

This ranch was kept by Curly Marshal, an old frontiersman, and said to be a government scout during the war, and afterwards an Indian scout under the employ of the government.

He was a desperado, and made his living in nefarious ways. This ranch consisted of a double log house in which were kept whiskies, provisions and feed for horses, and was probably established in 1869.

Marshal erected a frame box house near the log house, intending it to be used as a dance hall. He had made arrangements with some women of ill-repute to come from Wichita and aid him in running the hall. The women had not yet put in an appearance; public sentiment was against the starting of such a house, and used all means possible to prevent it.

This Last Chance was the favorite resort of the desperado and horse thief.

Curly Marshal was a fine type of physical manhood, standing about six feet in height. Physically he was perfection as a man animal, weighing perhaps about 250 pounds, muscular, well-built and well proportioned. In appearance he bore the type of the frontiersman; in dress neat, but pertaining to the western style of rowdyism.

Together with his extensive acquaintance on the frontier and on the western plains, and the numerous travelers on the trail, he expected at the Last Chance to establish a good business. His physical courage, indomitable will, and unerring marksmanship with the revolver, led him to believe that he could over-awe public sentiment.

In our next chapter we will show the reader wherein he was mistaken.

CHAPTER XII.

Watching the "Last Chance"—Burning the Dance Hall—Busey Nicholson Captured—McCarty Fights to the Bitter End The Final Result—Curly Marshal Attempts to Rebuild the Dance Hall—His Threat—An Encounter with Newt Williams.

As I mentioned in the preceding chapter, the night was extremely dark, which was to McCarty's advantage, for had he taken extra caution he might have escaped to Texas in safety. As I have said before, Anderson was killed on Monday afternoon about four o'clock; that night soon after dark, a posse of fifteen or twenty men went to the "Last Chance" ranch intending to get McCarty, as it was generally supposed he would make that his headquarters for the night.

These men went up to the ranch and demanded of the proprietor a right to search the ranch for McCarty, but the proprietor would not give his consent and this fact led them to believe that McCarty was hiding there.

The posse of men were not to be foiled, and rode away in the direction of town; about two hundred yards from the ranch is a ravine, running in a southeast direction, and finally terminating in Bluff Creek. This creek in its winding course, almost makes an island here, and the ranch is situated near the center of the ground in this enclosure.

Some of the men went to this ravine, the greater part of them remaining to watch the ranch, while two or three went to town. The remaining men were detailed here and there behind the bluffs and closely watched the movements at the ranch. They supposed McCarty would try and make his escape and by close watching they could get him. After waiting for sometime all was quiet at the ranch; I presume the inmates were wrapt in slumber; when the men from town returned to the ravine, they brought with them two pails of coal-oil, also a couple of bed quilts.

A part of the men went quietly, and cautiously up to the new frame house, which I have referred to, as being built to be used as a dance hall, and after saturating the quilts with the kerosene and throwing the remaing oil on the house, the quilts were fastened to the sides of the house with pins, and then, quick as a flash, the burning match touched the quilts and all was aflame,

A noise was heard in the building and soon the door was opened, and the inmates began taking out the counter and rolling out the several barrels of whiskey. In doing this they saw the crowd of men and began shooting at them, the firing was returned by the crowd, and was kept up for some time. Fortunately none of the party were hurt, but two of the ranch men, that were rolling out the whiskey barrels were hit with buck-shot fired from the crowd, but were not seriously hurt.

The light from the burning building made it almost light as day, and had McCarty been there he could easily have been seen; and as he failed to make an appearance, the crowd went back to town, after leaving two men in the woods near the ranch, to watch until daylight for McCarty's appearance.

As soon as the day had dawned, some one brought me a warrant for the arrest of McCarty, charged with murder. I soon had the necessary men to accompany me in my search for the fugitive. Men were sent in all directions, one went to Douglas, Butler County, the home of Anderson, for the purpose of informing his relatives and friends, of his death and the manner in which he met it.

On Tuesday night about ten o'clock, forty men from Butler County, arrived at my house. Their errand was to assist in capturing the murderer who was yet at large. I told them we had all the men necessary, and men who were well acquainted with the country over which we were compelled to travel, and also men who were acquainted with the parties who were supposed to give McCarty assistance.

After remaining a short time and getting something

to eat, they started on their return home, and after traveling about eight miles, they went into camp for the balance of the night.

We scoured the country in every direction, rode over hill and plain, up and down the banks of the streams, through ravine and hollow, but all in vain. Our chase was a long weary one to both horse and man, and we were utterly worn out from want of sleep and rest. The search was continued until Wednesday, when we returned to town giving up all hope of his capture. But upon returning to town, we learned that his hiding place had been ascertained by the men remaining to watch the proceedings at the ranch.

It seems the citizens wanted possession of the ranch, and as it was a little risky to attempt to get it by force, they laid a plan in which two men were sent to a rock quarry, which is in the territory, and on the opposite side of the creek, from the ranch, and in coming towards town they were to stop at the ranch and get some whiskey. Upon arriving at the ranch they found, to their good luck, only two men in possession of it.

They asked for a glass of whiskey, and when the bar-tender turned his head to get it, they drew their revolvers and ordered a surrender. This little game of stratagem gave them the possession of the "Last

Chance," and also the men under the employ of Curly Marshal.

Soon after getting possession of the ranch, some of the men who had been looking for McCarty came, and while holding council as to what would be the proper thing to do, a man by the name of Busey Nicholson came in and asked for a drink of whiskey. He then turned to the crowd and asked where Curly Marshal was. Some one replied that they did not know, but they supposed he was in Wichita.

Nicholson then said a man had given him an order to get five hundred dollars from Marshal. He was asked who the man was that had given him the order for the money. He refused to tell, but finally after much hesitation, told them it was McCarty. The news created considerable excitement among the men, and now they were satisfied the game was theirs.

The next in order would be to ascertain from Nicholson, the hiding place of McCarty, and this, he utterly refused to reveal to them.

The minds of the people, had become so inflamed over the tide of affairs now existing, that they were determined that Nicholson should reveal McCarty's whereabouts or die upon his refusal. A council was held and a rope produced, and Nicholson was given to understand that unless he told them of McCarty's place of concealment and went with them to find him, he would be hung to the joists of the building he was in. He saw that a further attempt at concealment would be fatal, unless he was willing to forfeit his life, for that of his friend.

He could see depicted in the faces of the men, a look of resolution and indignant determination, fore telling, that what they undertook to do, they meant to accomplish. Their looks and manner intimidated him and he told all he knew concerning **McCarty**, saying he was on Deer Creek about twelve miles South of town. Upon hearing that information concerning McCarty's whereabouts had been obtained, I went directly to the ranch, and arrangements were made to start for McCarty on the following morning about four o'clock.

I was very tired and sleepy, having been deprived of a good nights rest for several days; I went home and soon after I had eaten my supper I went to bed, and told my wife to have a cup of coffee ready for me at two o'clock in the morning, and also told my brother to have a fresh horse in readiness at my command.

At the appointed time my wife called me, and having lost so much sleep, I felt I had hardly closed my eyes before they told me it was two o'clock. I said I would lie down again for an hour, and then I could get to the ranch in time to start with the crowd.

At three o'clock I arose and after drinking a cup of coffee I went to get my horse, which I found had broken his halter and got loose; I found him, however, without any difficulty, and was soon on my way to the ranch.

To my surprise I found the men had been gone from the ranch a considerable length of time before my arrival, and as I thought it would be useless for me to try to overtake them, so I concluded to ride along at my leisure in the direction they had taken. I had not proceeded far, when I saw the forms of the men coming in the distance and after going a short distance I met them.

It was afterwards reported and I learned from good authority, that their reason for leaving the ranch earlier than the appointed time, was that their fears were that McCarty would become alarmed at Nicholson's lenghty visit and would change his hiding place, which proved to be the case. Nicholson told me afterwards, that when the men arrived at the place designated by him to be the place of McCarty's concealment, and found he had fled, he expected every minute he would be shot.

When they found McCarty had changed his place of concealment the men scattered, going in all directions to hunt him; they had not proceeded far when they saw a horse in the distance, and quietly approached near enough to see it was his horse. It was not light enough to see McCarty and they quietly waited for the coming day, which had already begun to break in the East.

As soon as it was sufficiently light, they saw McCarty lying on the ground, sleeping with his head on his saddle and the lariat rope on the horse, tied to the horn of the saddle.

The men surrounded him and ordered his surrender, this of course startled him, but he soon realized the condition he was in and began shooting at the men with a Sharpe carbine. Here, it is said, one of the most daring and perilous acts took place, which has ever been recorded. McCarty's horse was tied to a thirty foot rope, the rope was tied to the saddle, McCarty stood near the saddle, and was trying to get his horse in order to make a run. In the mean time he kept firing at the men, and they kept firing at him. One man with more daring and courageness than his comrades possessed, saw what McCarty's intentions were, and ran between him and his horse and cut the rope. McCarty shot at him twice during this perilous act, but each shot missed its errand, and he was allowed to return to his comrades unhurt. McCarty finally got a shell fast in his carbine and in his effort to get it out, his right hand was hit with buck-shot, disabling the use of that hand.

I presume he thought as long as life lasts there is

hope, and tried to use his revolver in his left hand, but found he must surrender or be killed in attempting to run. He could not use his left hand to advantage and at last, hope left him, and he threw up his hands as a signal of surrender.

The men went to him and the report was that McCarty asked for mercy at the hands of the mob. The men left him in charge of one of the party, and they stepped a short distance away from him and held a consultation, as to what they had better do with him. Some were in favor of hanging him, while others favored shooting him, and some of the cooler men were in favor of taking him to the state and give him a trial for his life. While they were discussing about it, some one asked Fielder a brother to the man McCarty had killed, what he wanted done with McCarty. He told McCarty that ten minutes before, he could have killed him, but now, his conscience would not let him become a murderer. Some one asked which one of the revolvers McCarty had killed Fielder with, and after being told, he took it from the scabbard and holding it at McCarty's head, pulled the trigger, the bullet entering his head, killing him instantly.

After their deadly work had been accomplished, they turned, and left the body of the murdered man lying as it fell. His body remained unburied at the place of his death until Sunday, when the mother and brother of McCarty arrived in Caldwell and proceeded to the spot where the son and brother had met his death. The body was buried near the battle ground where McCarty received the fatal charge which ended his life.

A short time after the shooting of McCarty, eighteen men residing in the vicinity of Caldwell, received a notice purported to have been signed by "many citizens," notifying each party that their presence was no longer needed in Caldwell. It would be needless to add that the eighteen men, excepting two, took warning, and deemed it best for their safety to leave the country, which they did. The determination was to rid the country of all parties who expressed themselves as sympathizers with murderers, outlaws and desperadoes.

A short time after the death of McCarty, Curly Marshal began to make preparations to rebuild a dance hall, in lieu of the one which the reader will remember as having been burned to the ground by the infuriated people, there-by hoping to capture McCarty. Marshal was in Wichita at the time the hall was burned, and when that intelligence reached him, he started for the "Last Chance" alone, as he had to defer bringing the prostitutes that were to aid him in establishing the dance hall.

He remained here for a short time, and in the mean time inquired among his friends for the facts concerning the killing of McCarty, the burning of the dance hall, and the circumstances pertaining to the strategy used, by which the "Last Chance" fell into the hands of the posse who were watching for McCarty. Upon learning who the men were that demanded a "throw-up" of his bar tender, Marshal made several threats, one of them was that he intended to kill Newt Williams for the active part he had taken in gaining possession of the "Last Chance."

The reported threat reached the ears of the citizens, and also was reported to Williams. Williams was a man who feared no man, he was quiet and unassuming in his manner. He believed in having the laws of the land enforced for the prosecution of the criminal, and was a strong believer in the bible quotation, "an eye for an eye and a tooth for a tooth," and thought it was applicable to the murderer, desperado and highwayman. He did not court danger, loved peace, and was ready to use his influence to quiet disorder and in upholding the law.

He was courageous and daring in disposition; the reader will remember the daring feat he performed in liberating McCarty's horse, by cutting the lariat rope amid a shower of shot and the deadly fusilade of bullets.

Marshal's indomitable will led him to believe he could establish the dance hall, at the "Last Chance" and make his business a profitable one, even though public sentiment was very unfavorable for the erection of the building, and the purpose for which Marshall intended it to be used. The citizens deemed it unwise to allow Marshal to establish a dance hall and house of prostitution at the "Last Chance." The country now was infested with horse thieves, criminals who had rushed to the border of the Indian Territory to evade the laws of the eastern states. This class of people were the popular element in society at the "Last Chance;" they made the ranch their favorite resort, in laying off, after they had been on a thieving expedition, or had escaped from some frontier town, and succeeded in dodging the officers of the law.

This ranch was known by every horse-thief in the south-west, and they knew the proprietor and his associates were friends and associates of the out-law and desperado.

Marshal's extensive acquaintance with the class of people who were known to frequent the dance hall and visit the houses of prostitution, assured him that his business would be profitable in various ways. He also sold whiskey of the vilest kind to his patrons and friends.

He finally went to Wichita to get lumber to erect the dance hall. In his absence the citizens concluded to prevent him from establishing his house to be filled with the lowest class of prostitutes from the city of Wichita, and the citizens finally agreed that Marshall must live elsewhere or submit to the wishes of the setlers, who wanted peace and quietude to reign through out the vicinity in which they lived.

The time arrived for Marshals return from Wichita and the people were watching with much anxiety for his coming. One morning about ten o'clock, I was sitting in front of a store, in company with Newt Williams conversing about various things, when Williams said Marshal was to return to Caldwell that day, when looking up the road we observed Marshal coming with a load of lumber ; as he approached town I attempted to induce Williams to go into one of the stores out of sight, knowing that if Marshal undertook to carry his threat into execution there would be a shooting scrape then and there. But Mr. Williams fearing no man refused to go out of sight, but when Marshal reached town and arrived in the street opposite to where we sat, Williams arose and said ; "halloo, Marshal, I want to see you," and revolver in hand approached the wagon. Marshal stopped his team as Williams came up. Williams then said, "I understand, Mr. Marshal, you intend to kill me on sight;" having followed Williams toward the wagon, I now saw their was trouble at hand

and so I at once seized William's revolver, and at the same time a citizen on the opposite side of the wagon, seized that of Marshall.

The citizen seemed to get Marshal's revolver without difficulty, but William's clutched his revolver like a vice, and it was by a great effort on my part, that I was enabled to remove it from his hand.

The two men were now face to face unarmed. Marshal being a giant physically, was much more than an equal for Williams, but the dauntless courage of Williams, buoyed up by a spirit of right and backed by public sentiment made him as courageous as a lion. Few words were spoken, but Marshal was given to understand that it would be impossible for him to erect a building and run such a den of iniquity as he proposed in the vicinity of Caldwell.

While Marshal had been government scout he had many narrow escapes, and had shown himself brave behind the six shooter on many occasions, yet perhaps he had never been so completely overawed by public sentiment. There was but one alternative, and that was to return to Wichita with his lumber, and never again be seen in Caldwell. The characteristic bravado having deserted him, the tears of the conquered, unbidden, forced their way down his cheeks. He said if he might be permitted to leave the town, he would never again be seen on the South side of the Ninnescah River.

He turned his team around and drove to the North part of the town, unhitched and fed ; he then spent a few minutes hurriedly in closing up his business as best he could, went to his team and hitched up and was soon on his way to Wichita. In the few minutes allotted him in town, he had sold his ranch interests to Dave Terrill, who run it for some length of time as a ranch and supply store.

Curly Marshal returned to Wichita with his load of lumber, and I presume kept his word sacred, as he was never seen in Caldwell again. He spent several years in Wichita after this, and finally died by disease brought on by his intemperate habits and life of debauchery.

CHAPTER XIII.

Busey Nicholson Arrested on Charge of Stealing Cattle—All Parties in Search of Evidence—Search Proves Futile—Nicholson Liberated at Pond Creek Ranch—His Reported Threat—Proposes for Me to Meet Him at His Camp—Gives Me a Family Cow.

After meeting the parties who had been on the McCarty chase, and receiving from them the intelligence that it would be useless for me to go further as the course of the double murderer was ended. Thus, I was left to infer what I might. But I was led to conclude that the dreadful work was done, and that McCarty was no more. I turned my horse and went back to the ranch and on up to town with the crowd. After we reached town, I found that some of the cattlemen had got out a warrant against Busey Nicholson on the charge of stealing cattle. It had been reported and currently believed that Nicholson had a herd of cattle about forty miles below town, and that most of his herd were stolen stock. Armed with the warrant, and in company with ten or twelve of the cattlemen, most of whom had lost stock, I proceeded to Wild Horse Creek where the stolen cattle were reported to be. Before leaving town I had made the arrest of Nicholson, as he had been stopping in town most of the time. But he seemed anxious to prove his innocence to the cattle owners by going with them and me to where, report said, he was keeping the herd. The cattle owners were also anxious to go and see for themselves, whether or not there was any mistake about the matter.

I have often thought that if evidence conclusive of theft, had been obtained, that I would have been overpowered, and the prisoner taken, and his life sealed then and there. I have always questioned my wisdom in going with my prisoner and these men down into the Territory so far.

We arrived about noon, at the place where the cattle were supposed to be kept, but found no cattle or any signs of where any cattle had been kept. It seems that often men's minds become so inflamed, that they are hasty to decide a man guilty without evidence or reason. About half the crowd were willing to hang the prisoner as a matter of example, without the remotest signs of guilt; while the other half seemed inclined to consider the matter in a much cooler light, and were willing to declare the prisoner "not guilty." But all parties were willing that I should turn the prisoner loose. The prisoner himself insisted that I should release him, as he would then be that far on his road to Texas, where he intended to go. But in my mind I was strongly averse to this proposition, for when men's minds become so inflamed, it is difficult to tell what they will not do, and were I to give him his liberty here, it was a question in my mind whether he would reach Texas in safety, or be over-taken on his journey and either be shot or hung to the nearest tree. I told Nicholson I would not turn him loose here but would take him back with us as far as the Pond Creek Ranch, which was fifteen miles distant. This was a traders ranch located on the Chisholm Cattle Trail, and men who were recognized by the U. S. Government could use it as a trading place; cattle drovers on their drives from Texas to some shipping point in Central Kansas, would lay in a supply of provisions here.

After we had eaten our dinner we started on our way towards home; Nicholson and I were riding a short distance behind the other men, our conversation pertaining in a measure to his arrest, when he suddenly turned to me and asked my reasons for not releasing him. I told him I did not think it would be a wise action on my part, for were I to liberate him here, my fears were that he would not reach Texas, as some of the men had shown a disposition to hang him and I knew them to be men of a determined will, and as an officer of the law, I would do my full duty in defending and protecting a prisoner in my charge; and were I to turn him loose here it would seem almost like placing him in the hands of a mob. I thought he would be safe when we arrived at Pond Creek Ranch and there he could go to Texas in company with some cattle drovers who would likely be there on their return from some shipping point. He would then be safe with his own countrymen, and in all probability they would protect him from further trouble. Nicholson seemed satisfied with my reasons and we rode quietly along, Nicholson conversing pleasantly about his home and friends in the "Star State."

Occasionally a coyote or jack-rabbit would cross our path of destination, at which some of our party would show his skill as a marksman. We proceeded on our travel without further adventure and arrived at Pond Creek Ranch late in the evening; there were a number of cattle drovers there to stay for the night beneath sheltering trees, and after passing the evening in the ranch we went to our respective places to rest. Soon after lying down on our blankets, we were in slumber-land and no doubt each dreaming of his happy by-gone days.

The next morning we were to start for Caldwell and before our departure I released my prisoner, gave him his revolver, and after bidding him good-by and wishing him a safe return to his native state, we started on our journey and arrived in Caldwell safely, and found after our absence of a few days, the people had again become quiet after their excitement over the McCarty tragedy, but how long peace and quietness is to prevail remains to be seen, and we fear it is like the rushing of the tide which recedes for a time, only to start with renewed and greater force.

The following summer, Nicholson came up the trail with cattle, going through Caldwell to Abilene for the purpose of shipping the cattle, which belonged to a cattleman in Texas, Nicholson acting as the boss drover of the herd. These large cattle owners seldom go through with the herd as the drive requires from two to five months traveling, and is attended with much exposure. He usually takes the train after the cattle have arrived at their destination, meeting and shipping them to some eastern cattle market. After the employees are hired for the drive, a boss is selected by the owner and he is given charge of the herd, and is usually known by the name of "boss herder."

After arriving in Caldwell, Nicholson, it was reported, had made threats to the effect that he intended taking my life. I became aware of the threat, and upon meeting Nicholson in town I asked him if he had said he would shoot me and why he had made such a threat. He said if I would come out to camp the next morning early, he would explain the circumstances to me.

Their camping place was about a mile and one-half

north of town, and they were holding the cattle there for a few days for the purpose of resting them and giving them a chance to graze. I hesitated about going to the camp, for I did not know what his intentions were and thought his purpose was not a good one, and this was done to get the advantage of me. I said nothing about it and the next morning I was undecided as to what I had better do; I finally concluded to risk that his intentions were all right, so saddled my horse and rode out to his camp. I had taken the necessary precaution, however, to see that my revolver was in good shooting order. Upon my arrival at camp, I found him eating his breakfast in company with several of the herders and was greeted with the usual good morning. I got off my horse and waited patiently until he had finished eating. Then he got his pony, saddled it and asked me to ride out to the cattle with him. I consented and we rode quietly along talking about everything excepting that which had prompted my being there. There was a man herding the cattle and we rode up to him, Nicholson telling him to go to camp and get his breakfast.

Now, thinks I my time has come, we were there on the open prairie alone, and my thoughts were not very bright, but by his manner I did not consider I was a dead man yet. He asked me to ride with him through the herd and look at the cattle; we were almost through the herd when we came opposite a large Texas cow.

He drew rein and stopped his horse, "now," said he that cow is a gentle, well broke animal and is a good milk cow; you can take her as yours, she is not mine, but I will make it satisfactory with the owner; I have often wondered if I could ever repay your kindness to me, for if there is any one to whom I owe my life it is to you; for had you not been so considerate when I was under your arrest, in all probability, I should not be alive to-day. I have never threatened your life, and I hope we part as friends." I was perfectly surprised and well pleased with his manner. The cow was driven to my place by two of the herders and was all Nicholson represented her to be.

CHAPTER XIV.

Cowboys Carousal—The Unseen Midnight Duel—Attempt to Awaken the Dead—Cost of Burial.
Manner of Interment.

It has been said that "when whikey is in, wisdom is out," and this maxim has too often proved true in the case of the cowboy and herder. How often has whiskey been the cause of their trouble, and while under its poisonous influence they have been prompted to do many things, which had they been in their sober moments and in full control of their senses, would have caused them to shudder with horror. The world to-day is strewn with wrecks of men, who under the North-east storm of intemperance have been driven to the rocks.

Whiskey has been the ruin and downfall of many a promising young man who had left his parental home with father's blessing and mother's prayers, anxious to mingle with the outside world, and to participate in the great struggle of life; how bright were his anticipations for the future, how radiant his hopes, alas, only to be blighted.

Whiskey has caused the best of friends to part in anger who have been continually in each others society for years, and shared each others burdens and whispered words of comfort in times of sorrow and bereavement, and finally when under the influence of the social glass, some disagreement probably of a trivial nature, causes one friend to fall at the hands of the other, and and upon regaining his natural senses he finds he is a murderer, is branded a criminal in the sight of people for taking the life of his dearest friend; he gives way to his grief and is inconsolable.

Would that he could recall the effects of that drink, and say, "it had not been;" ah, it is too late, any act committed, or word spoken yesterday, cannot be buried with the past. We may say, we forgive, but to forget, never. The act has been accomplished, the words have escaped from our lips, and time, alone, can obliterate them from our memory.

In the latter part of June, 1872, a party of about twelve men, with a large herd of cattle from southern Texas, passed Caldwell on the trail, and going about a mile north of town, went into camp.

They arrived at Caldwell in the fore part of the day, and as the cattle were weary from their long tedious drive, the men concluded they would rest one day and night, lay in a supply of provisions and proceed on their journey early the following morning.

In the afternoon some of the men came in to town

leaving the balance of the herders on duty and after buying the necessary articles wanted for their journey onward, the men indulged freely in drinking whiskey and playing cards.

Caldwell is the first town, in which whiskey can be bought, after leaving the state of Texas, consequently the boys get very thirsty for a drink of the ardent spirits, and the result is, as soon as Caldwell is reached, the saloons and grocery stores are visited, and a good supply of wet groceries is bought and often they receive an overdose of that article, called whiskey.

Such was the case of the parties referred too and after remaining in town until night, all returned to their camp, except two of the boys, who were by this time largely under the influence of liquor and were having, to use their expression, "a high old time."

As the evening shades began to draw near, and the twilight hours were rapt in stillness, and the moon beamed forth in her beauty, occasionally the cowboys' yell could be heard to ring out in the clear night air. They kept on drinking and reveling until near the midnight hour, and then they seemed to realize the lateness of the hour and got on their ponies and started for camp.

What scene took place after leaving town, is yet a

mystery and will always remain so, unless a voice from the dead tells the awful story.

Only the twinkling stars of heaven, and the moon in solemn awe, looked down upon the ghastly scene, which took place upon that fateful ride to camp.

Soon after the midnight hour, two shots fired simultaneously, were heard by the herders at camp; nothing was thought of it however, as the presumption was, that the boys were returning from town, and it was not an unusual thing for them to fire their revolvers.

No attention was given to the supposition and all was still again, with nothing to break the stillness, but the occasional lowing of some animal in the herd near by.

When the "wee sma hours" of the morning began to dawn, the cook arose and began making preparations for breakfast. He could see by the light of the coming day, the two forms of the cowboys, lying on the ground a short distance from camp. He supposed they had taken off their saddles, turned their horses loose to graze, and had lain down to sleep. The night had been a beautiful one, and the green grass for a bed and their blankets for a covering made an excellent place for sleeping.

When breakfast was ready, someone called to the

CATTLEMEN AT DINNER.

boys to get up, and as they did not seem to hear, one of the men went to arouse them from their drunken sleep. Can the reader imagine his horror, when upon touching them, found they were dead, each with a bullet through his heart.

As I stated, it was a mystery, and the facts will never be known, but after a close examination of the boys and their surroundings, the men came to this conclusion. After leaving town they became involved in a quarrel, one threatened the other's life, and quick as an instant the other pulled his revolver from its scabbard and holding at the heart of his adversary, pulled the trigger, both boys shooting simultaneously at each other. The result was, that both were shot through the heart, dying instantly.

It was a life for a life, they had died together and met death in a similar manner.

The men hired a man in town to bury the bodies, paying him twenty-five dollars, and the herd was started north. The man made a box out of crude pine boards, put the boys in it, and buried them about eighteen inches under ground. They were denied a decent burial.

Such was the fate of two young men, who, to-day

might have been living honorable lives, had they refrained from taking the first drink, and perhaps, a mother's prayers goes out for them to-day.

CHAPTER XV.

Oliver refuses to pay a discharged employee—I go to Oliver's Camp and serve papers on him—One of Oliver's herders killed—Oliver pays the employee and costs accrued—In pursuit of the murderer—My horses and wagon stolen.

The fame and notoriety which Caldwell and vicinity had won, was not confined to this immediate country. The flow of immigration from the East set in toward the Arkansas River, the largest river in the state, and finding the most beautiful country their eyes had ever rested upon, they stopped built their dug-out on the slope of a ravine, a cottonwood cabin on the hill, prairie grass stable close by and called it home. They were right in calling it home, as what they lacked in social enjoyment they made up in hard labor. With civilization also came horse thieves, hard characters and peril. The claim hunter from Missouri with two fat horses lay on the prairie with the picket ropes tied to his feet to be sure that he would be in sight of his team when the morning sun beamed out across the broad sea of prairie grass and resin weed.

More settlers came as time passed, and with them brought more horses and a bit of extra strong rope, also a double barreled shot-gun. Then there was peace and afterwards a coroner's inquest held over the body cut down from the spreading branches of the mammoth cottonwood tree.

Some guilty one had to suffer at the hands of the Vigilant's Committee, or in other words be used as an example for the good of others. While I do not uphold the method of the Vigilants, yet it is the only way lawlessness can be subdued in a new country. This country was fast assuming a point in which were two factions, the one belonging to the side of the law, the other against civil government. A few settlers took no part in the contests for the right, being on neutral ground; such people attended strictly to their own business, and they were seldom molested.

On the morning of June 5th, 1872, papers were placed in my hands to serve on one Oliver, a cattleman from Texas, who had passed through Caldwell on his way to Abilene to ship cattle from that place. He was then camped about twelve miles North of town on the trail. It seems Oliver had hired a man in Texas to drive cattle to Caldwell, and agreed upon arriving there to pay him in coin.

When Caldwell was reached the employee demanded his pay, and Oliver refused to pay in coin but said he would pay him in currency. The reason why the employee was not satisfied to accept currency instead of coin, was probably owing to the fact that at that time there was a small premium on coin, and as their contract stated that he was to receive coin, and as that was the only kind of money used in Texas, he would accept no other. The employer was willing to pay in coin but as there was no bank at Caldwell, it was impossible to pay the debt in coin, but moved on toward Abilene, when he was stopped by legal papers.

I took the necessary papers, and in company with the employee went to serve them on Oliver. I supposed we would have trouble with Oliver, for the class of men that worked under him were tough looking fellows, and I presume were as tough as they looked. We rode out to Oliver's camp and arrived there at noon; the herd was slowly grazing in the distance and enjoying their noon rest. The cook was getting dinner and the rest of the men were lying under the wagon in the shade, the horses quietly feeding on the green grass near the camp.

I told the employee he had better remain a short distance South of camp, for I did not know but his going to camp would create a disturbance between the parties concerned. He was willing to comply with my wishes, and when we got within sight of the camp he got off his horse, sat upon the grass near it, and prepared to wait until I should return.

When I rode up to the wagon I asked to see Mr. Oliver, and that person stepped from among the rest of the men and came to my side. I read the papers to him and he said, "all right, I will go with you as soon as I have had my dinner." He asked me to stay with them for dinner, and ordered that my horse be taken and fed.

It seemed he had noticed tnat a man was in company with me and had stopped a mile or more from camp, and he asked me if the man on the prairie was not the man he had refused to pay; I told him it was the man that had been under his employ; Oliver told one of the herders to go out and tell the man to come to camp and get his dinner. I objected to this, but finally said I would not oppose it if he would promise me he would not mention their trouble; he consented and said he would not say anything concerning their trouble.

The herder went for the man and they soon returned to the camp together, and to my surprise and satisfaction, their trouble was not mentioned during our stay at the camp or on our journey to Caldwell.

Oliver willingly went back to town with us, and we arrived there late in the afternoon. The man Oliver, could not have trial that evening, as it was too late after we got to town to do anything about the case.

The town was not supplied with a place in which prisoners could be kept, and it became my duty as an officer of the law, to remain with Oliver over night, and to have him in court the following morning. I gave Oliver his freedom to go about town, but kept an eye on him so he could not give a slip and return to his camp. We went to bed about eleven o'clock, and Oliver slept very sound, and I presume I did too, for when I awoke the next morning, it was about sunrise and we both got up and dressed and went and got our breakfast.

About seven o'clock a man came from Oliver's camp and said two of his employees had got into a dispute about something, and their trouble terminated in a fight and the result was, one of the men was killed.

This was new trouble for Oliver and worried him considerably; the affairs at his camp were in a terrible plight. One of his employees dead, another fleeing from justice, with the mark of Cain stamped indelibly upon his brow. Oliver's cattle had no doubt, strayed far from his camp, and all this with his previous trouble with his employee, confused and disturbed his mind wonderfully.

His cattle and the recent trouble at camp, demanded his immediate attention, and consequently he was in great haste to return to his cattle and ascertain the cause of the murder of his employee.

Oliver told me he would pay the money due the man, and also pay all costs that had accrued relative to the suit. This was satisfactory to the man, and after paying him the money and settling the costs, he was allowed to depart in peace.

Oliver went hurriedly to his camp, and after getting the facts concerning the murder, he, in company with others, started in search of the murderer.

The search was long, interesting and fruitless. The murderer eluded their grasp; they traveled in pursuit for some time, and at last utterly worn out from fast riding and exposure, they returned to camp.

The cattle were soon on the trail again and were driven to their destination, by a sadder set of cow-boys, since death had claimed one of their comrades.

Hardly had the words been spoken which liberated Oliver, and sent him to view the death scene at his camp, than a horseman was seen in the distance, riding in full speed and coming towards town. As he neared the little group of bystanders, we saw it was my brother, who was making his home with me, and in his haste, he told us my horses, harness and wagon had been stolen the day before by two unknown men.

The reader may better imagine than have me attempt to describe with what surprise and consternation I received this startling intelligence.

My one great fear had been realized ; I had watched my horses with great care and anxiety, and thus far they eluded the hands of the horse theif.

My horses were my main dependence, and now I was left without a team in a new country, and my condition financially speaking, was such that I could not buy me another team. I had paid $550 for them in Pottowattomie county, previous to my coming here. After paying my little all for them, I could not well stand the loss.

They were large Illinois horses, sorrel in color, and weighing perhaps twelve hundred pounds, and were considered as one among the best teams in Sumner county.

In my next chapter I will relate our experience in chasing the thieves over the western country, and the incidents pertaining to the long, weary chase.

CHAPTER XVI.

My Brother's Story—His Capture and Release—Thirty-five Men Start in Pursuit—Trail of Wagon and Horse Found—A Buffalo Killed—Great Thirst Prevails—Description of the Lariat.

I will relate to the reader as near as possible, the facts obtained from my brother concerning the stealing of my team and wagon.

On the fifth day of June, 1872, my brother took my team and wagon about four o'clock in the afternon, intending to go after a load of hay which we had cut and stacked a couple of miles from home.

When he was about one mile from home, he noticed two horsemen coming in the distance and riding in the direction he had picked out as his intended route. Upon nearing the wagon they stopped and inquired of him where they could find a good crossing on the creek. He was near the creek, on the west side of it, and as he turned his head to show them a fordable place, they drew their revolvers on him and demanded the team and wagon.

He told them they had the advantage of him, but if they would lay off their revolvers and step a hundred yards from the wagon, he would fight them and if they came out victorious they could have the out-fit. They laughed at this idea, and told him they did not propose to fight for it when they could have it without. He knew they had him at a disadvantage and realized that further remonstrance would probably make matters worse, so he submitted to their wishes.

One of the men got into the wagon while the other rode in front, and the one in the wagon told him to follow in the same direction the horseman had taken, which was toward the setting of the sun. They traveled until near midnight, when they stopped and asked him if he had any money with which to buy his breakfast. He told them he did not, and one of them gave him one dollar and told him he might get out of the wagon and return home.

He got out of the wagon and started to retrace his steps toward home; he walked very slowly for the first hundred yards expecting every minute to receive a shot from their revolvers. After he had walked a couple of hundred yards he ran until he came to a ravine, then stopped and listened, to see if he could hear the rattling of the wagon going on in the distance; he waited a few minutes which seemed hours to him, and soon the sound was heard.

There he stood, alone on the plains with no human in hearing, and how lonely and solitary he must have felt. The night was dark and he had only the twinkling stars to light him on his way. In the distance could be heard the howl of the coyote, which sounds very lonely in its nature; their howling made him feel and realize his far away condition. He did not know how far they had traveled before stopping.

He looked in the heavens and saw a bright star in the eastern horizon and used it as a guide by which to travel; he walked in its direction until about three o'clock in the morning, when he came to a ranch kept by Major Andrew Drum, who on learning the circumstances connected with his long walk, told one of his herders to get a horse for him to ride home and he would get hime something to eat. After he had eaten his breakfast, he got on the horse and Mr. Drum generously told him to tell me I could take the horse and ride it to hunt mine. He arrived at home about six o'clock in the morning.

I have mentioned before, that I was in town the time he came home, and as soon as possible he rode into town to tell the news.

The people stood spell bound while he was relating it, and as soon as he finished, about thirty-five men volunteered to go with me and try and find the horses and if possible, catch the thieves.

The ladies of the town began preparing eatables for

us to take with us, and the proprietors of the stores kindly offered us any thing they had in the line of provisions. Mr. C. H. Stone asked me if I was in need of any money; I told him how much I had and he gave me twenty dollars, saying I might find I was short of funds before my return. He also went to the stable and got a horse and saddle for a young man, and told the man if he did not think he would go and stay with me until I found my horses or gave up the chase, he did not want him to go. He said he would stay with me and never murmur ; he kept his resolve and proved to be an excellent companion, and made the arrest of one of the thieves.

We started from town about nine o'clock in the morning, on the day of June the sixth, and went to my house to see if my brother knew the men who had stolen the team. He was lying down on the bed and was sleeping soundly when I called him and told him what I wanted. His long walk during the night together with his loss of sleep had caused him great weariness, and when I roused him he seemed so bewildered that I could not make him understand what I wanted to know. He had told my wife all about it before lying down, and she told us all we wished to know.

When we had traveled but a short distance, a mile perhaps, we saw a man plowing, he wanted to know where we were bound for; we told him our business and he said, "by chinkins you shust take one of mine horses and let me have one of yours, for mine will stand the trip better than your horse," and we traded with him and were soon on our journey as before.

We traveled in the direction my brother said they went, and at noon stopped a few minutes to rest our horses and get something to eat, which was eaten hurriedly and we were again on our travels.

We had not proceeded far until we came to a low, marshy piece of land, and upon examination a wagon track was found, also a large horse track. One of the men asked me if it was my horse's track; I examined it and to my gratification I found it was. I am a blacksmith by trade and I had put the shoes on my horses, hence could easily identify the tracks made by my horses.

We followed the trail of the team and wagon until near the middle of the afternoon. The tracks showed we were not very far behind, and we did not travel very fast as we thought we would need the horses' strength and swiftness during the latter part of the chase. Asa Overall and myself were riding a short distance ahead of the balance of the men, and in nearing a ravine we saw some dark looking objects which we thought were horses; we turned towards the men and motioned for them to remain quietly where they were, while Overall and I would ascertain what it was.

Upon second thought, I concluded to deploy the men and make a charge towards the ravine. When we got nearer we could see what we supposed to be the horses' heads and after getting within one hundred yards from them, two buffaloes jumped up and ran across the prairie land. When we saw it was buffaloes instead of horses, Overall and myself ran after them. We pursued one of them about one-half mile and shot at it and succeeded in killing it. We now had a chance to get some delicious steak, and we cut several nice pieces of meat off the hump, tied it to our saddles, and started towards the men, and after resting our horses a short time, we started on our journey. We could easily follow the wagon track now, and after traveling until about dusk we came to a spring of water.

This was the first water we had seen since noon, and you may presume, how our party relished a drink of the pure sparkling water. We concluded to camp here, as the spring afforded us all the water we wanted, both, for ourselves and horses, and the grass was good here, and would make excellent grazing for our horses.

After lariating our horses we made a fire and prepared something to eat. Perhaps it would be well to explain to the eastern reader, what this word "lariat" means. It is derived from the Spanish word "lariata," and means a lasso, or rope with a noose, and is used by the Spaniards in catching wild horses. In the West on the frontier, the lariat rope is carried by all cowboys or plainsmen, and its principal use to them is simply to make their horses secure, or from straying from camp.

To lariat a horse, using the common term of the words, consists in tieing one end of the lariat rope around its neck and the other end is either tied to the saddle or an iron pin, which is driven into the ground, thus making the horse secure and, also giving it the freedom of roaming and feeding to the extent of the rope. The lariat is also used by cowboys or herders to lasso cattle, horses, or anything which commands the throwing of the rope to gain its possession. Some are very skilled in the use of the lasso, performing feats which seem very difficult.

CHAPTER XVII.

The Anonymous Letter—Provisions Getting Low—The Trail Shows but a Few Days in the Advance—Description of the Buffalo "Wallow"—The Thieves are Spied—Arrest of One Man—Waiting for Smith to Come to Camp—His Appearance and Refusal to Surrender—Smith Receives Several Shots, and Rides for Life.

After selecting a beautiful piece of sward for our couch, we took our saddle blankets for covering and our saddles for pillows. Both horses and riders were weary. At first the horses grazed upon the fresh green pasture, but fatigue more powerful than hunger, soon claimed the mastery, and in a few minutes our little group, horses and men, were wrapped in the sweetest of slumber. One man was left however on detail until midnight, to watch that nothing molested the horses.

Daylight was beginning to make its appearance in the east when our little party began to arouse themselves. Being the first to awake, I arose to a sitting posture and took a hasty survey of our situation. The appearance presented by this sombre looking group of sleepers strongly reminded me of scenes during the war when, after a battle the bodies of the dead had been collected for interment.

Breakfast disposed of, we saddled our horses and waited until it was sufficiently light to see the trail when we would again pursue in search of team, wagon and thieves. We had not long to wait, and soon we were galloping over hill and plain, feeling very much refreshed after our good sleep and rest.

Our provisions were running low; we had started with a sufficient supply to last us several days, when we hoped and expected to overtake the outfit by that time. We knew the thieves could not travel with any speed as long as they kept possession of the wagon. We intended, upon finding the deserted wagon and harness to return to Caldwell, and I would take the stage for Wichita, and there take the train and go to Ft. Larned. I expected to find the thieves at Boyd's Ranch, located about three miles east of Ft. Larned.

I have forgotten to mention this fact, as we were preparing to leave my home, a boy came to me and gave me a letter, stating this news, "Tom Smith, and ——Dalton have stolen your team and their destination will be Boyd's Ranch."

We had traveled a part of two days, and as yet nothing had been seen of the wagon or horses. I did not like to start home without some trace of the thieves, but our provisions was so limited, and now, we had nothing to eat but buffalo meat and coffee. I did not like to leave the trail and go home with nothing to how for our trip, and I told the boys, I would keep in pursuit, if any of them would remain with me. They replied in one chorus that they had come with me to find my team, and they would stay with me as long as I thought it was necessary to continue the search; and after shaking hands, signifying, "I'm with you until the last," we concluded to keep traveling and follow the trail until we found the wagon, and then we could make further arrangements, and offer suggestions as to what would be the best manner to gain possession of the thieves and stolen horses.

I have before stated that I received a letter telling me which way to pursue after the thieves, but as this letter was an anonymous one, I did not know but what it was used as a rule to throw us off from the direct course taken by the thieves, so our squad of thirty-five men divided into several different posses and started in different directions. The party of whom I was the leader, numbered seven men, namely, Ballard Dixon, Asa Overall, Jim McGuire, —Sullivan, —Dobbs and —Franklin. Some of these men are to-day honorable residents of this county, while some are peacefully sleeping the sleep which knows no waking.

The different parties of the squads, after traveling

for several days without any trail or signs of encouragement, returned to their homes.

We followed the trail until noon, and then stopped for a short time and made a fire out of buffalo chips, and proceeded to boil some coffee and fry some buffalo meat. Our horses were lariated to our saddles and were grazing on the green buffalo grass. We were very hungry, and it took a good supply of buffalo meat to satisfy our appetites, and our dinner consisted of buffalo meat alone, save a few swallows of coffee.

When the meat was cooked, we helped ourselves to the mess. One of the men looked at it, and remarked, he would rather starve than to eat meat which had been laid on buffalo chips and cooked. He sat quietly by, while we, old frontiermen, took hold with a relish and cleaned the platter.

We were soon in the saddle again, and traveled until nearly dusk. The country here was full of wolves and buffaloes. We could see great herds of them in the distance and the night air was filled with the howls of the gray wolves. We lariated our horses near camp, and guarded them all night, as we were afraid the wolves would prowl around the camp, and might possibly, scare our horses and cause a stampede, and then we would be left a foot on the broad prairies and many miles from home. I will relate an incident which occurred at supper time. Our supper consisted of buffalo meat, and cooked in the same manner in which it was cooked for our dinner; the man who would rather starve than to eat meat cooked on buffalo chips, had began to get pretty hungry, for he had had nothing to eat since morning. I roasted a nice piece of meat and was sitting near him, and after watching me a few minutes, he said, "George, give me a piece of your meat, I believe I can eat it." I willingly shared it with him, and after that he did not complain of cooking with buffalo chips. We were glad to have anything to eat, and it did not matter to us in what manner it was cooked.

Soon after starting on the following morning, we found where the thieves had camped the day before; from the appearances it had been their noon camp, and this gave us renewed strength and brightened our prospects. At noon, we found where they had killed an antelope, and from the appearances they did not seem to be in any hurry, for the grass had been eaten close to the ground by the horses. We hastened our speed, and were satisfied we would soon overtake them, unless they abandoned the wagon.

We traveled as long as we could see to follow the trail, and between sundown and dusk we stopped for the night on a high prairie land, and we were without water, unless we would use it out of the buffalo wallows. We used it however, and also watered our tired hores at one of the wallows. The wallows are to be found throughout the buffalo country, and are about eight feet in diameter and from six to eighteen inches in depth, and are made by the male buffalo in the spring when challenging a rival. The ground is broken in pawing, and if the challenge is accepted, as it usually is, the combat takes place; after which the one who comes off victorious, occupies the wallow of fresh upturned earth, and finds it gives a cooling sensation to his hot and bleeding sides. During the shedding season, the buffalo resorts to his wallow, to aid in removing the old coat of hair. After a heavy rain these wallows become filled with water, the soil being of such a compact character as to retain it. True, the water is not of the best quality, particularly if the water has been of long standing, and the wallow used by the buffalo as a summer resort, but on the plains a thirsty man or beast will not take these facts into consideration, but will make the best of his situation, and will drink and use the water for cooking purposes.

The night was a cloudy one, and after midnight a slight rain had fallen, which made it difficult to follow the trail. After we had proceeded on our journey about twenty miles, we came to a dim road, and could see by their wagon tracks that we were not far behind the thieves. Some of the men had a pack horse, so we changed our saddles, putting them on the horses we had been leading. I told the men that had no lead horse if they were afraid of hurting their horses, they could ride at their leisure, but we, who had fresh horses would ride faster. They all agreed to stay with me, so we started on a run and rode very rapidly for about five miles, when we came to some good water, and we decided to rest our horses and cook something to eat.

We cooked some buffalo meat, boiled some coffee and after eating our frugal meal, we prepared to proceed on our journey. We rode at a pretty good gait, and about four o'clock in the afternoon we came within sight of the Arkansas River. When we were within one mile and a half of the river, we found the land was broken by hills and ravines. We entered a ravine and halted until we could lay plans to get a view of the country beyond the hill over which the trail crossed and entered the valley.

I finally conceived the idea of tieing a bunch of weeds together and taking them with me and when I was near the top to roll the weeds in front of me, thereby keeping myself from being observed by parties in the valley, in case there should happen to be parties there — and would also afford me the chance to make observations beyond me.

I took my bunch of weeds and started for the hill and soon I lay down and crawled upon my hands and knees, carefully pushing the weeds in my advance. Upon my arrival at the summit of the hill, I was surprised to see a wagon in the valley and three grazing horses near by. I could not determine whether the horses were mine or not, but imagined they were the outfit we were after. I saw the river was very high, past fording, and the outfit could not cross, and neither could we so I went back to the men and told them what I had seen and what my surmises were. We decided to go into camp and a couple of us went to the summit of the hill and watched the movements at the wagon.

After remaining on the hill until dark, we entered a ravine, and followed it in its windings until we were within about one hundred yards from the wagon. We also got so near one of the horses, that we could have taken it very easy, but I did not care to get the horse until we were ready to get the horses, wagon and thieves. We went back to camp and we remained in the ravine until about three o'clock in the morning. By this time our horses were considerably rested and had had an abundance of green feed. We were now ready to attack the party and made our arrangements in this manner—two of the men were to take their horses and were to follow the thieves in case they made a run, the balance of the men were to creep on their hands and knees until we were within a few feet of the wagon.

When all was in readiness we followed the ravine until we were about one hundred yards of the wagon; the men on horseback remained in the ravine, while five of us crawled within about fifty feet of the wagon; The grass was about eighteen inches in height and was wet with dew, wetting our clothing through to our bodies and making us very uncomfortable. The night was damp, and together with our wet clothing and chilled bodies, made us wish morning would soon dawn. We quietly waited for daylight to make its appearance, and the hours seemed to drag slowly by. I kept raising my revolver and looking to see if I could see the sights on it, and at last, after examining it I found I could see well enough to shoot. The men were placed in such positions as to surround the wagon, and when the first signs of the coming day made its appearance, I quickly jumped to my feet and commanded the thieves to surrender. Not a sound was heard in the direction of the wagon; I again gave the command, but I received no response. I began to think there was no one in the wagon, and that the "birds had flown," but I made one more effort and yelled surrender. This time a man's head made its appearance, and I ordered him to lie down, he fell like a log and remained perfectly quiet. I then told him to get up, but to hold his hands above his head while he was getting out of the wagon; he did as I ordered, and I do not think I ever saw a more frightened man than he was. He looked around and saw five men, armed with guns and revolvers. I told him to tell the other man to get up and to hold his hands above his head, the same as he had done. He replied there was no one in the wagon. I told him if he did not tell the man to get up, I would give him a load of buckshot. Asa Overall was standing in such a position, that he could easily see into the wagon, and replied to me, that there was no one in the wagon but the man who had already surrendered. We closely surrounded the wagon and the man began begging for his life. I told him he would not be hurt provided he would answer all questions asked him. I asked him where the other man was; he hesitated a few minutes, then said, he took his horse, swam the river, and went to Boyd's ranch. He also said the other man's name was Tom Smith, and that he had gone to the ranch to get some provisions for them.

Dalton, the prisoner in our possession, was a nice looking young man, about twenty-two years old and less than medium height. He did not bear the looks of a desperado, nor had he the looks of a criminal upon his face. I do not think he was a hardened criminal, as he had not lost his looks of humanity. He was very much frightened and feared he would have to forfeit his life for the crime committed by him.

Two of the men took Dalton to our camp in the ravine, while the balance of us arranged ourselves around the wagon; we hid in the grass and waited for Smith to make his appearance. We were very hungry and thirsty, but did not think it best to go to the camp, so we concluded to wait for Smith. About ten o'clock we saw him in the distance; when he reached the Arkansas River, he took off his coat and swam his horse across the swollen waters, about 400 yards from the wagon ; after he had reached the opposite bank he stopped, put on his coat again and rode slowly toward the wagon, apparently as though his suspicions were aroused, that all was not right at the wagon.

I intended to let him come up to the wagon and then order his surrender, but I saw one of the men was about to rise, when I immediately arose upon my feet and ordered him to surrender. Smith took in the situation at once, and turned his horse rapidly and gave a yell like the Indian on the warpath. As he turned I fired at him with a double barreled shot gun. The shot did not seriously hurt him, as his coat was a very heavy one and the shot did not penetrate through its thickness. We found out however, that two of the buckshot struck him in the right shoulder and several of the shot took effect in his right arm the fine shot did not penetrate through the coat.

As he turned his horse he took from his belt a dirk, and began to use it on his horse instead of a spur, and the horse and rider were soon out of the range of our guns; hence the only way to get " our man" was to give chase and run him down, or trust to Providence to place him in the hands of the law.

In my next chapter I will relate to the reader, our long, weary chase and the final result of our pursuit after the thief.

CHAPTER XVIII.

In pursuit of Tom Smith—Arrival at Fort Larned—A sergeant and six soldiers accompany us to arrest Smith—Description of Boyd's Ranch—The Search—Smith arrested and shackled—Crossing the swollen waters of the Arkansas River—Smith falls from his horse and is nearly drowned—Our Homeward March—Great Hunger Prevails.

As quickly as I could I ran to the wagon and cut the rope which fastened one of my horses which the thieves had stolen, and mounted the horse and in haste proceeded after the thief. The land was a level prairie for about one mile, consequently was greatly to his advantage. My horse was rapidly gaining on his in the race, and I intended when I was near enough, to throw the lariat rope and jerk him from his horse. But in this scheme I failed, for Smith was riding for some hills and there he would have the advantage of me, for he could watch for me, he being concealed under the hill, and upon my approach he could shoot me. I saw what his intentions were, and had about given up the hope of getting him, when I saw one of the men who had been watching the prisoner, coming on the run, and he too saw what Smith's scheme was, and he ran between

Smith and the hills causing Smith to turn his horse in the direction of the river.

I turned and rode back to the wagon to get a saddle leaving Asa Overall in the chase. When I got to the wagon I found one of the men ready to go with me, and as soon as possible we were in the pursuit. Smith swam his horse across the river, and was riding at full speed on the opposite side. We did not stop to consider the perilous act that lay before us, but hastened on until the river bank was reached. I knew my horse to be an excellent swimmer. We did not take the necessary time to go to the ford, but entered the river at the nearest point within our reach. When my horse jumped from the bank into the river we both went under water. I had taken off my hat and held it in one hand, while with the other I took hold of the horn of the saddle. We had no difficulty in crossing to the opposite side, and as soon as we could conveniently, we got off our horses, pulled off our boots and emptied the water out of them, put them on again and immediately started for Fort Larned, which was located about nine miles from the river.

I had a couple of ten dollar bills in my pocket, which of course were wet, so I took them out and partially dried them before we reached our destination. We rode very rapidly until we reached Fort Larned, and we expected to find Smith had arrived there in our advance, but upon making inquiry we could find no one who could give us any information concerning him.

We were very hungry, having had nothing to eat since the evening before, and we concluded to go to the quartermaster's store and buy some provisions. While we were in the store a soldier came in and told the quartermaster that Tom Smith had been on the other side of the river, and had been attacked by a band of Indians; also that he had been shot at twice, one of the charges taking effect in his arm, and his horse had also been shot. He gave us the necessary information we wanted to know, for he further said, that Smith was going to Boyd's ranch to get a fresh horse, and wanted some of the men to go with him and they would give them a fight. We did not pretend to know anything about Tom Smith; but as soon as we had eaten a few bites of lunch set before us, I went to the commanding colonel of the fort and informed him what my mission was, and requested him to let a squad of soldiers accompany me to Boyd's ranch located about three miles East of the Fort.

The colonel sent his orderly to the sergeant with a command to take six soldiers and go with me to make the arrest of Tom Smith. I accompanied the orderly to the sergeant's headquarters, and he soon had six men in readiness. We also had the company of an old scout who expressed a desire to "see the fun." The scout had two fine horses and offered me the services of one of them; I was very much pleased to get a fresh horse, as mine had already begun to show signs of great fatigue.

I looked at the horses, one of them was a beautiful black, while the other was a smooth, sleek sorrel. I suggested that he let me ride the sorrel, but he said I had better take the black one. I did not think he was possessed of the qualities which require great speed, but thought a scout would certainly have good running horses, so I decided to ride the black horse.

When arrangements were made and all were in readiness to start, the scout told me to hold my horse, so that his could run with mine. I made reply that I thought in order to race with him, I would have to use the spur instead of holding my horse back with the rein. He warned me to hold my horse and not let him get the advantage of me, in the start.

No sooner had I taken my seat in the saddle, than my horse was all nerve and dashed away, over the broad prairie on the run; the balance of the men soon gained ground however, and were riding near my side.

When we were about two miles from the ranch, we saw a man leave the ranch, crossing the ravine and go North. Our party halted and I took the scout's field-glass and looked at the man, but could not satisfy myself that it was Smith. But fearing I might be mistaken, I suggested that the sergeant take three soldiers and get the man; and I would take the remaining three soldiers, the scout and the man that came with me from camp, and proceed to Boyd's ranch and search it. As the sergeant and soldiers left us, one of them, a Dutchman, turned to me and said, "sposen he shoots ven we go to arrest him." I told him if the man made any resistance and attempted to shoot, for him to be prepared to defend himself and get the first shot.

Our party arrived at the ranch and rode to the south door, got off our horses, and entered the ranch. We found to all appearances, that the bar-tender was the only person there, and I asked him if he knew where Tom Smith was; he replied in an indifferent manner that he did not know anything about Tom Smith. I told him I knew better, for Tom Smith was seen about noon going in the direction of the ranch, and also, that Smith said he was going to the ranch. The bar-tender said we could search the ranch if we wanted to. Two of the soldiers went to the back door and stood guard, while one remained at the front door. Perhaps it will interest the reader to have a description of the ranch. This ranch was well known throughout the West, and by some it was presumed to be the hiding place for criminals who were being searched for by the law. The ranch was about twenty feet in width and forty feet in length; the bar-room was in the southwest corner, the balance of the west side was partitioned into small rooms in which was a bunk or bed, to accommodate one man. A hall run through the entire building, and the East side was arranged in similar manner to the West. Opposite the bar-room was a room in which was kept saddles and guns.

I told the bar-tender to light a lamp and I would proceed to search the building. The scout took a position in the hall, about midway between the North and South doors. I have forgotten to mention that the building was lighted with only two small windows which were in the South end. The bar-tender got the light, and I told him to go into the room in advance of me; we searched the entire building and our search proved to be a futile effort. As we returned to our soldier friends t the door, they informed me that the soldiers had arrested the horseman and were going in the direction of Fort Larned. The bar-tender offered us a drink of whiskey; I did not indulge, but the other men seemed to think their livers were torpid and needed a tonic and indulged freely, and I presume they felt much better, physically, after drinking of the stimulant.

We got our horses and started for Fort Larned, and overtook the sergeant when we were about one mile from the fort. As I rode near the group I saw they had Tom Smith, or in other words, "our man." I turned to Smith and made this remark, "It seems that time makes a change in circumstances very quick." He said, speaking to the sergeant, "Do you allow a man to talk in such a manner to one whom you have under arrest." The sergeant replied, that he was arrested under my orders, consequently was under my control.

I took the prisoner to the Colonel's office, and when the Colonel came to the door, he said to Smith, "Mr. I think you are caught this time," Smith said I was only a constable and had no authority to arrest him. I showed a commission of Deputy U. S. Marshal, and colonel told Smith I was a U. S. officer and he was in duty bound to help me in making the arrest. He then asked me if I wanted shackles for the prisoner. I replied that I did and he gave me some shackles. I went to the blacksmith and had them properly fastened on Smith. I also obtained a pair of shackles for Dalton. The colonel offered me the services of six soldiers to accompany us on our return to camp, near the Arkansas River; I did not think it was necessary, for our prisoner was securely shackled and I did not think the circumstances required any additional help, other than what our own men were capable of doing. The colonel then asked me if we had a good wagon tongue and a piece of extra strong rope, intimating that if Smith gave us unnecessary trouble, we could put an end to his earthly career by hanging him to the wagon tongue. We were to travel over a prairie country almost devoid of trees, the only trees to be seen were very scattering and grew on the banks of the streams; hence in order to hang Smith, we would probably have to use the wagon tongue, but our intentions was not to commit violence to either of our prisoners, but to take them safely home and give them over to the law, and let them have trial and abide by the decision of the court.

Smith became very indignant over the colonel's jesting remark, and angrily told the colonel he would not dare to use such insulting language in his presence, provided he was free. The colonel replied in a very indifferent tone, saying, "I think when you are a free man again, you will have served a few years in the penitentiary, and I hope you will be capable of following a better trade and one in which you can make a more honorable living than by stealing horses." I presume Smith thought the colonel was "joking on facts," and that it would be best for him to keep still, so he made no reply; but his expression showed a terrible struggle with the inner man, in which to gain the mastery over his rebellious spirit, and quell the rage which was being manifested.

The colonel sent several soldiers to a mound a few miles South of the Fort, ordering them to remain there until we had reached the camp, and if we wanted their assistance we were to signal them and they would lend us a helping hand.

As we were on our way to camp I told Smith if any of his friends came to his rescue and offered to do us any violence, that he could easily quiet the trouble, and if he did not he would most assuredly suffer at our hands; and if necessary we could fight our way through. He said there would be no trouble for there was no one at the ranch. When we were about four miles from camp, Smith's horse was to much exhausted to carry his weight so Franklin let Smith ride his horse; we had to lift him in the saddle and he had to ride side ways, for his feet were shackled together, therefore preventing him from using both stirrups of the saddle. Franklin and I took a "turn about" in riding and we reached the river without any adventure worthy of mention.

The river was yet past fording with a wagon and really it was not safe to cross it on horseback, but we were good swimmers and our horses were, also, so we concluded to risk it and endeavored to cross to the opposite side. The Arkansas River is a very treacherous and swiftly-flowing stream; the shifting sands is a great barrier, and changes the intentions of many who attempt to cross this perilous water, unless they have great inducement or duty which causes immediate attention, and urges them onward across the muddy, foaming waves.

We belonged to that class of people that duty urged onward, and we cautiously entered the rapid running water. Franklin took off his clothing, and tied it securely to the saddle on the horse Smith was riding, and he was going to try and get Smith's horse to swim across to the opposite side. It was too weak however, and we left it standing on the sand bar. My horse was heavily loaded; besides my weight I had a two bushel sack filled with hard tack, twenty pounds of bacon and five pounds of coffee.

As we entered the water I took the bridle reign of the horse Smith was riding, and led it until we got within twenty feet of the opposite bank, when our horses began to whirl. It seems we had unconsciously rode into the whirl, and no sooner had we got within its reach, than our horses began to whirl with the tide and had not the boys come to our assistance with ropes, in all probability we should have been drowned.

The men at camp saw us coming and came down to the river to watch us cross it, and were thoughtful enough to bring a couple of lariat-ropes. When they saw our situation, one threw a lasso over the head of Smith's horse, and the other threw one end of a rope and I put the loop over the horn of my saddle. Then all on the bank lent a helping hand and we were out of our difficulty.

Smith, however came near losing his life; as the horse started out of the whirl, Smith accidently fell backwards, and had not the shackles caught on the horn of the saddle, he would have been buried beneath the bounding billows of the Arkansas river, and thereby escaped the shameless way in which he met his death, a few days after our arrival home. The shackles held him fast and he was dragged out of the water.

It was about six o'clock when we arrived at the camping place of the thieves, and we concluded we would go to our camping place in the ravine. We hitched my horses to the wagon and Smith was helped to get in, and then we started for camp. Upon our arrival there I put the shackles on the boy prisoner, and we prepared supper. We were very hungry and had not eaten any bread for three days, and it tasted very good to our appetites. Our supper consisted of bacon, coffee and hardtack; and we ate very heartily. Smith was very morose during the evening and did not seem inclined to talk.

My companion and I were very tired after our days work; I was feeling jubilant over the fact that we had good success in capturing the thieves, and obtaining my horses again; I imagine I felt as proud as the man whose wife presented him with twin babies; this man had lived the greater part of his life in a new country, and his greatest desire was to see the country populated.

The men who remained at camp during our absence, were to act as guard over the prisoners and horses. We feared an attack might be made by Smith's friends, but we were prepared for an active defense in case they had come to our camp. Each man in our party was armed with a shotgun and two revolvers, and two of the men had a Winchester rifle apiece, and the men were a determined and active set and I believe would have given the friends of Smith a warm reception, had they attempted to molest us.

After lariating our horses securely in our midst, and posting the guards for the night, each one of our little party first satisfying himself that his fire-arms were in good order and loaded, spread his blanket on the ground, and with his saddle for a pillow, the sky unobscured by tent or roof above him, was soon reposing comfortably on the broad bosom of mother earth, where, banishing from the mind as quickly as possible, all visions of horse-thieves, soldiers, etc., sleep soon came to the relief of each, and we, all except the guards, rested as peacefully and comfortably as if at home under our own roofs or that of our mother's home.

The next morning daylight found us in readiness to start for our homes in Caldwell. Our hard tack had to remain behind, however, on account of its not being fit to eat. In crossing the river, it had been thoroughly wet, and the following morning when we went for our hard tack for breakfast, we found it had increased in size and had a powerful smell about it, and it was not facinating either; so we left it "to perish by the roadside," and we started with no provisions, but coffee, salt and bacon.

After riding all day we went into camp early in the evening, as that would be the last watering place for fifteen miles; hence we concluded it would be advisable to camp near a good supply of water. Our supper consisted chiefly of water with a little coffee in it, and a slice of bacon for each.

The next morning as daylight was breaking in the east we proceeded on our journey. We did not see any game, and now our bacon was consumed; we watched thinking we might get a chance to kill a buffalo, but we were unfortunate and did not see a buffalo on our return trip. We traveled all forenoon without any water, and at noon we came to a buffalo " wallow," which furnished us a drink. The water was very muddy and filthy looking, and Smith told us to take a prickly pear leaf and pu it into the water, and it would settle it so we could drink with some satisfaction. We did this and it cleared the water very nicely, all the dirt adhering to the glutionous part of the leaf. I did not drink any of it until Smith drank a good draught of the water, then as it did not seem to injure him, we drank until our thirst was quenched. We made some coffee and rested our horses until about two o'clock, and we rolled out of camp and began traveling over the plains.

CHAPTER XIX.

One of the Thieves Escape—Arrival at a Cattle Camp—Arrival in Caldwell—The Prisoner Given Trial and Pleads Guilty Great Excitement Prevails—Smith on the way to Wellington, to be Confined in Jail—Smith taken from the Constable by a mob—Smith's Body Found Hanging From an Elm Tree—His Manner of Death and Burial.

Those unfortunate persons who have always been accustomed to the easy comforts of civilization, and who have never known what real fatigue or hunger is, cannot realize or appreciate the blissful luxury of a sleep which follows a days ride in the saddle, of half a hundred miles or more. After riding until nearly dark, we selected our camping place on the banks of a small tributary of the Chikaskia River. The water stood in small pools and was very warm for drinking purposes. One of the men dug a hole about eighteen inches deep in the sand, and it was soon filled with much cooler water than we found in the pools.

Our horses were lariated near the wagon and they were soon contentedly grazing on the green verdure. We made some coffee and had to content ourselves as well as we could, without any provisions. The low hanging clouds gave us warning that a rain storm was approaching. We gathered some dry limbs and brush to keep a bright fire throughout the night; the brightness of the fire made our watch more cheerful, and the hours seemed to pass more swiftly.

Ballard Dixon and myself, acted as guards during the fore part of the night. The prisoners had been submissive, and did not give us any uneasiness; yet we concluded it would be safer for us to guard them closely. About midnight Asa Overall and McGuire came to our relief, and said they would stand guard the balance of the night. We were sleepy, tired and hungry.

Relieved from our sense of responsibility, and feeling confident that our comrades would perform their duties as guards, which gave me strong assurance of the prisoners safety, we sought our blankets and were soon rapt in slumber. The night was dark, and the little fire kept by the guards, blazed very brightly, showing the dim outlines of the horses picketed near the wagon. Before I lay down to sleep I looked about me to see if all was well, and being assured that men and prisoners were sleeping, I felt renewed confidence and slept profoundly during the after part of the night.

I had been confident during our traveling with the prisoners, that they would make an effort to secure their liberty should there be the slightest probability of success. Their past career justified me in attributing to them the nerve and daring necessary to accomplish their freedom. How well my presumptions were grounded, the reader will know as this chapter progresses.

At daylight I arose, and the first thing I did was to go to the wagon and see if the prisoners were there; you can imagine my amazement when I saw Dalton had made his escape. I called to the sleeping men and told them of his flight, and then went to see if the horses were safe. I saw that Dalton had taken the precaution to take his own horse, and when I came back to the wagon the men were in a group, discussing the subject which was uppermost in the minds of every one in camp. I listened to the various theories and surmises advanced by them and derived but little encouragement from their expressions. I hastily saddled my horse and started in pursuit of our prisoner, but who was now at liberty and a free man. A slight rain had fallen during the night and as he had escaped after the shower, I could readily follow his trail. I noticed by his trail that he rode away very rapidly and after following the trail for about three miles, and not knowing at what hour he had escaped, I concluded it would be useless for to follow him. We were only a days drive from Caldwell; the men were getting tired and great hunger prevailed, and I was certain we had the thief who had instigated the theft and was probably the cause of Dalton's taking the active part he did in stealing the horses. My opinion was, that we had better let Dalton go and start toward home as quick as possible.

When I returned to camp the men had made some coffee, had the horses harnessed and were ready to "roll on." We found the shackles that Dalton had worn were too large for him, and we supposed he had pulled off his boots, slipped the shackles over them and put his boots on again; thus freeing him provided he could elude the guards, gain his horse and ride away.

We had now been two days without provisions, and were almost ravenous; at times our thirst was so great that we could scarcely talk above a whisper. We had hoped we might kill sufficient game to satisfy our wants, but our efforts proved futile; we traveled onward however, realizing we would soon reach Caldwell where we could obtain the necessaries of life. We drove as fast as our tired horses could endure, and about noon we came to a cattle camp; the cowboys had eaten their dinner and were preparing to drive the cattle on toward their destination. The men remained about a quarter of a mile from the camp, while I went to it to see if we could get something to eat. The boss herder said they had a good supply of provisions, but he did not want so many men to come to his camp. I saw that his suspicions were aroused, and I suppose he thought we were a band of thieves or highwaymen. I showed him my commision as Deputy United States Marshal and made him acquainted with what I had done; he then said to have the men come and get some dinner.

He called the cook and he soon spread before us a beautiful dinner, and it would be needless to add, that we did it justice as far as our ravenous appetites were concerned. I asked the boss what our bill was, and he said "you are welcome to all that you ate, and if he should ever catch the man who had stolen anything from him, he would take the stock and return home, and he would bet that thief would never steal again." We rested about two hours to let our horses graze, then we proceeded on our journey and arrived at Caldwell about four o'clock.

The people were very much surprised when they saw us; I was driving the team, and Smith was riding in the wagon with me. As the men at town saw us coming, they kew it was our outfit before we reached town. My team was well known throughout the country, as a team of their weight was seldom to be seen in the West. The horses were a span of matched sorrels and commanded attention wherever they were to be seen.

As I drove into town the men threw up their hats, and yelled "hurrah for the boys, they have the team and also captured the thief." This caused great excitement, and I feared the prisoner would be taken and hanged. I hurriedly took Smith up the stairs over Thomas' store, and secured the services of some trusty men to guard him. I went immediately to the Justice and told him the facts concerning our capture of Smith, also that the people were manifesting much excitement and indignation over our return, with Smith in our possession.

The Justice told me to send for my brother as quickly as possible, and let Smith have his trial and be taken to Wellington, the county seat, that night; for in case he remained in Caldwell, he had an idea that Smith would be lynched by a mob. My brother was sent for and arrived in a short time ; I went to Smith and asked him if he was ready for trial, he replied that he was. I took him to the office of the Justice, and was followed by a crowd of excited men. When Smith was asked by the Justice if he was ready for trial, he answered in the affirmative, and my brother was called to the witness stand. His evidence was, that Smith was one of the men who came to him on the fifth day of June, and demanded the team and wagon, also that he was commanded, by Smith, to drive the team for them, and that after traveling about twenty miles, he was released from bondage and given one dollar and told to return home. After hearing my brothers testimony, the Justice asked

HENNESSEY, O. T.

Smith if he was guilty of the crime as set forth in the evidence; Smith replied, "I am guilty."

The Justice ordered that I take Smith to Wellington immediately. I was fortunate in getting Mr. I. N. Cooper to let me take his team and wagon; and I secured the services of Perry Haines, Dan Carter and Dr. Black, to accompany us with the prisoner, to Wellington.

We started from Caldwell about sundown. The wagon was supplied with three seats, and two persons sat on each seat. I. N. Cooper and Dr. Black sat on the front seat, Cooper driving the team; Dan Carter and Smith occupied the middle seat, Dan sitting on the right side; leaving the hindmost seat to be occupied by Perry Haines and myself. We did not anticipate any trouble unless the excited crowd should follow us from town, but we would occasionally glance back, and was satisfied we were not followed.

As we were nearing the Chikaskia River, Smith put his hand on Carter's shoulder, and was slyly letting his hand slip near his revolver, which was in a scabbard, in the belt worn around Carter's waist. I happened to glance in that direction, and saw Smith's hand within six inches of Carter's revolver. I caught the revolver before Smith could get it, and told Carter that it was not safe to carry his revolver there, and that I would keep it for him.

Darkness had overtaken us before our arrival at the crossing on the Chikaskia River, known as the stage crossing and located on the claim of J. A. Ryland.

As we neared the river, Smith pointed at the bunch of timber on its banks and the remark, boys I never expect to pass that clump of trees; how well his assertion proved a fact, the reader will learn in the conclusion of this chapter. Whether he had a premonition of his death, I cannot say, but he seemed willing apparently, to meet his death. Before leaving Caldwell he wrote a letter to his brother Charlie, at Wichita, and placed in it forty dollars; telling his brother he did not expect to live long enough to need the money.

When we arrived at the river bottom, we emerged into a road densely grown with tall grass, weeds and brush; as we entered this our team was stopped, and the forms of about one hundred men gathered around the wagon. Some of the men began to feel for the prisoner; the only way to distinguish Smith from our party, was by finding the man who wore the shackles. As they were doing this, Smith raised to his feet and said "I am the man you are after." I told him to sit down and keep quiet; he did as I directed and at that instant a revolver was placed near my face, and the possessor of it told me if I said anything, I would be shot. I pushed the revolver from my face and told the man not to be so careless, as the revolver might go off. He said he was not careless, and if I did not keep quiet it would go off. A couple of men took hold of Smith and he again rose to his feet; I commanded him to sit down. In an instant a double barreled shot gun was placed in such a position that I could easily see the shining barrels, and I was told if I said one word I would be shot. I saw it was useless to try and defend the prisoner, and to keep him from the hands of the mob. I did not care to run any chances for my life, as our party was so outnumbered by the mob, and the shining barrels of the shotgun looked as large as stovepipes, so I concluded it was safer to keep quiet.

Smith was taken from the wagon, and a couple of men took our horses by the reins of the bridle and led them across the river; and then the men informed us that we would be shot if we attempted to cross the river again, until morning.

I concluded the best thing to do was to drive on to Wellington, the county seat of the county, and report to the sheriff. We arrived at Wellington about sunrise and I immediately went to the sheriff's office, and informed him of the probable hanging of Smith by the mob. The sheriff said it reminded him of a circumstance in which a drunken Irishman was left at a station because he was too drunk to get on the cars; his partner, a Paddy, went to the conductor and told him there was a passenger on board, who had been left behind.

We went to the hotel and had our breakfast, and soon the news was spread over town, and the hotel office was filled with people, anxious to learn of the circumstances.

I was very sleepy and tired and concluded to seek a little rest, while the team was eating and resting before they were driven to Caldwell. About ten o'clock I awoke and Mr. Cooper was satisfied that his team was ready for our return home, so we harnessed them to the wagon and started for Caldwell. We arrived at the Chikaskia River about the middle of the afternoon, and found Smith's body hanging to a limb of an elm tree; a Justice and ten or twelve men were holding an inquest over the body. We waited until the verdict was given by the jury, which was to this effect; that Smith was taken from the constable by a gang of desperadoes and horse-thieves and hanged, for fear he would divulge the secrets of the order to which he belonged.

Whether or not they were former associates of Smith, and feared he had divulged their secrets to the officers, or if the hanging was done by a party who had organized themselves into a vigilance committee, remains a mystery to the community. Smith may have recognized some of his former associates, which caused his eagerness to escape from our hands, but the unfortunate man had fallen into the hands of an infuriated mob, and met a shameful death.

Smith was hanged to a tree whose branches spread their protection over the road, and afforded to the weary traveler who had stopped to rest beneath its spreading branches, a cool resting place, sheltering him from the heat of the noonday sun. The limb from which Smith was hung has long since decayed, and to-day the tree may be found, but the limb which supported the body of Smith may be designated by the rough knot in the side of the tree which nature has caused to grow over the place, after the limb had decayed and fallen to the ground.

Smith was buried across the river, almost opposite from the place where he met his death. A large sand hill was selected as his burial place. The grave was dug on the summit of the hill, the body, with the shackles still upon the feet, was placed in an open grave and sand thrown over it, and all that remained of Tom Smith was lost to view.

I suppose if Dalton by chance, heard of Smith's sorrowful death, he felt that he had been very fortunate in making his escape before we reached Caldwell. Dalton had made a confession concerning the stealing of my horses. His story was that Smith had been hired by

Curly Marshall, whom the reader will remember as the proprietor of the "Last Chance" ranch. Smith was to receive twenty dollars when the team was delivered at Boyd's ranch. Smith got Dalton to help him get possession of the horses. Dalton said Smith and himself had secreted themselves on several occasions to get the team, They wanted to get it from my brother, as it was generally known that he did not go armed at any time, consequently they could get the team without any trouble. They watched their chances, and finally succeeded in obtaining possession and the reader knows the result; and the ignominious death of Smith. How sad to think that the small sum of twenty dollars was the cause of the crime, and the sad ending of one of the parties concerned.

I suppose the twenty dollars Smith put in the letter to be sent to his brother, was the money due him at the ranch for stealing the horses.

Dalton said Smith belonged to a large gang of thieves which infested the southwest, who made their living in no other way than by stealing horses. The thieves were scattered throughout the southwest, some staying in Wichita others at Newton, while those who were in this part of the country, made the "Last Chance" ranch their favorite resort; others made Boyd's ranch their headquarters. The country South and West was a vast expanse of land where isolation and wildness brooded. The landscape was unbroken by house or fence, and thus afforded a hiding place for outlaws and criminals who were evading the laws of our great common wealth.

These thieves and desperadoes often visited the frontier towns, and laid in a supply of whiskey. They were often brought before the public minds, by some daring feat they would perform, or by a free use of the six-shooter in which some unfortunate man was the victim.

CHAPTER XX.

Charlie Smith's Threat—The "Last Chance"—The Horse Race—Smith attempts to put his threat into execution—Our new friends—Arrival in Butler County.

A short time after the hanging of Tom Smith by a mob or vigilance committee, a friend of mine came to me and informed me that my life was in danger. It seems Tom Smith's brother Charlie of Wichita, Kansas, had said he was coming to Caldwell, and would kill me on sight. My friend gave me a description of Charlie Smith, and told me I had better be cautious and not let Smith get the advantage of me.

About two months after the conversation with this friend, I sold some hay to the proprietor of the Pole Cat Ranch. This ranch is located on the cattle trail about thirteen miles South of Caldwell, in the Indian Territory, and is named after the stream upon whose banks the ranch is built.

One morning I took my team and wagon and started down the trail with a load of hay for the Pole Cat Ranch. I stopped at the Last Chance Ranch to buy some corn to feed my horses until my return home. A man by the name of Dave Terrill was proprietor of the Last Chance; here I will tell the reader what an odd sign this ranch had for the purpose of advertising its business. Near the front of the log house was a board upon which was printed the "Last Chance." This inscription was in such a position as to be read by those leaving the state, while on the reverse side of the board was the inscription "First Chance," which was to be read by those coming from the Indian Territory. The full meaning was that on going South the ranch was the last chance the traveler had to get a drink of whiskey until the line of Texas was reached, and it also afforded the first chance the weary traveler had encountered since leaving the Lone Star State.

After this slight digression from my story, I will return by saying as I entered the door of the ranch I passed by a man who answered the description given me of Charlie Smith. I watched him very closely and in a few minutes Terrill took me into the back room and asked me if I knew who the man was. I told him I thought it was Tom Smith's brother.

He said I was right and that Smith had arrived there that morning and had made arrangements to stay there a few days. Terrill said Smith took a fifty dollar bill out of his pocket and said he would kill me before he would have to pay that for board.

Terrill asked me if I had a gun; I replied in the negative, and he said I could have his shotgun, that he would load it, and go out of the back door and take it down to the ford of the creek for me. I told him not to load it, but bring the ammunition; also that I wanted buckshot. I got the corn, went to the wagon, (on the way I again passed Smith who was sitting in the door) and drove to the ford where I found Terrill with the gun. I examined it closely and loaded it, and proceeded to Pole Cat Ranch.

I kept a good lookout for Smith, but he failed to put in an appearance. That evening I called at the Last Chance, gave Terrill his gun and again passed Smith. I was satisfied he would not hurt anyone unless he was under the influence of whiskey, and I concluded he had been intoxicated when he threatened my life, and was too cowardly to put his threat into execution, unless he was made courageous by a few drinks of whiskey.

I saw him again in a few days but he said nothing to me, and I began to think it was unnecessary for me to anticipate any trouble, for he seemed wholly unconcerned about the threats he had made. Sly whispers came to my ears concerning his intentions, and I deemed it best to be prepared at all times, so that in the event he did attempt to take my life I would not be taken unawares.

During the summer months I frequently saw Smith;

he made the Last Chance his headquarters, and during his stay in this part of the country he made frequent visits to Wichita and other cities. What his business was we did not know; he was considered a "gentleman of leisure," but before this book closes the reader will read much of his history, and of the disgraceful way in which he met his death.

Sometime in the fall when the leaves were about to clothe themselves with the yellow of autumn, and the flowers which had dotted the prairies with their pretty faces as they peeped from beneath the tall waving grasses, had long since died and had been buried under the trodden turf, I happened to be in town when Smith was drunk, and a friend of mine came to me and warned me of the threat Smith had made on that morning, saying that if I came to town that day he would shoot me. The friend urged me to go home with him and remain at his house for a time, and perhaps Smith would leave town and go to the Last Chance.

I did not like the idea of offering myself as a target in which Smith might show his skill as a marksman, so after considering the proposition my friend had made, I concluded to do as he suggested. I went to his house and after remaining until about ten o'clock, I had no desire to remain longer in secretion, so I went up town and found quite an excitement was raised over a proposed horse race.

In the selection of judges for the race, Smith, Jones, James Short and myself were chosen. Smith and Jones were to judge at one end of the race course, while Short and I were to judge at the other end. After the race was ended, our decision was called for. Jones and I gave our report, but Smith and Short did not say anything concerning the race or what horse had come out victorious.

The crowd dispersed and the majority went to town, some to indulge in a glass of whiskey, and others to loaf and pass the hours in social enjoyment. We had not been in town but a short time, when I heard Jones sing out in clear musical tones, "George can you see?" I looked around and saw Smith coming in the direction where I was standing, with his hand in his pocket. I drew my revolver from the scabbard and held it in my hand near my side. As he came near I heard the click of the hammer of his derringer, as he raised it preparatory to shooting and I watched his arm, and the first movement he gave I intended to shoot him. He approached and stood within a few feet of me for several moments, but the suspense made the moments seem like hours, and I drew a long sigh of relief when he turned and entered a saloon. The saloon proprietor had been watching the proceeding and as they entered the saloon door he said, "you coward why did'nt you shoot him?" Smith's reply was that he only had one load in his derringer, and if it by chance refused fire or if his aim was not true, I would have the drop on him and would cut him to pieces, as I had a dirk in my belt.

He certainly was a mind reader and a good judge of human nature, for my calculations were the same as he represented them to be. I had found a splendid dirk belonging to a cowboy, and I had brought it with me intending to return it to him should I happen to see him in town, and if Smith had shot and missed me I certainly would have used the knife to the best of my ability.

This circumstance led me to believe that my supposition was correct, concerning his cowardice. I was quite sure he would not attempt to put his threats into execution, unless he was favored with the advantage.

He came to live with a family who were living about one half mile from my claim, and it had become generally known that he had threatened my life, and the neighbors were very uneasy concerning my safety, with Smith living on an adjoining claim.

One morning a man with his wife, a wagon, horses and household furniture, drove to my house and wanted to stay with us. He said they had no place to stay and if we would let him live with us a few days, it would be doing a great favor for them. I asked my wife her oppinion about sharing our house with these people, and she seemed to be in favor of giving them the privilege of remaining with us, and remarked that she would be glad to have their company. So it was decided that they should stay with us. We unloaded the wagon and cared for the horses, and before we returned to the house, the man told me why he came to my house. He said it was reported among the neighbors, that Smith had come to live near me so he could have the advantage of me on my trips to town, as he could waylay me and shoot me from ambush. The neighbors had conceived the idea of having him move to my house and accompany me on my trips to town, and perhaps Smith would give up his project.

Everything run along smoothly for a few days; we found the company of our new friends made life very interesting and pleasant for us. Our neighbors were very few and scattering, and my wife yearned for company, and now she was delighted to have these friends with us. The threats Smith had made reached her ears, and she was in continual suspense and anxiety, so great were her fears concerning my safety, that she would scarcely give her consent to have me leave home.

Words of warning and new threats made by Smith, were whispered in my ears, and at last I became tired of being hounded by this ruffian and forbearance had ceased to be a virtue with me, and I asked myself the question, will my manhood allow me to remain quiet, while this man with his threats and insinuations, makes my life one of suspense and peril? No, I would not be classed as a coward or submit to his threats any longer and as it has been said by an illustrious man, "procrastination is the thief of time," hence I concluded I would get my shot gun and horse, and proceed to his stopping place and we would determine which of us could remain here or emigrate to a healthier clime.

I was getting my horse in readiness when our friend came out and asked me where I was going; I replied in an indifferent manner, hardly able to control my agitation, that I was going to take a ride. He noticed I was not in my usual condition of mind, so he entered the house and inquired of my wife, if she knew where I was going. My wife replied that she did not know positively, but her supicions were, that I was going to order Smith to leave the country, and requested him to say nothing to me concerning the matter, and she would try and use her influence to detain me from going on such a perilous errand.

My wife came out where I was and pleaded and begged me not to go ; her words convinced me of the rash step I was about to take, and of the dangerous role I was about to play; and after much hesitation and consideration I told her, her words had probably saved my life, and although many years have passed since she was laid beneath the sod, yet I remember distinctly her pleadings, and I feel like asking God to bless her. Had I gone to see Smith he would have killed me or I should have become a murderer.

My wife's health began to fail; she had not been very well since the Indians had shot Fred Crats, and this, together with the suspense she had endured since Smith had come to Caldwell, sometime in July, had been very trying on her nerves and constitution, and she finally persuaded me to rent our farm to the friends that were living with us, and we moved to Butler County, where my father was living.

After our arrival in Butler County, I received a letter stating Smith's disappearance from Caldwell, and telling me to watch for him. In several days I received more letters concerning Smith's disappearance; I gave them no further thought, as I did not think he would follow me. I destroyed the letters and did not say anything about it to my wife, for I considered the fact, and saw it would disturb her peace of mind and could not add any to her pleasures.

We were well pleased to return to our relatives, old neighbors and many friends, and hoped my wife would be greatly benefited by the change.

CHAPTER XXI.

The Drought of 1874—The Grass Hopper Raid—My Return to Caldwell in 1879—Taking Photographs of the Cowboys—The Appearances and positions assumed.

The mind of the reader will now accompany us in our ramblings, and note the sorrows and misfortunes which attended us. The autumn months were gone and grim Winter has taken their place. It is now January, 1874. The new year is gladly welcomed and hopes are entertained by us, that this will eclipse the preceeding years, in the prosperity and development of our State.

In the Spring of 1874 I rented my father's farm, and took my brother as a co-worker in the business transaction. I made a contract with my brother, giving him a share of all the crops raised on the farm. We had into cultivation one hundred and fourteen acres of land. All productions of the soil grew most luxuriantly, and gave promise of a bountiful harvest. In June, I bought the interest my brother had in the crop, giving him about three hundred dollars for it. Previous to this, the corn we had planted was waving its green guidons of prosperity in the wind, but in the latter part of

June, rain was needed very badly, for the last rain had fallen in May. Vegetation began to wither and die, and the clouds were daily watched by the people, hoping to save the remaining crops, which had up to this time continued to hold their verdure.

The early settlers, like all pioneers were poor, and many of them unaccustomed to rough western life; therefore they were discouraged over the prospect of the coming drought.

The ground became hard and dry, and the heat of the sun's rays parched and dried up the grass and herbage. The streams and water courses were almost devoid of water, in some of the creeks the water had entirely dried up and the cattle were driven for miles in order that they might find a pool in which to quench their great thirst.

The old saying, that "misfortunes never come singly," was verified; the suffering occasioned by the continued drought was increased by the appearance of the grass hoppers. On August the first, the sun was darkened by the clouds of grass hoppers, which came from the north-west, from the Rocky Mountain region, miles in width and scores of miles long.

The greater part of these pests passed on, but the small portion of them that did alight, almost covered the earth, in some places making drifts from two to four inches deep. Then the remaining vegetation disappeared, and every green thing shared the same fate, and disappeared from the face of the earth.

The crops did not diminish their appetites and the leaves and twigs were eaten from the trees and shrubs. Fields and gardens were devastated and left bare. The earliest planted corn was the only crop the farmers harvested, and it was thought by some that this was not an act of mercy by the grasshoppers, but a necessity compelled them to leave it, for it was too tough for their mastication. The plague continued through the summer and fall. The continuation of the drought caused want, much suffering and distress among the people. Immigration began to be reversed, and many who were able financially left the country; those who would not, and could not leave, were compelled to appeal to the charitable public for aid. Our sister states responded generously, and car loads of corn, flour, potatoes and clothing were sent to the relief of the almost famishing families.

On the fifth day of September, the first rain since May, was gladly welcomed by the people. The summer had been an uncommon hot and dry one, and in the fall many were stricken with death, and the ague, commonly called chills and fever, was a prevailing desease throughout the country.

In September, the illness of my wife terminated in her death, and I was left prostrated with grief with four motherless children, the youngest a babe six months old. In my hours of affliction, my sister kindly came to my aid and took my family of little children home with her, and filled a mother's place in caring for them. She kept them about two months, when her health began to fail, and finally she told me she could no longer keep the children for her health was not sufficient to care for so large a family of little ones. I told her if she could keep them a short time I would try to find a home for them, or make arrangements to bring them home. This she willingly did, and I was perplexed and undecided what to do. I was placed in very straitened circumstances and could not pay money for their keeping and I was not competent to take them home, and alone share the responsibility of filling the place vacated by the death of their mother, and give them the attention and care which children need in their early youth.

After giving due consideration to my conflicting thoughts, realizing my situation, I thought the best thing for me to do was to get married and then I could have my children at home.

I will not weary the reader by relating the experience I had in finding a suitable companion, or of my courtship and marriage; suffice it to say, I found a most admirable woman and we were "made one," and on our way to our home stopped at my sisters and got the children.

I was well acquainted with the lady I married, and my suppositions were that she would make an excellent wife and mother, and since living with her for fifteen years I have realized that she possessed excellent qualities and filled the place of a mother in my home.

The following spring I again rented my father's farm and the season was a very favorable one, consequently I reaped a very bountiful harvest for my labor. In the mean time I traded my land near Caldwell for a farm in Missouri. I did not care to change my location, so made another trade; this time I obtained land in Butler county.

Soon after trading for my Butler county farm I took possession of it and we were living quite comfortably and laying up a few pennies for old age.

My health began to fail and I was advised by

AUTHOR'S RESIDENCE, CALDWELL, KAS., 1881.

the physicians to change my locality, and said in all probability I could be greatly benefited by the climate of Colorado. Acting upon their advice I traded for land in Colorado, and fully intended to go to that healthful climate; but circumstances over which I had no control prevented my going on my proposed trip.

Late in the fall I purchased a daguerreo car and started west, traveling through small towns, stopping several days in a place to take photographs, and in this method I paid my traveling expenses.

I traveled through the winter months and finally reached Caldwell in April, 1879. I opened out a photograph gallery and did a profitable business among the "cowboys," who were anxious to get a photograph of themselves in "cowboy" style to send to their friends living in the eastern states. Some of their styles were novel in the extreme. Some of the boys would wear a large sombrero and have several revolvers hanging from a belt worn around their waist, others would be represented in leather leggins, two large Texas spurs on their boots, revolvers in hand and looking as much like a desperado as their custom and appearance would admit. Often I would be required to take a photograph of a "cowboy" and his horse; some of the attitudes were very ludicrous and displayed wonderful equestrianism; while some of their positions has a dignified appearance, yet the observer would notice the dignity was assumed for the time being.

After remaining in Caldwell a month I received the appointment of Constable to fill a vacancy, and in the spring election I was elected to fill that office.

I found that during my absence from Caldwell many changes had taken place, and in the meantime Caldwell had not stood still, but kept on enlarging her borders and taking in every thing that came within her reach.

The seasons had been favorable for several years previous and immigration began to flow west as it had in the early seventies. The railroad had now reached Wichita, sixty miles north-east of Caldwell, and the farmers found a ready market for grain. Cattle were shipped from Wichita instead of from Abilene.

The Indian territory was now the home of the "cowboy," and this vast grazing ground was filled with cattle. The Texas cattle and ranch interests took on vast proportions, and the "cowboy" of yesterday finds himself rated in commercial circles at twenty-five, fifty, one hundred and two hundred thousand dollars.

More permanent and costly homes are being built, and a new Kansas is being developed, and the drought and grass hopper raids are a thing of the past.

CHAPTER XXII.

A party in search of horse thieves—Listening to the tales of an old buffalo hunter—Arrival at Kiowa—A man killed by Indians—A log house used as a fort—Twenty-one Indians killed by one man—Reinforcements, and preparations made to follow the Indians.

In the latter part of August 1872, I received a letter from a party at Wichita, Kansas, stating that forty-four horses had been stolen from some employees of the railroad company, and also some government horses from Fort Larned and the report was that five thieves had stolen the entire outfit, and were traveling south and would probably take the horses to Texas.

A party of eight men were organized to go with me to search for the thieves and horses. Several of us had conceived the idea of going on a buffalo hunt and now we concluded to take a wagon with supplies sufficient to last us several weeks, also a good supply of ammunition and in case of a failure to capture the thieves, we would take our proposed hunt.

The first day we travelled about thirty-five miles, and went into camp near a spring of water. We found we were very tired and hungry, for we had not stopped to get anything to eat since morning. Our camp fire was built and preparations were made to get our supper.

We had, in our company, several men who might be called "tenderfeet." They had recently come from the east and were not accustomed to rough western life, and especially as to the exposures of the camper and buffalo hunter.

We old frontiersmen were willing they should be initiated in a romantic way, and learn as much as possible of life on the frontier, and be able to fully understand and appreciate this life to its fullest extent, they must take "some bitter with the sweet," and must not complain if the larger proportion of it is the bitter.

Our crew was a jolly set of men and the first night we enjoyed ourselves hugely. After supper we listened to the tales told by an old buffalo hunter, of adventures among the Indians, and learned much of the art of killing the buffalo. Perhaps many of the readers will presume there is no art in being a successful buffalo hunter, but in this you would be mistaken, for it is certainly an accomplishment to be successful nine times out of ten in causing these monarchs of the plains to fall from a shot fired from your carbine.

They are difficult to kill by shooting them in the head, as the form of the fore-part of the head is oval shaped and will glance a ball, and then their forehead is covered with such a thick mass of hair and so closely matted, that it is seldom a bullet penetrates through its thickness, consequently the experienced hunter never shoots at the forehead, but aims just behind the shoulder, the shot generally taking effect in the lungs, which either causes its death or disables it until a ball can be planted into the heart.

After digressing from the principal part of my story I will now resume to the "stopping place" and endeavor to interest the reader by relating the many facts which occured during our trip.

The next morning we were in our saddles, and on our way, ready and eager for what might be in store for us. The general direction taken by us was nearly due west. We were riding along without interruption or incident to disturb our progress, until we had traveled ten miles perhaps, when we suddenly came upon some government soldiers who were on their way from Fort Reno to Fort Larned and we made inquiry of them as to whether they had seen any men with horses travelling south-west. They replied in the negative. We were now about five miles east of Kiowa, this was a small supply ranch and located on the territory line about fifty-five miles west of Caldwell.

We arrived at Kiowa about nine o'clock in the

morning, and to our amazement found but two remaining families in the ranch and one of the men, Mosley by name, had been killed by the Indians. Upon inquiry we found that the northern Cheyennes had passed through that country about daylight on their way from the Indian territory to the reservation in the northern territories, recently occupied by that tribe, and in traveling they killed or would take possession of all stock found on their route, and also killed a number of persons and caused much suffering, many homes were devastated and houses and stables burned by these "Government Pets."

The women and children were very much frightened and one of the children, a boy about six years of age, had handled one of the guns to good advantage when the Indians attacked the house that morning.

The families had assembled together in a log house, and soon after Mosley was shot, Leonard realized that he must fight to the bitter end, and contrived a plan of getting the drop on the Indians, by climbing upon the joists of the house and picking out one of the pieces of wood, used as chinking between the logs, and by putting his gun through this opening he could use it to a great advantage. His wife staid below and loaded the guns for him to shoot, and how well he succeeded in keeping them at bay and their final hasty departure was told to me by an Indian trader; he said the Indians told him Leonard killed twenty-one Indians, and that all his shots were true and each Indian was shot in the head.

A short time after this we found the dead body of an Indian, and, as the trader had said, he was shot through the head, the charge taking effect just above the right eye.

While we were thus engaged in conversation about the murderous work of the savages, five men came up to us and informed us that they were Kansas State Militia men. The man claiming to be lieutenant, was acquainted with W. B. King, my former partner, and an old buffalo hunter. King introduced the lieutenant to me, and upon the information given him, by King, that I was a Deputy U. S. Marshal, I observed a change of countenance in the man, and also noted his actions were those of a man who was not at ease; and his conversation ceased entirely.

It was now about noon, and after eating our dinner we held council to know what was best to do. The Indians had gone into camp about two miles from Kiowa, and their tents could be plainly seen by climbing to the top of the house. They had chosen as their camping place, a fine location in the Horse Shoe bend of the Medicine Lodge river.

After our consultation it was considered by all that we had better remain where we were until night, and for the men to take their families to some canyon for safety, and we would go to the Indian camp and surround it. Their location was greatly to our advantage, the banks of the river, where the Indians were, was about four feet high, and it was about two hundred yards across the bend. Our intentions were to surround the camp by remaining under the banks, and use this as a fortification, and by firing upon them we presumed it would not be a difficult matter to drive them from their camps and ponies.

When we made it known to the families what our best judgement was and what our intentions were, we found they were very much opposed to it. Their plan was, for a couple of us to go and get the soldiers to come to their aid and for those remaining to secrete themselves in the houses and be prepared in case another attack was made by the Indians.

It was finally decided that the plan was a favorable one, and Nute Williams and myself were selected to go for help. We saddled our horses and were soon on our journey. After traveling about five miles we came to the Cedar Mountains; we rode to the top of them and by looking through our field glass, we could see the Indians, and by watching them a few minutes, we saw they were taking down their wigwams and preparing to move; we remained on the mountain until we saw them start in a south-west direction, and after they had traveled as far as the eye could see, we were satisfied they would not molest our new found friends again.

Our horses were very much fatigued and we concluded to remain where we were until morning. We went down to the canyon and there, in the valley, found excellent grazing for our horses, and also a good camping place, with plenty of cedar limbs to build a fire.

At dawn on the following day, we were ready for our journey to Kiowa and upon our arrival we related what had been seen by us. Upon receiving this information the party were in favor of following the Indians and attacking them, with the exception of Nute Williams, King and myself; our reasons were that they had now one night's travel in advance of us and we did not consider it a wise project to interfere with them, but as the majority of the party were in favor of pursuing them, we finally agreed, but very reluctantly, to accompany them.

We found the few scattering people were willing to join us in an enterprise which promised to afford them an opportunity to visit just punishment upon their enemies.

The frontiersmen of the Kansas border, stirred up

INDIAN CAMP AT KIOWA.

by the numerous massacres committed in their midst by the savages, favored our project, and we made arrangements to start immediately.

CHAPTER XXIII.

In pursuit of the Indians—The appearance of the Lockwood family on the trip—The "Arkansaw Traveler"—The sound of the coming buffalo—Keeping the buffalo from ruining the corn field—Strange actions of the State Militia men.

No person who has not lived on the frontier and in an Indian country, can correctly realize or thoroughly appreciate the extent to which a frontiersman becomes familiar with, and apparently indifferent to the accustomed dangers which surround him on every side. It is but another verification of the truth of the old saying, "familarity breeds contempt."

After the necessary preparations were made, we proceeded on our journey. Our party would have been a good sketch for the artist pen. I was riding near the head of the column of marching men, and as I would occasionally glance backward toward the line of gallant men, it was with much difficulty that I could refrain from laughing out loud. The sight was equal to any circus parade I have ever seen. Old Mr. Lockwood was thus represented; he rode on a mule without a saddle, or, to use a common expression, he rode "bareback;" on his head was a cap made of a coon skin; he wore a pair of Indian moccasins on his feet; his "weepen" was an old musket and had the appearance of taking an active part in the Revolutionary war. One of the Lockwood boys was armed with a muzzle loading rifle, and the other, a double barreled shot gun, with only one lock on it; both of the boys were bare headed, and were without shoes or boots and like the old man Lockwood, they rode "barebacked." They were very anxious to get started and their manner was very amusing. I imagined they would be equally as glad to get home again, especially if there would be any fast riding to do, or if the Indians should give us a chase. We wanted them to get all the fun there was in it, as we rode rapidly for about five miles. Our "bareback" friends seemed to enjoy the ride very much, and as we advanced in the distance they could be noticed in riding "sideways." We kept riding at pretty good speed until about noon, when we stopped and went into camp. We were now about seventeen miles from Kiowa.

After we had drank a cup of coffee, and were comparitively rested after our ride, we decided it was useless to try to follow the Indians, as we had now traveled one half day and had seen nothing to encourage us in our pursuit, so we turned our faces in the direction of Kiowa.

The "bareback" riders did not seem to be in as much haste as they had been before dinner, and after traveling a little in the advance of them we stopped and waited until they overtook us; then we told them they must ride with us, as there was danger in remaining so far behind us for some of the Indians may possibly have remained and were hunting buffalo, and in case they should happed to see them, they would, in all probability, be scalped by the savages. They rode near us for a little while, and it was soon noticed they began to lag behind again; finally they got off their mules and walked. To have a little amusement one of the men asked them why they did not ride and keep up with the crowd. One of them replied: "We would as leave be killed by the Indians as to be split into by a mule." This created a laugh, and as we knew there was no danger of being "killed by the Indians" we rode on and left them, but was soon overtaken by the old man, who said he "could stay with us, for he was as tough as the mules back, and if the mule could stand it to be rode barebacked, he could stand to ride it so, as he was the oldest." We indulged in another hearty laugh and lessened our speed, for, at our rate of rapid riding, there was certainly great danger of the old man getting "split into" before we would reach our destination.

We arrived at Leonard's ranch about five o'clock in the afternoon. After supper we talked of starting on the morrow in search of the thieves, but some of the party were not favorable towards going any farther as we had been delayed for several days, and in all probability, the thieves had nearly reached Texas, and, after a lengthy conversation, we concluded to give up the chase, and then after letting our horses rest for a couple of days, we would hunt buffalo, and return to Caldwell.

Our new friends, the Lockwood's, told us they had not seen any buffalo for three or four weeks, and we would have to go some distance west to find them.

Old man Lockwood lived about one-half mile south of Leonard's ranch, and he was an oddity to be sure. He had ten children and had formerly come from Arkansas, and in my mind, the old gentleman and the farmer represented in the "Arkansaw Traveler" are very similar persons in appearances. The song entitled "The Arkansaw Traveler," was a favorite piece of music in the home of the Lockwood's. The old man and his family were living on a claim, and he had planted a considerable part of his land to corn, and the crop gave every evidence of a bountiful yield of corn in the coming Fall.

We camped at Leonard's the following night and I

shared my blanket with King; our bed was made on the green, mossy, buffalo grass and after lying down we were soon in the land of dreams. It was just that uncertain period between darkness and daylight on the following morning, and I was lying enjoying the perfect repose which only camp life offers, when I was startled by a shake from the hands of King; he told me to put my ear to the ground and I could hear the sound of the coming buffalo. I did so, and I could distinctly hear the sound, and the very earth seemed to quiver beneath their tread. King said they were probably about three miles away, and that their course was in the same direction taken by us on our Indian chase.

When the sun was about one hour high we looked in the distant west and saw a moving cloud of dark objects, which, upon closer observation as they came nearer to our camp we could easily determine what the black looking objects were. It was the largest herd of buffalo I had ever seen, and they probably numbered by the thousands.

When we saw their course was towards Lockwood's claim we thought we would mount our horses and endeavor to keep these huge monsters out of the corn field.

In traveling, if not grazing or alarmed, the buffalo usually move in single file, the column generally headed by the champion of the herd, who is not only familiar with the topegraphy of the country, but whose championship in the contests entitles him to become the the leader of the herd. He maintains this leadership only so long as his strength and courage enable him to remain the successful champion in the many contests he is called upon to maintain.

In traveling they follow their leader "through thick and thin," to use a common expression, and it is useless to attempt to change their course after the leader has advanced in the chosen direction.

We took our guns and went to the corn field and succeeded in turning their leader in his course. We shot and killed a number of them as they would pass us on their travels, and before a great while had a good supply; in fact we had a sufficient amount to load our wagon, and it would be unnecessary to go further on a "buffalo hunt" as we could have all we wanted without hunting for them.

It was about noon before the last buffalo passed the field, and after they got beyond the hill, located about one mile east of the Leonard ranch, they stopped traveling and began grazing quietly along with as much ease as though they were thousands of miles from human habitation.

We were well pleased with our mornings work, and

concluded to go to the ranch and get dinner, and then we would remove the hides from the buffalo slain by us and select the pieces of meat we wished to take home with us, load up our wagons, and prepare to start towards home the following morning.

While one of our party was getting dinner, one of the party rode out to the dead buffalo and cut a fine piece of delicious steak from the loin, and we enjoyed our dinner very much. It was the first time our "tender foot" friends had tasted buffalo meat, and they relished it exceedingly well.

The five men who claimed to be State Milita men were still with us, and after our dinner was over I noticed they had congregated together in a group and seemed to be talking in undertones, and the man who claimed to be a lieutenant, had been intently watching our movements for several days.

Soon after this incident King and I went to water our horses and prepare them to ride to the buffalo herd in company with the other men of our original party, and in conversation with King I told him I did not think the men were Militia men, but my fears were that they belonged to a set of horse thieves. The horses they were riding were above an average sized horse, and I could not help but think that they were stolen stock.

King laughed at my apprehension and said I must be mistaken, for he knew the man claiming to be the lieutenant and he did not think he was of that character. The reader will hear of them in my next chapter, and of how my fears were confirmed.

CHAPTER XXIV.

The Colonel and Mrs. Leonard Shoot a Buffalo—The Wounded Buffalo Gives Them a Chase—A Laughable Episode-The Return to Caldwell—Lockwood's Mules are Stolen—Arrival in Wichita in Search of the Thieves—An Exciting Race After the Thief—Capture of Thieves and They Receive Sentence.

In opening this chapter I must refer to incidents in the preceding one, and the reader will go with me in imagination to the scenes which took place during our dinner hour, and at a time when we were saddling our horses, preparatory to going to the buffalo herd. The herd was on the opposite side of the Medicine Lodge River, and was about one mile from the ranch which is located on the east side of the river; consequently the buffalo were on the west side of the ranch and also across the river. Here I witnessed one of the most laughable incidents which has ever occured within my knowledge, and yet it was occasioned with much danger to the parties concerned, and after the danger had passed we enjoyed the sport with the originators of it.

As we prepared to go to the herd, Colonel Connoble, one of our party from Caldwell, asked a lady if she would like to ride out to the herd and if she would he would unload our spring wagon, and he would drive out with the team. She replied that she would like to see the buffalo, so it was settled that they should go in the spring wagon. The Colonel unloaded the spring wagon and with a lady on the seat with him, and with his trusty gun by his side, they proceeded to the top of the hill and there they could get a good view; also a splendid shot at the loitering buffalo.

After gaining the summit of the hill they noticed a large, shaggy fellow near them, and the Colonel drew his gun and shot it. To his surprise and gratification the buffalo fell and to all appearances was dead. The Colonel was very much pleased with his good luck, and was telling the lady he "had always been considered a good shot." As he drove to his game he was feeling very jubilant and made the lady think she was highly honored to have the privilege of riding with "Col. Connoble."

When he had driven within fifty yards of the buffalo, it suddenly jumped up and started for them on the run. The Colonel turned the horses as quickly as he could, and the first cut with the whip the horses received, Mrs. Leonard tumbled backwards into the spring wagon, her feet were resting on the spring seat, and in her efforts to regain her position, her feet were kicking the

Colonel in the back, while he was bent in the shape of of a rainbow striking the horses at every jump.

For about three quarters of a mile the country was a level prairie, and the race was an even one; the Colonel's hat had fallen off his head and his iron grey locks were flying in the wind. He did not take the time to glance backward to see if the enemy was following him, but looked onward and had his thoughts on every thing except the woman bumping up and down in the back part of the wagon.

The buffalo began to gain on the horses, and had either of the horses stumbled and fell, the buffalo would have been the victor, and the spoils would certainly have belonged to him.

We had been watching the race, and now as the buffalo was gaining ground we saw something must be done, and done quickly, too, or the wagon was liable to be upset by the angry antagonist. We started and our intentions were to run between the buffalo and the wagon, thereby changing his course, as he was sure to attack the first enemy seen. We run our horses between the fleeing party and the pursuer, and as I passed the buffalo I drew my gun and fired a shot at him, and we finally killed it.

The Colonel did not stop but supposed the angry buffalo was in pursuit of him, and he kept running the team up hill and down; and when the banks of the river was reached he dashed on, splashed through the water and did not draw rein until the ranch door was reached. All this time the lady was lying in the back part of the wagon and was laughing to her hearts content.

We followed in the direction taken by them and arrived at the ranch soon after they had reached it. We indulged in a good laugh over their funny escapade, and the lady told the Colonel she did not care to go on a hunting expedition with him again, and that he should have known better than to drive up to a buffalo until he was certain it was dead. The shot fired by Colonel Connoble only stunned the buffalo for a few minutes and had maddened it. The buffalo are very vicious when they are wounded and will always attack the enemy unless they happen to be shot in the loins, disabling them in such a manner as to interfere with their locomotion.

Breakfasting before the stars bade us good night, or rather good morning, daylight found us ready for our homeward march towards Caldwell. I will not weary the reader by describing our journey, but will say we did not meet with any adventure or incidents worthy of mention.

About six weeks after our return home the old man

Lockwood came to Caldwell, and informed me that four of his mules had been stolen, and his suppositions were that they had been taken to Wichita. I engaged the services of Neut Williams to accompany me in search for the thieves and stolen property.

We left Caldwell on the evening of the same day I received the warrant, and after traveling all night we arrived in Wichita the next morning about daylight. The night was a beautiful one and the moon shone her mellow light over hill and dale, and seemed to cheer us on our way. The distance to Wichita was about sixty miles and we had to ride at a rapid gait in order to arrive there and search the stables before time for feeding the horses. We had an idea the thieves had either sold the stock or would start early for some other town in which they could dispose of the mules at a bargain.

Soon after our arrival there we made inquiry concerning the stock, and then went to the several livery stables to look for the stock we were hunting. Finally after we had wasted considerable time in looking through the barns we went to West Wichita and there upon entering a feed stable we noticed a man run out of the back door. We gave pursuit and fired several shots at him, but he made good use of his lower extremities and soon reached the Arkansas river. This did not check him but he jumped into the water and was soon on the other side, then in his flight he started down the river and was soon lost from our view.

We could not ford the river on our horses so we hurriedly ran to the bridge, a few yards above us, and we were soon on his trail. We followed the river bank for several hundred yards and finally found him in a brush heap, where he supposed he was hidden from sight. We arrested him and took him back to Wichita and put a guard over him, then went in search of the other thief. We searched a number of houses where we supposed he would be found and failing to meet with success we went into a saloon and there found "our man." The man proved to be lieutenant, and one of the men represented themselves as state militia men.

We took them to the jail for safe keeping and then searched for the mules; by this time old Mr. Lockwood was with us and he was very much pleased with our success so far, and when we found the mules he was happy.

Court was in session in Wichita and the men were given trial and found guilty and sentenced to the penitentiary; one for the term of five years and the other for seven years. The curtain closed upon the scene and the prisoners were left to meet the fate the judge had decreed to be theirs, and I presume in after years they realized the truth of the familiar saying, "The way of the transgressor is hard."

A short time after this incident a U. S. marshall went to Texas in search of the thieves of whom we were in pursuit when we reached Kiowa and there found the ill fated families and the murderous Cheyenne Indians of which we gave mention of in a preceding chapter.

The stolen horses were found but the thieves had escaped, and no clue could be found which would lead to their capture. Two of them were arrested by me and assistant. These men were the same whom the reader will remember as having received their sentence at Wichita for stealing Lockwoods mules.

The men claiming to be militia men were none other than a band of thieves and they had in their possession at the time we were at the Leonard ranch, horses which had been stolen from a man living near Belle Plaine, Kansas. Some time previous I had had a description of the horses and was offered a reward for the capture of the thieves and horses.

The horses were probably sent to Texas or taken there by three of the party, while the "Lieutenant" and one of the men stood near the vicinity of the Leonard ranch watching a chance to steal Mr. Lockwood's mules. The much wished for opportunity came, the mules were stolen and the reader has learned of the result and the sentence of the "Lieutenant" and the "state militia" men.

CHAPTER XXV.

Indians on the war path—The frightened settlers flee to places of safety—Fortifications built at Caldwell—Men organized into a force to protect the town—Four freighters killed—The finding of Pat Hennesey's body by W. E. Mallaley—
The rude funeral.

In opening this chapter the reader must turn backward with me to the year of 1874 and to the month of July, the fifteenth.

The year 1874 was a most disastrous one to Kansas at large, but doubly fatal to Sumner county. During the years of 1872 and 1873, thousands after thousands of immigrants were attracted thither by our delightful climate and magnificent soil, so that by the spring of 1874 there were no less than 8,000 actual settlers within the county limits.

In the preceding chapter I have related to the reader facts concerning the drought and the grasshopper raid, and have, briefly, pictured the suffering and distress which was occasioned by these visitations and now, to add to the already stricken people, rumors were afloat that the Indians were making trouble at Fort Reno. This is a military fort, kept up by the government and is located about one hundred and ten miles south of Caldwell, in the Indian Territory. The northern Cheyenne Indians had threatened an outbreak, and rumors had been afloat all spring and had occasioned much uneasiness among those, who pictured in their imagination, the savage arrayed in war paint and feathers.

On July the 15th report came to Caldwell, that two freighters had been murdered, and the third one burned alive by the Indians, a few miles south of Caldwell.

This startling news created quite an excitement on the border and many were very much frightened and caused much anxiety for the frontiersmen concerning the safety of their families.

On the evening of July 15th, Agent J. D. Miles arrived in Caldwell from Fort Reno. He came with his family, driving as fast as his horse could run, and halted in Caldwell long enough to say the reports were true, that the Indians were on the warpath and that he and his wife were fleeing for their lives.

The wildest consternation prevailed among the people. A few old soldiers organized themselves in a body and prepared to protect the town. Scouts scoured the southern border. Many were the hearts that sank when they heard the shot fired from a gun or revolver, and the warning cry, "The Indians are on the warpath, run for your lives," awakened them from their slumbers.

Couriers went from house to house and from town to town carrying the dreadful news. In most cases the people availed themselves by putting into use any wheeled vehicle in which to convey themselves and families to supposed places of safety.

Major Miles arrived at Wellington about midnight and gave a report similar to the one he gave in Caldwell. About twenty men, old soldiers and citizens, armed themselves and started to help protect the town of Caldwell. Men organized into a force also came from Oxford, Belle Plaine, Sotuh Haven and Guelph.

The fleeing settlers met in Wellington and camped there in a body. Hundreds were camped upon the banks of Slate Creek about one-half mile from Wellington.

The remaining citizens of Caldwell were prepared to defend themselves in case of an attack and fortifications were built of barrels and boxes which were filled with dirt and placed in such a position to serve as a protection against the wiles of the noble redman. The military companies never saw service, as the hostile Indians were not accommodating enough to come nearer than sixty miles to Caldwell.

Many of those who deserted their homes returned in a few days, and many others, having turned their faces toward the east, never saw fit to return to their new homes, while others returned after several years thinking the danger, which the frontiers were subject to, was now passed, and peace and contentment would be the controlling element.

The year 1874 was calamitous in more ways than one. The Indian scare drove hundreds of people from our county, and occasioned the loss of much property. The drought made crops a failure, and the grasshoppers finished what little vegetation remained; the granaries were empty and the coming cold, bleak winter was staring the people in the face, woe, despair and discouragement was depicted upon their countenances, and had not the charitable public sent them succor and aid many would have perished from hunger and cold.

The consequence of these disasters were that a large proportion of the settlers lost faith in the state of Kansas, and the tide of immigration was reversed from what it had been. Many were so poverty stricken that it was common to see a horse and a cow harnessed together to pull the wagon and a few household goods, including a feather bed, upon which six or eight children were seated; the load being too heavy for the poor old horse and cow to pull the man was compelled to walk, in order that he might be able to shake the Kansas dust from his feet forever. **We will presume these** people were seeking the provender in the home of "wifes people."

Those that remained by dint of skillful management and stolid endurance, have held the fort and are to-day, valuable, honored and wealthy citizens of our county. Many others after enduring the hardships of the frontier life, have been laid to rest, and are now peacefully sleeping their final sleep.

It is strange, indeed, how panic stricken the people will become, and rush pell mell to supposed places of safety. Many of the old veterans who have braved the fusilade of bullets and the clash of the saber, in the late civil war, were among the first to rush from their country, and let the noble redman have entire possession, had he wanted it, and like our "Robinson Crusoe" be the monarch of all he surveyed.

The "Indian scare" did not extend on the border alone, but reached far in the interior of the State. The excitement almost reached Topeka, and in the counties of Sedgwick and Butler the excitement was nearly equal to that of the border counties.

I was living in Butler county at the time and the people there were terrorized with the reported outbreak. Everyone seemed to think his place would be the first attacked by the murderous Cheyennes on their departure from their homes in the Indian **Territory.**

I was in the field cutting oats, when the news of the outbreak reached Augusta, and a man came running to my place and gave me the warning. He was very much excited and begged me to go and find out if the report was substantiated by facts; he said that the people had congregated themselves together in Mr. Brodies corral, and they had sent him to me to request me to go and ascertain if the report was true, and to report to them immediately. Their reasons for wanting me to act as scout was because I had traveled the road to and from Caldwell so often that I knew of places in which I could secrete myself and thereby escape from the hands of the Indians.

I told the man I would go provided he would take my place as one of the binders, and that I did not have any faith in the report, and I knew how excited the people would become under such circumstances, for I had a little experience myself, about a supposed Indian outbreak at the time Fred Cratts was shot, of which the reader will remember.

I took my horse and started on my errand and after proceeding about ten miles I met a man who had just came from Wellington. He reported how the affairs were there and that upon investigation there was nothing of it, and upon hearing this news I went back and found some of the people hid in the brush near their rendezvous.

I related to them what I had heard and they quietly went back to their homes in contentment.

In Summer county, the people had scarcely returned to their homes and got settled again to their usual routine of living when the second alarm was given. The report even went so far as to say South Haven had been burned and the Indians were now on their way to Caldwell, and were burning buildings and killing people on their route. One man said he had just came from South Haven, a town twelve miles east of Caldwell, and had seen the burning buildings and the farmers' haystacks afire; this created another rushing of the people, and it was soon found out that the report was false, and South Haven had not been burned and an Indian had not been seen within her borders, or nearer than sixty or eighty miles.

The report of the murdered freighters however was true. Whether they were surprised while encamped and killed by the murderous Indians is a mystery and has not been fully determined in the minds of the people. There were many theories advanced relative to the murder, and at this late date many of the old settlers regard the theory advanced that the freighters met their death at the hands of the Indians, as a myth.

One good reason for their doubts is this: Had the Indians been on the warpath and killed the parties, in the manner in which one of them was found, it would be reasonable to suppose that his scalp would have been taken by the Indian by whom the man was killed. According to the belief of the Indian tribe, a warrior's bravery is known by the number of scalps taken, consequently it would be reasonable to suppose that the warrior would have added this scalp as a trophy of his greatness.

In the month of July, 1874, Pat Hennesey in company with three companions were engaged in hauling government freight, consisting of various kinds of provisions, from Wichita, said freight to be delivered at some government post located on the Caldwell and Fort Reno trail.

When the freighters arrived at Buffalo Spring, a ranch whose proprietor was Ed Mosier, they concluded as it was early to go into camp, to travel on and they would probably reach the location which is now known as Bull Foot Ranch. These ranches are located on the stage line running from Wichita southwest into the Indian Territory and are in distance, about eight miles apart. probably darkness would over take the freight ers before arriving at Bull Foot Ranch, and they con cluded to camp for the night on the divide, about one mile from the ranch.

What happened during the night will probably never be known, save by the parties who were present.

This we know that the freighters met a sorrowful death at the hands of some murderous fiends.

I will give the reader the facts concerning the finding of Pat Hennesey's body by Wm. E. Mallaley, who kindly gave the writer a correct statement of the sad affair. Mr. Mallaley is an honorable resident of Caldwell, and is an extensive cattle dealer and owns considerable real estate property,

Mr. Mallaley in company with Indian agent J. Miles of Fort Reno, and J. A. Covington, his wife and others, were on their route from Fort Reno to Caldwell, and upon their arrival at the Red Fork Ranch, they were told by the ranchman that the Indians had been making trouble between that point and Caldwell, and cautioned them of the impending danger of traveling on the trail.

The company were not frightened however, and after watering their horses proceeded on their journey. They had traveled about eight miles, when they saw the remains of a wagon at the east side and perhaps a hun-

W. E. MALLALEY.

dred yards from the trail. They also saw a pile of corn and oats still smouldering; the fire had almost consumed the wagon, leaving the corn and oats still burning. Mr. Mallaley thought he spied a man's feet protruding from the pile of smoking grain. Contrary to the wishes of the party, Mr. Mallaley went to the ruins to ascertain if his suppositions were correct; to his horror he saw he was not mistaken. The shoes were not burnt from the feet, and he took hold of them and pulled the blackened and charred remains of a man from the pile of smoking grain. The flesh had been almost burnt from his legs and arms, and the body presented a most sickening appearance; the intestines were dragging from the abdomen.

The body was examined to ascertain the cause of the unfortunate man's death. One bullet hole was found to have penetrated the left leg, just above the knee. A close examination was made of the wagon and the party came to the conclusion that Hennesey had been tied with his hands, to one of the hind wheels of the wagon and his feet to the other, then the body was covered with corn and oats, taken from Hennesey's wagon, and the whole set on fire. The result was as I have given it. Some of the party were in favor of leaving the body and others did not want to leave it unburied. But it was decided to bury it, and preparations were made to dig a grave. They had nothing to dig the earth with except an ax; which Mr. Mallaley took and cut the earth, while the other men cleared away the earth with their hands.

After digging the grave as deep as they could with the ax, the dead man was laid in it and the men filled the grave by throwing the dirt in with their hands.

The party found provisions and pieces of harness scattered around the wagon. Nothing was seen of the other freighters by Mr. Mallaley, but when he arrived at the Buffalo Springs Ranch, upon inquiry he found that Mosier and a companion by the name of Bill Brooks had taken a wagon from the ranch, and proceeded to the place of the massacre, and taking the bodies of the three freighters, had buried them near Buffalo Springs Ranch. In what manner they met their death Mr. Mallaley did not ascertain. He asked Mosier and Brooks why they did not get Pat Hennesey's body and bury it at the same time they got the other bodies. They replied they did'nt have time. Mr. Mallaley received the information that the three freighters were killed about fifty yards from Hennesey, and east of the trail. He did not see the teams which belonged to the murdered men.

Pat Hennesey's grave is in the Oklohomo country, about ninety miles South of Caldwell. An enterprising town has been laid out near the place which marks the spot on which the murder was committed, and the town bears the name of Hennesey, in honor of the unfortunate Pat Hennesey, whose rude funeral was solemnized by the presence of four parties. There was no shroud or coffin, no priest nor tolling bells.

Pat Hennesey left a widow with four children, living near Manhattan, Kansas. The family were left in destitute circumstances.

In later years a stone was placed at Hennesey's grave with the following inscription, "Pat Hennesey, killed, July 13, 1874."

CHAPTER XXVI.

The Stage stock is stolen—The secret told to A. M. Colson—
He organizes a party to pursue the thieves—A fight with
buffalo hunters—A flag of truce—Great hunger prevails among the party—A jack-rabbit shot and
divided—The thieves are spied—The
fight—The escape of the thieves—
Capture of seven mules
and three horses.

A short time after the death of Pat Hennesey, word reached Caldwell that the Stage Company had lost nearly all their stock and a reward of $400 was offered by the Stage Agent, John Williamson, for the capture of the stock. About the time the Stage stock was stolen, Bob Drummond also lost a fine race horse and a pony; the presumptions were that the thieves who had stolen the Stage Company's horses, had also stolen the race horse. Numerous horses belonging to the settlers were missing, or had "strayed too far" from civilization so that all traces of them were lost.

The Stage line was owned and controlled by the South-west Missouri Stage Company, and its starting place was Caldwell; and Fort Sill, a place 180 miles away, was its point of destination. Stage ranches were located all along the line, furnishing fresh horses for traveling and supplying food and shelter for both man and horses.

Near the latter part of July, Dr. J. M. Burkett, a doctor and druggist of Caldwell, called A. M. Colson, a resident of the town, into his office and told him to get up a crowd and try to capture the thieves, who were to pass the Devore place, twelve miles west of Caldwell, with the stolen stock at about nine o'clock the next morning.

Mr. Colson asked Burkett of whom he received the information. Burket declined to reveal the name of the informer, but finally, after asking Mr. Colson to "never give it away," he told the secret and stated that the thieves had been holding about thirty-five head of horses and mules in the "black jack" near Turkey creek, located in the Indian Territory about seventy-five miles South-west of Caldwell. Burkett said the thieves would pass Devor's place with the horses and continue North-west in their travels, their destination would be either Larned or Fort Dodge. Upon receiving this information, Mr. Colson concluded to get up a party and go to the place designated by Burkett and endeavor to capture the thieves and get possession of the stock. He immediately went to the North of Caldwell, to the Chikaskia river, and engaged the services of some of the settlers and all together mustered up a crowd of seven men, namely, Frank Barrington, Alex. Williamson, Bob Drummond, —— Force, John Williams and A. Livingston; the men were detained from starting until quite dark, and, after traveling for some, time they reached Fall creek where they were joined by Ballard Dixon and George Perringer, citizens living on Fall creek. The night was extremely dark, the company of men got bewildered in the darkness and after traveling for some time up hill and down they concluded they were lost and the best thing for them to do was to stop here until daylight; here Ballard Dixon and George Perringer forsook the party and returned to their homes. The little company of men began to make preparations to rest until morning. They made themselves as comfortable as their circumstances would allow and slept on the prairie, using mother earth for their bed; as soon as it was sufficiently light enough to view the surrounding country they saddled their horses and started on their journey, and soon after they arrived at Major Andrew Drum's ranch, where the party ate breakfast; here they were joined by "Buffalo" King and soon after by Sheriff John Davis from Wellington, with a company of ten men. Upon their arrival at the Devore place, they were surprised to learn from one of the family, that the thieves—three in number—had passed there the day before, driving and leading ten head of horses and mules. The question was asked: where are the other twenty-five head of stock?" It was presumed that the original stock had been divided, a party of men each taking a bunch and going in different directions, their intent was, it is supposed, to dispose of the stock, get their money and return to Caldwell.

The party who were in pursuit of the horse thieves started in a North-west direction, following the Ellsworth cattle trail. Perhaps it would be well to give a description of this cattle trail. As the tide of civilization crowded West, and settlers settled here and there on their farms of 160 acres of land, the Chisholm trail was in the center of a civilized country, hence the trail must be disposed of and a new one established further west. The new trail made connection with the former one at Pond creek, Indian Territory, and angled across the the country in a North-west direction; its destination was a town located near Larned, on the Kansas Pacific Railroad. This town was called Ellsworth, and the trail was designated by the cattle men as the "Ellsworth trail."

After the men had traveled a short distance they rode upon a herd of buffalo and each man endeavored to kill the greatest number of these mighty monarchs, until the horses were very much wearied from the chase. The party were unwise in doing this, for by doing so they had lost the trail of the thieves. They did not realize the condition of their horses until after the chase was over, then they saw the disadvantage they were in and rode slowly on; some of the party, however, walked a greater part of the way. When they neared the Chiskaski river the trail was again found and the party traveled on. We will not attempt to follow them in their many turns, but will say that the trail was again soon lost, and the party traveled a part of two days without trace or track of the thieves. It had been ascertained by the men upon starting from Devore's, that the thieves had a wagon along with the outfit; this could be easily followed as long as it was kept in the road, but after leaving it the tracks were difficult to discover. The party left the Ellsworth trail and traveled in a North-west direction and traveled for two days with the trail of the stock thieves. The party had started with a good supply of whiskey, and so long as that article lasted the men were ready and eager to push on after the thieves, but when the last drop had been drained, the spirits and energy of the party began to wane, and one by one the men left until the little band numbered but ten men. Five of these men were from Wellington: namely, John Botkin, Neal Gatliff, Joe Thralls, John Davis, the sheriff, and one whom I have forgotten. The five men who started from Caldwell were : W. B. King, A. M. Colson, Frank Barrington, Alex. Williamson and — Force.

This band of ten men were determined to follow on, and succeed, if possible, in catching the thieves and getting possession of the stock. They arrived at Kingman about noon and ate dinner at that place ; this was the last meal they ate until four days afterwards. After they had been without food for one day and a half, Mr. Colson shot a jack rabbit ; a fire was quickly made out of buffalo chips, and some of the men removed the hide from the rabbit, then the rabbit was laid on the buffalo chips and roasted ; the party had no salt, hence the rabbit was to be eaten without that article of seasoning. As the meat lay frying on the fire, Neal Gatliff looked on with utter disgust and remarked " he could'nt eat it, fried on buffalo chips." There would be no trouble attended to this, for the remaining nine men were ravenous and could quickly dispose of Gatliff's portion, but when the rabbit was cooked, it was divided into ten pieces and distributed among the ten men, who ate it quickly and wished for more. Gatliff ate his share without a murmur.

From Kingman the party traveled west until they reached Sand Creek, where they struck the trail of the thieves again. This time they had found a camping place of the thieves, which showed the fact that they had used pieces of a wagon for fuel, for the men found burned remnants of a wagon bed with pieces of old iron scattered around the recent camp fire.

The little party tired, hungry, and almost utterly worn out from exposure and fatigue traveled on, and, when they neared the Nennescah River bottom, the eyes of the men scanned the bottoms, and at last an exclamation of surprise escaped the boys, when one of them said, "Boys, there's our outfit," and in looking near a draw two men were seen going toward the camp, about which a number of horses were grazing. At this agreeable intelligence, the men were elated, because of their good luck, and nervous because they feared the thieves would become aware of their presence, and make a hasty departure. The party decided to run, and if possible, obtain a position between the two men and the camp. Their plans once laid, the party dashed on the run toward the camp, but the two men reached the camp before the party could head them off. The men at camp began to fire at the party, and a general battle ensued, in which both parties indulged. After trying to get possession for nearly a half day, the party from Caldwell took a handkerchief and made a flag of truce and run it up so that it could be seen by the men at the camp.

This had the desired effect, and the men consulted over the matter; finally they had a meeting, when to the surprise of both parties, they saw they had had a wrong impression, for the men at camp were a party of buffalo hunters who mistook the ten men for Indians. The affair was settled without further trouble. The party of ten men said the buffalo hunters stood them off, and it was strange that none of the men were hurt by the numerous bullets that were flying.

The party had now lost one-half day of valuable time and another half day was spent in finding the trail of the thieves, which was found but soon lost again. They were near a draw or ravine and the men got off their horses and hunted in the ravine to find where the wagon had crossed. The only manner in which the trail could be found, would be to part the tall grass of rank growth. This the men did, and succeeded in finding the tracks made by the wagon through the damp ground. The party were now west of the Ellsworth cattle trail and south of the Nennescah River, and were traveling in a north-west course. It would be wearisome to follow them in their many changes of directions, hence will not attempt it. Now we find them pursuing a different course. The party had conceived the idea of striking the Medicine Lodge and Wichita wagon road and there the trail could be followed, or the tracks could be easily seen in case the thieves crossed the road. They crossed Elm Creek near Medicine Lodge; it was here Mr. Colson killed the jack rabbit which was divided between ten hungry men. How ravenous their appetites must have been as they had now been several days without provisions. No doubt they relished their frugal meal. The horses had become weary and exhausted from hard riding, and it was necessary for the men to walk a part of the time in order to rest the weak and tired horses. W. B. King walked a greater part of the time as his weight was about two hundred and fifty pounds, and his horse was almost too weary to travel and carry the weight of Mr. King. A man could outwalk the poor, tired beasts and it would be useless to urge them in a run.

When the party reached the sand hills near the Arkansas River, and an abundance of wild plums were found growing on the sand hills, as the men caught sight of the fruit, they hastily left their horses and began picking and eating the plums; they had now been one day and a half without any nourishment and nearly four days without a sufficient supply of food to satisfy their appetites.

After eating all the plums their appetites craved, the men once more resumed their weary chase. The signs of the thieves' camping places satisfied the party of men who were following them, that they were getting nearer and nearer to the object of their search and for whom they had suffered the privations of hunger and thirst in order that the thieves might be captured.

When the men came within sight of the Arkansas River, a settlement was within one mile and a half, and the men, with the exception of Mr. Colson, wanted to go to one of the houses, and try to obtain some provisions. Mr. Colson told the men he was in favor of keeping on in the chase, for the signs were that they were not a great distance behind the thieves. He also said he thought he could get along without provisions for about twenty-four hours longer, and he was certain that by that time they would have the thieves in their possession; finally Mr. Davis, the sheriff, agreed to Mr. Colson's suggestions, and said he would favor pushing on in search of the thieves. After much talking, it was agreed to take a vote on the question, whether they were to travel on in pursuit of the thieves, or go to the houses and obtain food. The result was, four of the men went to a house to get provisions, two men to the Arkansas River to get a drink of water, leaving four men to wait until their return. While the four men were talking they noticed about three-quarters of a mile away, some stock, resembling horses, grazing on the grass. The horses were watched and in a short time a man came out of a ravine and drove the horses under the hill out of sight. These actions aroused the suspicions of the men, and they concluded they were the thieves, which they knew from the recent signs, could not be very far in their advance.

The men waited for Williamson and Force to return from the river, then they said, "Colson, you are the lightest, you run and get the other men," Mr. Colson started to get the men who had crossed the river and gone to the settlement; when Mr. Colson reached the bank of the Arkansas River, the men that he wanted were on the opposite side, probably one-half mile from Mr. Colson. He hallooed to them but could not make them understand him. He tried to inform them what his errand was by the signs and maneuverings which he underwent for their benefit; he would take off his hat, wave it, beckoning for them to come to him, then he would turn his horse quickly and dash off, thinking thereby to inform them what he meant and what he wanted; the men stood and looked in amazement and wondered if Colson had gone crazy, or what was the cause for his strange movements; finally John Botkin came across and together with Colson went through performances similar to what Colson had, and, after much difficulty these men succeeded in inducing the

three men to cross the river, when Colson informed them that the thieves were near and were making preparations to travel again.

The five men rode as rapidly as they could in the direction where the thieves were supposed to be camping. As the party neared the wagon they saw the other five men of the party ride up to the wagon and began firing at the thieves. After several shots had been fired, the five men rode up to their party; the firing was returned by the thieves, who had by this time jumped into the wagon to which two mules were harnessed. One of the party had been slightly wounded in the affray, and the other two applied the whip to the frightened mules, and they left the party far behind. The horses could not endure fast running, and, in fact, they could not run faster than a good man on foot. The party of the thieves were pursued however by three or four of the party, and, becoming alarmed, they quickly untied the two horses which they were leading; the thieves made their escape. One of the horses was the race horse which had been stolen from Drummond. Their horses being fleet runners, it was not difficult to escape from the party of men, as their horses were too tired to travel far. The party tried to obtain fresh horses in the settlement, in order to give the thieves a chase. Some of the settlers that had heard the firing, had started to see the fight. These men were met by the thieves, and were informed that the party after them were horse thieves, and the men could not for some time change the opinions held by the settlers, hence a horse could not be procured until it was too late to give the thieves chase.

Three of the men hunted and gathered together the mules and horses that had taken fright during the firing of the guns. The stock had been hobbled, but they had become so frightened that it was with much difficulty that the boys could accomplish their errand and bring the stock to a halt, sufficiently for them to be driven back from whence they came. Information was received that the names of the thieves were— Williamson, "Hurricane Bill" and "Red," this man was a blonde with red hair and moustache, hence his name "Red;" what his real name was I never knew, nor did I know that of "Hurricane Bill." These men had been temporary residents of Caldwell. "Hurricane Bill" and — Williamson were in the wagon and escaped on the two horses. It was supposed by many, that the wounded thief gave the information which implicated many of the residents of Caldwell as accomplices in the stealing of the stage company's stock. It was rumored that the wounded man was rounded in by some of the party and to them made a confession, implicating Charles Hasbrook, Bill Brooke, one arm Charlie Smith, Jud Calkins, Dave Terril and others. He also gave the names of the two men who had made their escape. "Red" reported they were to receive three hundred dollars for stealing the stock. It was afterwards reported and published in the newspapers that the stealing was instigated by the Southern Kansas Stage Company, thinking in this way the Missouri Stage Company would become discouraged and throw up the contract for carrying the mail, and they would step in and fill it for them. The Southwest Missouri Company bid in the contract at eleven thousand dollars, while the Kansas company had been receiving a much larger sum, and the last bid made by them was seventeen thousand dollars; the Southwest Missouri Company was given the contract, and the result was their stock was stolen near the beginning of the first trips made by them through the Indian Territory.

The party were elated over their good luck in securing the stock, and of the information received, they probably concluded the information received from the thief was more profitable to the community than the harm which he had done, and, as the party were tired, thirsty, hungry and much fatigued, the vigilance of the guards proved not sufficient to keep the prisoner, it was reported he escaped from the crew of sleeping men. The men returned home after an absence of ten days; the party divided at Slate Creek; the Wellington men returned to their homes, while those living in Caldwell, traveled in a southeast direction, and reached home on the tenth day after leaving Caldwell.

CHAPTER XXVII.

A Vigilance Committee—The Sheriff and Two Hundred Men Surround Caldwell--Capture Dave Terril, Jud Calking, Charles Hasbrook, Bill Brooks and Charlie Smith—The Prisoners Taken to Wellington—Three Prisoners are Hanged by a Mob--A Banquet Given by Agent Williamson—Four Hundren Dollars Divided Among Ten Men.

The numerous deeds of lawlessness and horse stealing in the south-west portion of Sumner county had occured so frequently that in order to suppress it something must be done by the citizens of the county. To catch a thief, try him by a process of law was a slow method to render justice to the law breaker, besides costing the county a large sum of money. A quicker and surer way of meting justice to the horse thief was contemplated by the settlers. As a result the entire southwest part of the county was organized into a vigilants committee, whose purpose it was to rid the country of horse thieves, and if necessary to accomplish this they would indulge in dealing with the thieves according to the rules and regulations of the law over which Judge Lynch presided.

The adage, "Where there is a will, there is a way," seldom fails to be realized. So it was with the vigilants;

they had an indomitable will, and a power behind the throne of Judge Lynch which always found the way to accomplish their mission.

The citizens at Caldwell knew nothing about the catching of the horses, until the men had returned from their trip after the thieves. It was not generally reported among the residents of the town. At a late hour in the night the town of Caldwell was surrounded by a crowd of men numbering about two hundred. The sheriff was in charge of the men, and it was soon reported what their object was. They were after the parties implicated in the stealing of the stage stock. After surrounding the town, the sheriff proceeded to make the arrest of the parties. Jud Calking was found at the City Hotel, of which he was proprietor; Hasbrook was found at the Last Chance ranch, located one and one-half miles south of town; Bill Brooks had taken refuge in a dug-out on the Fall Creek, where he was arrested by the sheriff's posse; Dave Terril was found three miles northwest of town, at the house of Deacon Jones; Charlie Smith was on Deer Creek, about twelve miles south of town. Smith was arrested the following day, and was taken while procuring wood for the camp. He was surprised to find himself in the presence of the sheriff's posse, who were standing with guns drawn, requesting him to surrender. Hasbrook heard the men coming and ran into a cornfield, which was immediately surrounded by the men, who waited until the approach of daylight when they arrested him.

The actions of the sheriff's posse caused great excitement among the residents of the town; some of them secretly left it and did not return for several days, while others left it never to return; whether they were guilty or not remains a mystery. A doctor had informed the sheriff of the information he had received when the men surrounded the town; the doctor requested the sheriff to place guards around his house, which he did; leaving five men as guards for several days, or until the doctor could pack up his goods and settle his business affairs in order that he might be able to leave the country. It seems the doctor feared the men implicated in the stealing, or their friends, might attempt to take his life. This fear occasioned great anxiety and fear on the doctors mind and as quickly as he could, he bid farewell to Caldwell and hied himself away to a healthier clime.

The prisoners were taken to Wellington and given a preliminary trial. Terril and Calking were liberated on a habeas corpus. Charlie Smith, Bill Brooks and Chas. Hasbrook, were found guilty and confined in the county jail to await the convening of court. These men remained in jail one night and a part of two days. The second night, the 30th of July, will be ever immemorial in the minds of the earlier residents of Wellington, and also to the settlers who were living throughout the country during the month of July, 1874.

About the twilight hour, horsemen armed with guns and revolvers, were seen near the town of Wellington; one by one the number increased until the crowd probably numbered three hundred men. Near the midnight hour the men marched with muffled tread to the jail in which were confined the three guilty men. The jail was broke open and the prisoners were taken out. The crowd quietly marched to the creek south of Wellington, probably one mile from the town, and the prisoners were hanged to a tree near the main road from Wellington to Caldwell.

It was reported by citizens of Wellington, who saw the mob as they marched through the streets, that the silence was unbroken by word or whisper, and the men resembled an army marching on duty. Everything was done in an orderly and systematic way; the foot steps of the entire crowd seemed to be marching to a "right," "left," "right," "left" order. The prisoners were marched between two men, each file having one of the three prisoners.

Hasbrook asked permission to speak before the hangmans noose was placed around his neck, but this request was denied him; where upon he began talking and requested that the awful manner in which he was to meet his death, be never reported to his parents, who were living in one of the eastern states. While he was talking the noose was put around his neck, and he was swung into eternity. Hasbrook was a young man possessed with great intelligence, had won the reputation as being a smart lawyer, and practiced in the courts of Sumner County until the time of his arrest and death.

Charlie Smith was a brother of Tom Smith, who had, some time previous, been hanged at Rylands Ford, on the Chikaskia River. He had only one arm, having lost the other either by an accident or in a fight with an adversary. The Smith brothers were respectfully connected with relatives in Illinois. It was reported that they were the illigitimate sons of one of Illinois' most noted men, officially speaking.

Bill Brooks is one of the men, who it is claimed helped to bury the two freighters, who met their death in company with Pat Hennessey. It was reported that Brooks pled for mercy at the hands of the mob, but he was to receive none and was hung with Hasbrook and Smith. It is the supposition that Brooks and Hasbrook stole the race horse and pony from Bob Drummond.

The men were left hanging until the following morning, when their bodies were cut down and taken to Wellington, when they were placed in the old court house.

The bodies of the dead men were laid side by side upon the floor, and to shield their gastly faces from the gaze of the passing people, a blanket was spread over the bodies, covering the faces.

They were buried in rude coffins near the old cemetery, and the graves are pointed out to the recent settlers as the last resting place of the three horse thieves who were hanged by a mob on Slate Creek.

But little remains to be told; suffice it to say this hanging had the desired effect; horse thieves took a leave of absence and quit their haunts in Sumner county. They learned, by the example of Hasbrook, Bill Brooks and "one armed Charlie" Smith, that the people were determined to suppress lawlessness, and if they continued in the practice of horse stealing, they were liable to meet a similar death to that of the three prisoners. The consequences were the thieves did not know who to trust and all men were suspicioned as belonging to the vigilants committee of the Southwest. So strongly were the people organized into this society, that in case of a necessity an hours ride would collect, without difficulty, a company of men numbering several hundred. Thus the reader will see with what uniformity the settlers worked together, to suppress lawlessness and to encourage men of law, energy and enterprise, to visit our country, settle down and cast their fortunes with us.

The stock belonging to the stage company was restored to the agent. The stock numbered seven head of mules and several horses. A short time after the capture of the thieves and horses, the agent for the stage company, John Williamson, gave a banquet at Wellington, inviting the ten men who had effected the capture of the mules; the four hundred dollars offered as a reward for the stock, was divided among the trusty and tried men, each receiving an equal share of the money.

This sum would not pay them for the horses they had ruined while searching for the thieves, notwithstanding the exposure, starvation and fatigue, which the men had suffered, while they were riding over the western plains; enduring the privations of the plainsman without food or drink.

The greater part of these ten men are still residents of Sumner county; by their energy and pluck they have accumulated a small fortune, and we presume their intentions are to live the rest of their years in "Sunny Kansas."

CHAPTER XXVIII.

T. Oliver Shoots a Shoemaker of Caldwell—Facts Concerning the Murder—Citizens become Enraged—Efforts to Hang the Murderer to a Sign Board—Men of Cooler Judgment Interfere—At Midnight He is taken and Lynched—The Burial of the Body.

Scarcely had the people of Sumner County, Kansas, settled down to the usual routine of life, scarcely had the excitement caused by the hanging of Hasbrook, Smith and Bill Brooks quieted, before we are again called upon to witness a dreadful tragedy, in which two men are the unfortunate victims. This time it was not the Texas desperado, the dreaded horse thief, or the duelist that has met death. It is the laboring man bending over his work, unmindful of the vengeance which is being kindled in the breast of the enemy, who wantonly murders his opponent.

It was a beautiful morning, the 20th of August, 1874; the sun broke in beauty over the undulating prairie. The day was exceedingly warm, the sun was hot, but its rays were tempered by a gentle breeze.

Men and women were going forth on some business errand, or were lounging lazily in the shade of the building, chatting socially and conversing of recent

MIDNIGHT AND NOONDAY. 261

events, when the crack of a revolver rang in the air, and the hushed and startled citizens looked this way and that in order to learn from whence came the sound and who was the victim and victor.

Very soon the mystery was solved by the appearance of a young man holding in his hand the still smoking revolver. Immediately a dozen or more of excited citizens were at the scene of the murder and had the murderer in their possession. The facts obtained concerning the shooting were these.

T. T. Oliver, a young man, a temporary resident of Caldwell, had been drinking whiskey and carousing alone in hours of dissipation until he met a shoemaker living in the town who also liked the influence of whiskey, whereupon they both entered the saloon and drank to the health of each, and the consequences were, that the two men became very much intoxicated and had a hilarious time together.

When the shoemaker was partially sober, he went to his shop and began to work at his trade. T. T. Oliver entered the shop for the purpose of buying a pair of boots. After priceing the different pairs of boots, he selected a pair which suited him and the men differed about the price, which Oliver said was too high. The shoemaker would not sell them as cheaply as Oliver offered to pay for them, consequently a dispute arose and a quarrel ensued.

Finally Oliver told the shoemaker he would not buy the boots, and, turning he went out of the shop. The shoemaker was thus free, so he began mending a pair of boots, giving no more thought of the dispute with Oliver. This person, however, was harboring an ill feeling against the shoemaker, and to avenge himself of the wrong which he supposed had been inflicted upon him, he resolved to kill his opponent. He walked back to the shoe shop, and looking in, he saw the shoemaker at work near the door. He quietly drew his revolver and pointing toward the unsuspecting shoemaker, sent a bullet crashing through his body. He saw the form of the shoemaker sway and fall, then he turned and left him writhing in the agonies of death.

The citizens' minds became inflamed over the cruel, cold-blooded murder. Had the victim been implicated in any manner by giving just cause for the action on the part of Oliver, the people would have viewed the murder with consideration, but the facts relative to the shooting were without just cause for the terrible crime, hence public sentiment revolted at the circumstance that so cruel a murder should be committed in their midst. A crowd of excited men took hold of Oliver and showed a determination to hang him to a sign board, but men of cooler judgment interfered with this project, by remembering the presence of the gentler sex and the children of the town.

Oliver was guarded by men of principles and good judgment, and had the murderer been removed from the town, in all probability, his life would have been spared, but the enraged people in the community were determined Oliver should pay the penalty of the crime he had committed, by dying the death of a felon.

About the midnight hour a moving of dark objects could been seen near the place occupied by the criminal. They enter the house, got possession of the man and went in an easterly direction; after going about one quarter of a mile they congregate in a group, and as the summer moon in full glory was rising majestically above the dark treetops, she looked upon a dreadful picture. The body of young Oliver was hanging from the limbs of a tree, his feet dangling in the air; his expression bore marks of a conquered hero, his face assumed a look as if calling for mercy at the hands of his enemies. The deed has been done, the law "an eye for an eye" had been filled."

The body of the murderer was left hanging during the night, and the spectral scene was looked upon by stars that have shown in the cloudless firmament—there was a wailing wind like a funeral dirge sweeping through the trees; sad, unearthly music it sighed and moaned, and whispered forth, dying away in faint prolonged surges over the distant prairies.

The body of the shoemaker was laid away to rest near the bodies of Fielder and Anderson.

The following morning after the dreadful double tragedy, the citizens repaired to the place of the lynching which took place on the little creek, a few rods east of Caldwell, and cut the rope which held the body swaying between the heavens and the earth, and placing it in a rude box, buried it beneath the grassy turf and the last sad rites were over.

Thus ends another chapter where whiskey was king and caused the untimely death of two of its victims.

Will the growing youths take warning and think wisely on the crimes committed within our county, and then resolve to "touch not, taste not, handle not" the intoxicating beverages, then we can truthfully say, intemperance does not exist.

CHAPTER XXIX.

Description of the First Election at Caldwell—Scenes at the Polls during the Election in 1872—Votes Challenged The Final Result—A Caldwell Stage Driver put a young lady into a swill barrel—The barrel is kicked over—The girl's appearance.

To make this history a complete work on the early days of Caldwell, I must record the early elections at that place. The first election held at Caldwell, was in the early part of November, 1871. The election was held for the purpose of electing township officers.

I do not think I would be exaggerating were I to say that all voted who were inclined to do so. I did not hear any questions asked relative to the residing place of the voter. I presume the only question asked was whether the voter was a resident of America. I know there were votes cast by men whose homes were in New York City, and other voters who lived as far South as Mexico. I do not think that any town polled a larger vote in its early infancy than did the town of Caldwell.

Everything went as merry as a marriage bell; whiskey was the most popular article in demand; the saloons and grocery stores had replenished their stock of wet groceries prior to the day of election. The day gave them a good business and added many quarters to their pocket-books.

An occasional shot was fired from a revolver in order that the day might be celebrated according to the western style of celebrating the day of election. The usual festivities of drinking whiskey, horse racing and target shooting was indulged in by the cow boys.

The silence would sometimes be broken by some one throwing an old oyster can into the air, when some one would fire at it in rapid succession, to ascertain how many balls he could put into it before the can fell to the ground; again was the can thrown into the air, giving another party a chance to show his dexterity with the six shooter.

After the votes were counted, the voters requested the newly elected men to contribute ten or fifteen dollars to a whiskey fund. The new officers donated the required sum of money, and all adjourned to a saloon where the money was squandered in drinking and gambling until the "we sma hours" began to dawn upon the scenes of revelry and dissipation.

On one or two occasions it took the participants several days to sober up. Some of the officers elected were men who very often indulged in drinking a glass of whiskey, and generally when the time comes for the officers to use their influence and authority in quelling disturbances of various kinds, they are found to be under the influence of whiskey, and unfit to fill their office in a manner becoming an officer.

The second election of township officers was held at Caldwell in the month of April, 1872.

Caldwell was the only town in Sumner County which did not contend for the county seat, consequently representatives from Belle Plaine and Wellington were sent to Caldwell to electioneer for their respective towns contesting for the county seat.

The voters at Caldwell favored Wellington as the location of the county seat for several reasons: First, it was the nearest town contending for the county seat; secondly, it was near the center of the county, and it was a fine location to make a prosperous business center.

The evening before election day the representative from Belle Plaine arrived in our little hamlet. It was readily seen that whiskey was his controlling element. He was feeling jubilant and had a good word for everyone with whom he conversed.

The men from Wellington were pleased to see the delegate from Belle Plaine, and the citizens of Caldwell treated him freely to whiskey. He was feeling pretty lively on the following morning; when the polls were opened he was escorted to the place of voting, and as he manifested a desire to challenge votes he was taken into the room where the election was held. He was very much under the influence of Caldwell whiskey, and I presume lost the tickets he had brought with him from Belle Plaine, for as soon as he entered the room he began searching his pockets for the tickets, and when he found he had lost them, he became very angry and said he had been robbed. This assertion created a laugh among the prominent men at the polls, which had a tendency to increase his anger. One of the citizens told him he ought to do something for his town, and in order to have a fine time he was told that Mr. C. H. Stone was intending to vote, and that he was not entitled to become a voter as his wife was living in Wichita. The gentleman from Belle Blaine said he would challenge C. H. Stones' vote, also that he would not let anyone vote who was not a legal voter. The township justice was acting as one of the judges of election.

When C. H. Stone came to vote, a couple of men led the drunken delegate to the judges, where he challenged Stones' vote; the justice asked the delegate his reason for challenging Stones' vote; the delegate replied, "that C. H. Stones' wife was in Wichita, and that Stone was not a legal voter." **The justice said to**

Stone, "what do you think of that?" Mr. Stone said, "I am one of the first settlers in the town, and consequently I intend to cast my vote." The justice said he would have to swear in his vote, and Stone replied, "all right," and held his hand up to receive the oath, when the justice said, "Mr. Stone, will you swear to treat the crowd of voters and not slight one man?" Mr. Stone agreed to the proposition, and his vote was cast into the ballot box. The judges of election adjourned the order of business for ten minutes, giving every man a chance to go to the saloon and get a drink. The majority thought the judge had found the correct method in which to determine whether a man was a legal voter.

In a few minutes the polls were opened again and men cast their votes into the ballot box with greater assurance of giving Wellington the victory, than the preceding voters had before getting their drink of whiskey.

The Belle Plaine man did not rally round the polls any more that day, and when the time appeared in which darkness hovers over the horizon, he had forgotten it was the day of election, challenging votes or of his stolen tickets, but was peacefully resting in a drunken sleep, free from the cares of this life, on the floor of one of the out-buildings.

He was left to his own thoughts and to sober up at leisure. The following morning he was ready to return to his native town, and expressed himself as enjoying himself immensely while in this vicinity, but notwithstanding this he seemed anxious to bid the citizens of the town farewell, and departed with the well wishes of the Caldwell people, for his future success in electioneering for county seats.

In the early days of Caldwell's history, long before the mighty steam engine came thundering over the prairie, the coaches filled with the immigrant and land speculator, whose destination was at some enterprising frontier town, a stage line run from Wichita, making connections there with the "iron horse," and carried the speculator, immigrant and traveler to the several towns which were in close proximity to the stage route. This line run southwest from Wichita and Caldwell was the end of that division; another division made connection with the Caldwell stage, and furnished transportation to some point in the Indian Territory. The stage carried the United States Mail and an occasional passenger, but very few availed themselves of this expensive manner of transportation. Money was considered a luxury by a majority of the pioneer settlers, and by many the fare from Caldwell to Wichita which was six dollars, was considered very unreasonable, consequently the settlers used their own teams and conveyances to travel to and from Wichita. There was those however who had to patronize the stage company, having no other means to travel except in this way.

The incident which I am going to relate, happened during the first few months after Caldwell's connection with Wichita by the stage line. The driver of the stage was a young man addicted to the habit of drinking whiskey. The settlers in and around Caldwell made the necessary arangements to have a little social pleasure, by giving a public ball, all men invited who cared to "trip the light fantastic toe" and the consequences were that the larger proportion of the crowd, were a class of disorderly and drinking people.

The stage driver was in town, on the evening of the ball, and he, being a lover of that fascinating art, known as dancing, concluded to avail himself of the present opportunity, and seek the company of some young lady to accompany him as a partner to the ball room.

He had been drinking since his arrival in town and the result was that when the hour came, for him to appear for the young lady, he was very much intoxicated. The young lady was working at the City Hotel.

The young lady declined to accept of his company,

on account of his drunkeness. He considered her refusal as an insult, and as a solace, he went to the saloon and sought to drive evil thoughts and care from his mind, by filling himself full of whiskey. He was so drunk the following morning that a new stage driver was in demand and the stage made its accustomed trip, but with a new driver however.

About noon some one went to the stage driver and told him if he did not stop drinking, and "sober up" he would be discharged as stage driver. This information had the desired effect upon the driver and about five o'clock in the afternoon, he was sober enough to go to the hotel and get his supper.

As he entered the door of the hotel, he saw the young lady, who had refused to go to the ball with him, go into the back yard, with a pan of dish water to empty into a swill barrel. He quietly approached unknown to her and as she was in the act of emptying the water into the barrel, he took hold of her feet and gently dropped her head first into the barrel swill, then turned and ran away.

I was standing in the door of the blacksmith shop, and saw the whole proceeding, and, in company with a man, who was also a blacksmith, I ran across the street

to get the girl out of the barrel. The barrel was over flowing with dishwater and refuse from the kitchen; the girl was kicking and struggling to get out of her predicament, when we arrived on the scene. Had I not understood the blacksmiths trade and been accustomed to handling kicking animals, I should have used much hesitancy in venturing so near the barrel. We saw it useless to attempt to pull her out, by the feet, so we tripped the barrel over, girl and all. She was nearly drowned, and wallowed around in the dish water and finally succeeded in gaining "terra firma" when she wiped the greasy water out of her eyes sufficiently to see us, she began to "read our title clear," and almost tore up the ground in her rage. We protested our innocence and related the circumstances to her; she kept up her abusive talk, until quite a crowd of people arrived on the scene. Some of the people laughed, and I could not help but laugh to see the girl standing with her dress bedaubed with dish water her hair filled with coffee grounds, potatoe parings and dirty grease. The men became very indignant over the affair and had not the landlady come to our rescue, confirmed our statement, we would have, probably, been used in a rough manner by the bystanders. But when they found the stage driver had put the girl into the barrel, they went to a saloon, found him, and the trouble was settled by treating the crowd to all the whiskey they wanted to drink.

CHAPTER XXX.

Cowboys Attempt to Take the Town—The Marshal Deputizes Six Men to Assist in Making Their Arrest—George Flat Alone Takes Them—The Sixshooter Does the Dreadful Work—The Coroners Jury Decide the Case.

Justice had been swift and certain in her dealings with the three horse thieves, hung on Slate Creek, one-half mile South of Wellington. After a period of comparitive peace and prosperity throughout Sumner county, we are again called upon to witness the scene of a double tragedy, which occured in the town of Caldwell, in the month of July, 1879.

Caldwell has become a notorious western town; her fame as the home of the cowboy, desperado and gambler, has been spread abroad throughout the land. People living in the eastern states, shrink with horror, and tremble with fear, when they first enter the town on a business transaction; the traveling salesman, commonly called the drummer, hastens to leave the town; he meets the hardware and dry goods merchant, the druggist, groceryman and saloon keeper greets them hastily, shows them the articles he sells, talks very glib and flattering for a few minutes, succeeds in making a sale, bids the merchant good-bye, and hies himself away to a more quiet town. All this is accomplished in a very few minutes; very often, however, before his departure, he witnesses a bloody encounter between the cowboy and marshal of the town, or a pitched battle between the citizen and a band of desperadoes.

The reader will accompany me to the town of Caldwell. The summer has gone, the first bright sunny days of July are here. The day is a balmy and breezy one, such as are usually seen by the residents of sunny Kansas. The evening zephyrs fanned the cheek of the blushing maiden, and made nature seem more lonely and pleasing to the aged. The children were running to and fro in their frolics, unmindful of what future had in store for them.

Near the middle of the afternoon two cowboys, whose names were Woods and Adams, came riding into town armed with several six shooters; they rode in front of a saloon, hitched their horses and entered the door of the saloon. They passed the time in drinking the vile stuff, known as whiskey. Soon their evil nature was aroused, and they appeared like demons in human form.

The quietness of the the town was soon broken by these inebriates, and the peaceful citizens were startled by the shots fired from the six-shooters of the cowboys. After filling themselves with whiskey, they proceeded to "take the town." They mounted their jaded horses and rode at full speed up and down the streets, firing their revolvers at what ever their evil dispositions dictated.

The constable of the town became tired of these things and proceeded to make arrangements for the arrest of the cowboys. The cowboy yell, and daring disposition they manifested, terrorized the constable and intimidated him to such an extent, that he was afraid to attempt their arrest unless he had a sufficient number of men to assist him.

He appointed six men to assist him, and among that number was George Flat, who was known as a man possessed with great nerve and courage; he was also an unerring marksman with the six-shooter; John Wilson was also appointed to act as a leader with George Flat. Wilson was considered a good man behind a six-shooter; and was a man with an indomitable will, and possessed that character pertaining to the order of the desperado.

The leaders, Flat and Wilson, went to the saloon and found the cowboys, George Wood and Jake Adams, in conversation with the saloon keeper. Wilson went around the building and stood near the back door of the saloon; Flat entered the front door; I stationed myself near the door opening onto the street, and was sitting outside the door talking to a friend. When Flat entered the saloon he went to the bar and called for a glass of whiskey; he placed his six-shooter on the counter and quaffed the whiskey; then one of the cowboys went up to the bar and called for some whiskey, and after drinking it gave a Texas whoop. This whoop is commonly called "a cowboy yell," but as the sandy complected Texan was the originator, its proper name would be a Texas whoop. It would be needless for me to attempt to describe it to the eastern reader; I presume all who have lived in the West are familiar with it. I will say this however, that the whoop has a blood-curdling sound, and terrifies one who is unaccustomed to its sound.

After the cowboy gave a whoop, Flat indulged in another drink, and answered the whoop in true Texas style. The cowboy drew his revolver on Flat who backed towards the front door; the cowboy followed with his revolver drawn within six inches of Flat's face. As Flat stepped out the door, the cowboy said "throwup;" as quick as a flash Flat jerked his revolver to the head of the cowboy, and as he was saying "I don't have to," fired several shots in quick succession; the cowboy's partner jumped out of the door where Flat was standing, and, I presume, intended to get one of the horses and make his escape; but his fate was sealed, for as he approached Flat, that person was on the alert, and he fired at the cowboy who reeled to the sidewalk and fell into the street in the agonies of death. The one Flat shot first, turned and ran out the back door and fell mortally wounded. He suffered from the effects of his wounds about thirty minutes, when death came to his relief, and ended his sufferings and checkered career.

The cowboy that was lying in the street was found to be dead; and upon examination, one of the fingers on his right hand was missing, it was found however, and the revolver that he held in his right hand, upon investigation, was found too, minus the trigger; and strange as it may seem, the hammer still remained standing, which proved the fact that Flat had shot the cowboy as he was in the act of pulling the trigger of his revolver, the ball striking his forefinger, tearing it from his hand, and on the same bloody errand tore the trigger from the revolver, leaving it cocked with the hammer standing.

Flat was very much excited after he had shot the men, and his intoxication seemed to leave him; he pointed his revolvers toward a plank in the sidewalk, and emptied both barrels, firing six or eight shots into one spot, in the sidewalk.

Great excitement prevailed throughout the town. The men rushed to the scene of slaughter; darkness had settled over the bloody scene, and excited men were questioning the propriety of the murder. Flat was so excited that he ran out into the middle of the street, and would allow no one to approach him. Finally I succeeded in getting near enough to talk to him. I told him the people upheld him in his actions, and I requested him to be quiet and not fire any more shots. He held out his hand and quickly withdrew it, then offered it to me again; I took his hand, and he asked me if I would stay with him. I told him I would, and that I did not apprehend any trouble. A crowd assembled, and among it were sympathizers of the dead cowboys. Some of the citizens feared an outbreak in which the sympathizers would seek to avenge the cowboys death, by shooting Flat or some of the assistants of the constable. Citizens were armed with revolvers and shotguns. Suddenly the report of a gun was heard, and the excited men rushed helter skelter and hid themselves behind buildings and boxes, and secreted themselves from the shower of bullets they expected would follow after the enemy had fired the first shot. Their flight was unnecessary, as the shot was fired accidently, by —— Hollister, who was approaching the crowd. On his way to the crowd he passed between the saloon and a building, and his shotgun was accidentally discharged. The crowd of men thought the shot was fired by friends of the dead men, and had Hollister been in the street, he would in all probability have received his death wound at the hands of friends, who would have been mistaken in their man.

As soon as the excitement was quieted, Flat entered the saloon of which Jim Moreland was proprietor; it was the same saloon in which the bloody encounter took place, and in which Flat had been the victor and double murderer; thus adding two more victims to his list of nine men, said to have been killed by him; he went to Moreland and accused him of befriending the cowboys and urging them on in their devilish work; his manner terrified Moreland, and he ran out of the saloon and went to his home.

Some of the citizens of the town, went to a barber who extended his sympathies with the cowboys, and who had been suspected of encouraging them in their daring acts and desperadoism. The barber ran into a restaurant followed by the inflamed men, a riot ensued, but no one was seriously hurt in the affray.

The dead desperadoes were herders belonging to some cattle outfit, located in the southwest part of the Indian Territory. They had probably been paid by their employer, and had come to Caldwell to have a fine time. The report was afterwards circulated, that they had rode until within ten or twelve miles of Caldwell, in company with a cattleman, and had informed him that they were going to kill some one before they left town.

The cattleman stopped for dinner at an acquaintances and told his friend that he must hasten on to town, and if possible, prevent the cowboys from putting their threat into execution. He recommended the boys as being hard workers, and quite unoffensive when at work; but their appetites for whiskey was so strong, that they would get on a spree occasionally; when their evil dispositions were brought to view, and their character assumed that of the western desperado.

Their last ride decided their fate, and drinking whiskey, had been the cause of their death. Their evil habit had caused them to go step by step toward the awful gulf of ruin, until they reached the brink, and not halting in their downward career, took the last step which landed them in the gulf of darkness, ruin and terrible death.

The morning sun beamed with brightness upon the spot, where the night before, a bloody tragedy had taken place. The town was unusually quiet; the people talked in undertones when referring to the double murder which had been committed in their midst.

An inquest was held over the bodies of the dead cowboys, and the jury gave in a verdict that the men were killed by George Flat in self-defence, acting as an officer in the discharge of his duty.

The citizens of the town, gave the remains proper burial in the old cemetery, northeast of the town. The remains were followed to their final resting place, by a few friends and associates, including a number of the citizens of the town.

Thus two more men are added to the list of victims killed by the power of rum.

CHAPTER XXXI.

Caldwell becomes a Railroad Town—The Town Incorporated and Officers Elected—The notorious "Red Light" and Proprietor—The killing of George Flat—Theories concerning the Shooting.

The period of triumph began in 1875. The grass hoppers and Indian scare of Sumner County, is being talked about by the world, meanwhile Caldwell is getting ready for a great future. In the summer of 1880, a branch of the Atchison, Topeka and Santa Fe R. R. was extended through the county, and Caldwell was the terminus of the railroad, thus giving her the name of a cattle town. Caldwell being situated at the head of the great Chisholm trail and so near the center of the grazing fields of the Indian Territory, found the trade of this vast interest poured into her lap. In the year 1880, the first shipment of Texas cattle was made from Caldwell. After the advent of the railroad, for a year or two the city was a pretty tough place for a peaceable citizen to live in, but as the "survival of the fittest" is a law of nature, it was not broken in this case.

Caldwell was incorporated as a city of the third class in July, 1879, and elected the following officers on August 7: N. J. Dixon, Mayor; J. D. Kelley, Sr.,

Police Judge; J. A. Blair, F. G. Hussen, H. C. Challis, A. C. Jones and A. Rhodes, councilmen. She also had marshals and a cooler. Then she began to grow as western towns grow, and with her prosperity came, the "Free and Easys" a brick hotel, bank and opera house, also the old "Red Light" and the Varieties.

The building known as the "Red Light" was a house of ill-repute; in connection with it was a dance hall. This building was erected by Woods of Wichita and that notorious character, Mag Woods, with ten or twelve prostitutes made it their abiding place. This house was the originator of much disorder, bloodshed, and deaths; whiskey was kept for sale in the building; after the cowboy had reached Caldwell after his long dusty drive, the proprietor of the herd would usually pay him his dues and in company with his companions he would visit the "Red Light," fill up on the vile whiskey sold there, then he was ready to "take the town." The citizens of Caldwell are, in a measure, responsible for the deeds committed in this house of prostitution. Had the officers and citizens never tolerated the erection of such a building, and given the necessary license for such a nefarious business to be carried on in their midst, the town would not have been compelled by the home and society to cleanse the name of Caldwell from the stain that had blotted her fair name.

About this time there were no less than ten or twelve saloons, and together with the "Red Light" house of prostitution, and with the society which assembles at such dives is it a wonder that the town was called a "tough" place" by people who were unaccustomed to such a state of society as that which existed in Caldwell at this time.

It was not an uncommon sight to see the women of ill-repute parading the streets, mingling with the innocent girls of the town and vicinity and luring many unfortunate victims to the "Red Light" where they were either robbed and pitched into the streets, or had squandered their money while under the influence of their vile whiskey, only to "sober up" and find they were "busted." Then their hatred for the place is being manifested in various ways; they began to shoot at sign boards, ride up and down the street firing off their revolver promiscously, and the final result is, either the death of the offenders or an officer is shot down while in discharge of his duties.

The "Red Light" was notorious throughout the west; Wichita lent her worst characters to become its inmates. The house and inmates is said to have accomplished the ruin of several of Caldwells brightest young girls, who to-day had they not listened to the "song of the tempter," might have been filling the exalted positon of a noble wife and mother.

How many happy homes have been destroyed, and innocent lives blasted, by the influence of this house of prostitution.

The cowboy is not a terror as many suppose him to be. They are inoffensive and social in nature; they are not bad men unless they are filled with whiskey. Many of them work month after month on the drive and right the herd through storm and sunshine, then they must have a "lay of" and the employer pays them their wages; they bid farewell to camp life and the familiar scenes of life in its monotonous cares, and hie themselves away to the frontier town to indulge in the luxuries which that little hamlet may possess. They meet with companions of former acquaintance visit the various saloons and gambling holes, probably lose the larger porportion of their money, then as a last resort, visit the houses of ill-fame and lose their remaining "little all." The dance hall affords them amusement, the air is filled with the echo of their lewd songs. Their drinking is continued, the fun grows fast and furious. The night is passed in debauchery and delights such as the "Red Light" offered. The early morning air is filled with the reports of the revolver fired by the drunken inmates of the house. Ever and anon can the unearthfy yell of the cowboy be heard by the citizens, who are aroused from their slumbers, by these lesser types of humanity.

The general consequences of such proceedings was that the cowboy would commit some serious offense while under the influence of whiskey and would either leave town with the marshal in pursuit of him, or he would be tried and fined ten, twenty or twenty-five dollars. His companions would generally come to his rescue, pay his fine, and after he was released, the cowboy together with his friends, would get the drop on the marshal, and to use the phrase familiar in the wild west would "take the town." "Taking the town" usually consisted in riding up and down the streets, shooting at sign boards, at the glass window fronts of the stores, ordering whiskey at the muzzle of the six shooter, riding their horses on the pavements and hotel verandahs and in fact they were at liberty to run things their own way. Sometimes the citizens would arm themselves and attempt to quiet the "boys," and generally a riot would ensue, a pitch battle would take place, often times ending in bloodshed.

For several years the drunken "cowboys" would "take the town" at their pleasure; the citizens finally became tired of this accustomed dramatic **performance,**

RANCH IN INDIAN TERRITORY.

and were determined to protect her officers and citizens from the desperate deeds enacted by the "wild and wooly cowboy." A marshal and an assistant were appointed and men were deputized upon special occasions to help the officers in discharging their duties,

The quiet manner which had been asumed heretofore in attempting the arrest of the desperado was to be a thing of the past, and now a new method was put into practice, which may be described in this manner: A wise officer before making the arrest would watch his chances and "get the drop on his man" by placing his six shooter within a few inches of the desperadoes head and demanded him to "throw up;" nine times out of ten the desperado will throw up his hands but occasionally a daring fellow will jerk his revolver from his belt and "throw up" with a bullet fired at the officer. It was not uncommon to see a "cowboy" with several "six shooters" in his belt, the belt carrying from fifty to one hundred cartridges. So the reader will conclude that in case of an emergency the "cowboy" is prepared for a fight.

The positon of a marshal is not to be greatly envied. He is in the midst of peril at all times and especially so when he attends to his duties. However successful he may be in the discharge of his duties, he can hardly expect to be a favorite amongst men or an ornament to society. There is always a class of people, who give their sympathy to the desperado, and are ready to keep the blame upon the officer, never realizing the the existing state of affairs,

The familiar saying, "Fight the devil with his own men" was confirmed in the case of marshal George Flat.

Flat was a drinking man and when under the influence of whiskey he was looked upon as a "holy terror." He proved himself to be a man of down right bravery and a shrewd observer of men and nature. He was very seldom known to be perfectly sober, and when sober was said to be as cowardly, as he was brave when under influence of whiskey. He was formerly from Texas and like most of the Texan's who visited Caldwell was a lover of strong drink and a frequent visitor of the "Red Light." His general associates were a rough class of people as well as a low class of humanity. When his temper was aroused he was as ferocious as a tiger, and had a strong spirit of revenge which marked his daily characteristics. He had an evil looking eye which betrayed the inner man. He was an expert shot with the revolver, combined with great dexterity and alterness.

His love for whiskey, and drunkeness made it necessary to discharge him from his office as marshal of Caldwell. A new officer, with three or four assistants, entered upon their new and perilous duties.

Flats discharge from office seemed to irate him to such an extent that the new officers seemed apparently, to be in great fear of him. He continued to carry his "six shooter" contrary to the city laws, and it was reported that upon one occasion, one of the deputy marshals ordered Flat to lay down his revolver. Flat replied that he could come and get it, and held his revolver toward the officer; he was in the act of reaching for it; Flat cocked the revolver and pointing it toward the officer, said "take it." The officer knew any attempt to "take it," would mean certain death for him; consequently he made no effort to do so. Flat was not afraid of the officers, and he knew the entire police force were afraid to arrest him. He continued to rule the officers with his supremacy, until one morning about half pas- one o'clock, in the month of June, 1880. Flat was walking along on the pavement in company with —— Spears, when the stillness was broken by a shot fired from a revolver; instantly the night air resounded with probably a dozen shots in quick succession, and Flat fell mortally wounded, his crimson life blood oozing from his wounds and staining the plank pavement he had so often trod, while endeavoring to assume the duties of an officer, and living simply as a citizen of the town. The night was dark, and beneath the light of the twinkling star in the heavens, Flats life ebbed away, and his body was carried by kind friends, to the home of his wife. I will not dwell on the sorrowful scene which took place, when the loving wife embraced the body of her husband; suffice it to say, the wife received the sympathy of the people in the community, in her hours of bereavement and sorrow.

The murder of Flat was very mysterious. The building opposite to where he was killed, was perforated with balls and the evidence showed they were fired from several different directions. A warrant was issued for the arrest of the marshal and assistants, and they were given trial; but no conclusive evidence could be found which implicated them as the murderers.

It was currently reported and believed, that the officers were afraid of Flat; none of them were courageous enough to arrest him, and they knew they did not dare to meet him face to face in a fight; and it was presumed by many, that a plan was laid in which Flat must give up to the inevitable.

They took him unawares and at a disadvantage; for he was walking quietly along not dreaming of danger, or his premediated death by the unknown parties who sought to kill him. One theory of the shooting had been that the police force had decided that Flat must die; and they had arranged themselves at different places along his route to his home, and at a given signal of one shot, by one of the officers, the balance of the officers were to shoot and kill Flat. It was well they took this precaution, for Flat would certainly fought to the last had he had a show for his life, and as it was, when he was found after death he had a death grip on his trusty revolver; before he died, which was almost instantly, he had the presence of mind to clutch his revolver.

CHAPTER XXXII.

Frank Hunt Slain—Who Fired the Fatal Bullet—The Theories Advanced—Description of the "Red Light Saloon"—George Woods the proprietor is killed—Charlie Davis the Slayer of Woods—Inmates of the "Red Light" seek "Richer Fields"—The Old Land Mark Gone.

The citizen of Caldwell who hied to his daily occupation at an early hour on the morning of October 12, 1880, was greeted with the phrase peculiar to the wild, wild west, "another man for breakfast." It was ascertained that Frank Hunt, acting as one of the assistant marshals of the town, lay dead at a dwelling house on Main Street.

No definite information could be learned concerning the shooting of Hunt. It seems he was sitting in one of the windows of the Red Light house of prostitution. The inmates of the house were on the floor dancing. The festivities were at their heighth, everything was going merry; the influences of whiskey was being felt by many, when sharp and clear on the night air was wafted forth the deadly crack of the revolver. Who, now was the victim who received the bullet? Who, now fired the fatal shot? The former question could only be answered by those immediately present at the Red Light. The latter question remains a secret to this day. The inquisitive mind would naturally wonder what was the cause and who the perpetrator of the deed. Theories were at once afloat; some thought that it was some friend of the notorious Flat, who presumption said met his death at the hands of the police force of Caldwell, while others thought it may have been the finale of an old, long standing grudge. Suffice it to say the mystery has never been unraveled. The only certainty was Frank Hunt was a corpse and the assassin was at liberty.

Hunt was one of the police at the time the notorious George Flat met his death, who rumor said was killed by the police force. Some attributed the killing of Hunt as a sequel to the killing of Flat.

But a few months had passed since the death of Flat. The early freshness of spring had passed away and the bloom and the glory of summer had departed. The time of the year when the apple trees are laden with their rosy treasures, and the summer darkness of the woods are varied by the appearance of the yellow leaves.

The autumnal moon shed her soft light upon the man, who with murder in his heart, cautiously approaches the open window of the Red Light dance hall;

he crouches low in the shadow, and when he reaches the exact spot or at the desired time, he holds the deadly revolver toward the visitor of the hall, pulls the trigger, then turns on his heel and walks quickly from the scene.

Hunt lived a few hours, suffering intensely but thought he was not mortally wounded. He clung to life tenaciously, and when he could no longer hope, he died without a murmur on his lips and succumbed to the inevitable fate of all humanity.

The scene changes once more. We are again called in imagination to the noted Red Light. Oh, the deeds of crime which have been committed within its walls of iniquity and shame. Many are the crimes and murders which have been caused by its immoral and vile influence.

Since its erection in 1879, we have witnessed many revolting scenes and much depraved humanity. This infamous den was erected in 1879 by George Woods, a noted man from Wichita, Kansas. The house was a two story building; the front was furnished as a saloon, of which George Woods was the proprietor. Upon the front window the following words were inscribed, "Red Light Saloon."

Mag Woods, the notorious woman known as Woods wife, was the proprietress of the dance hall, which was run in connection with the saloon. Wichita lent her worst inmates, to become inmates of this hall, and part of the population of Caldwell.

On August 18, 1881, a visitor and patron of the Red Light, by the name of Charlie Davis, had trouble with one of the female inmates, when George Woods interfered in behalf of the woman, which caused a quarrel between the two men. Davis pulled his revolver and shot Woods, killing him almost instantly. Davis got his horse and left town, going to the Indian Territory. A reward was offered for his arrest but he was never captured. George Woods was buried in the city cemetery and his wife erected a handsome monument to his memory.

For sometime after the death of Woods, the business of the noted Red Light was on the decline. The proprietor was now dead, and the visitors were few; as the tide of civilization came West bringing with it men of morality and influences of a christianized people. The citizens became aware of the immorality and bad influences brought about by this den of prostitution. They also saw that its presence caused the worst characters to visit the town, and their visits occasioned much disorder revelry and murder.

The citizens devised means to rid the city of the Red Light building and the female inmates; thinking in this manner to suppress much lawlessness, dissipation and bloodshed. In a short time the city authorities realized the building as a city nuisance, and the noted Mag Woods and her followers left the city, perhaps only to find richer fields in which to establish her infamous business.

The suppression of this den of iniquity had the desired effect; the visits of the rougher element of society became less frequent, as their old resort was no longer a land mark in the growing city, and their associates were gone to try their fortunes in the new country, in the direction of the setting sun; they too, turned West, in order that they might "grow up with the country," and amid their wild companions, seek the pleasures in the drama of life.

CHAPTER XXXIII.

George Brown appointed Marshal of Caldwell—The Arrival of Two Texas Men—They Drink Whiskey Freely—George Brown enters the Building Known as the "Red Light" The Marshal Shot and Killed by the Texans— The Flight of the Murderers—Sad Scenes at the Home of Marshal Brown.

In the year of 1882, George S. Brown was appointed City Marshal of Caldwell.

Brown was a young man of an exceptional good character, had a fair education, and unaccustomed to mingling with the rougher elements of society, especially of the drunken cowboys and daredevils which visited the western frontier towns. He was by nature, fearful of meeting the adversary or foe, but his characteristics showed him to be a true gentleman, a lover of peace, and his dealings with a man were in a quiet and unassuming manner.

The new marshal entered upon his duties amid the well wishes and congratulations of his friends. Had he dreamed of the destiny awaiting him, he would have recoiled with alarm, and shrunk from obeying the duties which he would be compelled to assume so long as he held the office of marshal, and endeavored to fill the office satisfactorily to the people.

The fate of the Marshals since the corporation of the city, had been anything but pleasing to the City Council. The rough element had prevailed, and the marshals must, under the circumstances, either give way to the desperado, or take the consequences if he endeavored to suppress riots, or in ordering the law-breakers to desist his free use of the sixshooter.

Marshal Brown was unfit to fill the office of Marshal. The man to fill the office should have been one who was accustomed to western life, and moreover, should be a man ready to lay down his life at any time, for no prophet could foretell the moment when the marshal would fall, shot by a law-breaker and drunken desperado. A man was wanted and needed who knew no fear, whose highest ambition was to be dreaded by man, and who rushed to the front of battle or where duty calls, with caution and determination to come out of the conflict victorious.

On the morning of June 22d, 1882, two Texans rode into the town of Caldwell. They put their horses in the livery stable, and immediately went to a saloon where they filled themselves with the vile stuff, known as whiskey. They soon made themselves conspicuous in the eyes of the citizens, by the various feats which they displayed with their sixshooters.

At last they seek the noted "Red Light," kept by

the notorious Mag Woods, and there they indulge in drinking more whiskey, and enjoying the society of the inmates of this vile den. They annoy the passing citizen by their profane and obscene language, and frighten the wives of the citizens who live in that immediate neighborhood, by the frequent firing of their sixshooters.

Finally the marshal goes to the "Red Light," and attempts the arrest of the Texas men. The proprietor informs the marshal that the parties are up-stairs, and the officer starts to make the arrest. Some of the inmates of the house had seen the Marshal coming in the direction of the "Red Light," and guessing his errand, the information was made known to the Texas men, who took a position near the head of the stairs, and waited for his presence to be made known to them by his asking them to "throw up."

The design of the house, and the plan upon which the stairs were erected was such that the Texans were concealed from the view of Marshal Brown, or any person that came up the stairway. When the marshal arrived near the head of the stairs, the attempt was made by him to arrest the men. Quick as a flash they fired three shots in succession at the form of the marshal, who reeled and fell to the landing below.

Quickly the Texas murderers ran down the stairs,

out into the street, and across to the livery barn, where they obtained possession of their horses, and rode rapidly in the direction of the Indian Territory.

Scarcely had the report of the deadly revolver died away before a crowd of excited citizens visited the scene of the murder, and viewed the remains of the dead officer. The news spread rapidly over the town, and the sister of Brown was notified of his death.

A number of the dead officer's friends tenderly carried the body to the home where the almost heartbroken sister awaited in sorrow to receive it.

The murderers of G. S. Brown made their escape, and are still at large. They were pursued by the citizens, but the twin murderers had the advantage, as they had left town before a posse was organized to pursue them, and while the citizens were scouring the adjacent country, the murderers were over the hills and far away.

The official life of G. S. Brown had been short. But a few short months before, in the early spring time, he took the office of marshal; scarcely had the freshness and verdure of spring passed away before he was called to lay down his life, and enter the quietness of a sleep in which there is no dreaming and from which there is no awakening.

The sister of Marshal Brown was very much affected by the death of a brother in whom she centered all her affections. It was a sad parting for her when she saw all that remained of her brother, buried deep within the bosom of mother earth. Fannie Brown turned in sadness from the grave; it was then she felt her loneliness, and knew of her broken home which awaited her coming. Her grief was almost unconsolable, and in the sad hours of her affliction, amid kind and loving friends she found extended sympathy and condolence.

Several years after the death of her brother, Miss Brown married an honorable citizen of Caldwell, and they are both to-day living in the city. The husband is classed among the influential business men of Caldwell.

CHAPTER XXXIV.

Must the Officers Be Hunted Down?—Who will Be the Next?—
A Remedy in which Law and Order will Prevail—"Bat"
Carr and Henry Brown Appointed to Fill the Office
of Marshal—Characters of the Men—They are
Looked upon as "Holy Terrors"—Peace and
Good Will Reign Supreme—"Bat" Carr
Removed from Office—Henry Brown
and B. F. Wheeler Appointed.

Since the direful tragedy of Caldwell in which Marshal Brown had met his death, the citizens were awakening to the pressing facts which were staring them in the face. Must the officers be hunted down, and shot like wild beasts in the forest? Must wantonly murders become daily occurrences were the queries of the law-abiding and law-upholding citizen? The questions were answered most emphatically—No. The pitcher goes often to the fountain, but it is broken at last. The longest lane comes to an abrupt and unexpected turning, or, the lane is a mighty long one that has no turning. The city laws and regulations must be upheld and supported, either by submissiveness on the part of the law-breaker, or at a cost of his life's blood. Life was becoming perilous to live; the officer and citizen were in suspense and anxiety. Who would be the next to die at the hands of the assassin? The elements of character displayed by the border desperado was terrible to contemplate. They rushed in the city, took the town, hunted the officers and shot them down, then riding as swiftly as the wind, they crossed the Indian Territory line, reached Texas and escaped the hands of the law of our enterprising and law-abiding citizens.

The desperado oftimes branded with the mark of Cain upon his brow, visits our quiet town, and before leaving it, he becomes a transgressor and usually eludes the officers by reaching the adjacent territory which is usually filled with criminals, out-laws and murderers. Once in the Indian Territory they are safe and free from molestation, but occasionally, however, they meet their match and they are taken in by the officers. The first thought of the law-breaker is, "How and where can I escape?" which is answered by the second thought, "Flee to the Indian Territory." Under the circumstances which were existing, a remedy must be found in which their plans can be outwitted. What was to be the remedy? At last the city mayor, A. M. Colson, together with the city councilmen, after devising various methods and different operations, they concluded to send for a marshal, who was recommended as a good man for that position.

The new marshal was a stranger in the city, but he soon won the admiration of the citizens by his pleasing manners and good discipline. He soon won the hearts of the children, boys and girls, and many times has he been seen crossing the street with girls five, eight and ten years old hanging to his side, holding his hands, chatting and laughing merrily with this pleasant man who proved to be a fierce, determined officer and a leader of men.

The name of the new marshal was B. O. Carr, and usually answered to the name of "Bat," given him by his intimate friends. He was a man weighing perhaps, one hundred and eighty pounds; was well proportioned, probably five feet, eight inches in height. His manner was pleasing to the ladies and agreeable to the gentlemen. His dress was without fault; he was usually seen dressed in a uniform of dark navy blue, with polished gilt trimming and brass buttons. On his finger he wore a handsome ring, set with precious stones; in his hand he carried a polished cane, and upon his breast a large silver star with the words, "Bat Carr, Marshal," inscribed upon it. He took special pains to get acquainted with the citizens, who, as they become more intimate with him, learned to respect and honor him for his good moral character. He was strictly temperate in his habits, and was generally found at his

post of duty. I have given a big description of the
new marshal, as he appeared daily in his costume and
manners, now I will endeavor to picture him when he
assumed the role of the conqueror. No character in
this history presents more peculiarities than that of
"Bat" Carr. His whole nature was enigmetic; his
traits of character were peculiar. He was, apparently,
at once the polished gentleman and the daring frontiersman, shrinking from and courting danger at the same
time ; large in his own estimation, yet modest and most
unpretentious among his associates. He was a lover of
peace. His heighth of ambition was to be feared by
men. He took great pride in having his name looked
upon with terror and dismay by the cowboy and desperado. He had a perfect knowledge of human nature
and could unravel the hidden mysteries of the plots and
schemes laid by the cowboys. Carr was looked upon
as a necessary evil to straighten the lower class of
humanity which paraded the streets of Caldwell.

His assistant was a man similar in character to
Carr, with the exception that he seldom smiled, was
sober, candid and determined in expression and mind,
therefore was not familiar with the children, or a man
with whom the ladies loved to converse. He dressed
neatly, was gentlemanly and won friends immediately
upon his arrival in Caldwell.

These men were efficient officers, and forcibly upheld the law at all hazards. They were ever ready for the desperadoes lawless conduct, and took delight in an engagement which they were determined to prove the most powerful in producing the intended effects. The result was, the officers were looked upon by the public, as men with force of character which was not altogether assumed. Their determined expression, energy and unerring shot with the sixshooter, won for them a name of fame, both at home and abroad. They were looked upon by the cowboys as a "mighty terror," and soon learned they meant business, and were not there for their health, consequently quietness reigned supreme in the city of Caldwell, where once the cowboy held full sway and possession, and was the monarch of all he surveyed. There was no trifling with these marshals; when aroused they were like the fearless tiger of the wild jungles of Africa. These men were constantly on the alert, and when a man was requested to "throw up," it was at the muzzle of a cocked sixshooter, and the offender could read the expression of the marshal, which meant, "surrender or die." While Carr was looked upon as a holy terror, strange to say, while he was the marshal of Caldwell, he was not called upon to kill his man, when arresting a man or suppressing a riot.

Marshal Carr and Henry Brown, the assistant, made a different town of Caldwell ; it was no longer known as a rough place, the home of the wild and wooley cowboy, the haunt of the desperado, and the favorite resort of the horse thief. These outlaws soon learned the conditions under which they could visit the town in which they were to respect the wishes of the citizens and desires of the officers, whose word was looked upon by the rougher element as law, and was not to be broken.

The result of this was, that Caldwell began to take rapid strides toward becoming an enterprising and influential business center ; she is becoming the metropolis of Kansas, and her future destiny is written in letters of gold. New enterprises are started every day, new buildings are being erected, new people arrive in the town to cast their fortunes with the frontier settler. Railroads, school-houses, churches and neighbors can be found now, where the Indian, buffalo, coyote and skunk held unmolested possession then.

The past of Caldwell has been dark and gloomy, the present shows the cloud with the silver lining, and the future is bright with promises that will be realized in a grand and glorious manner.

Marshal Carr held dominion over Caldwell's interests until December 2, 1882, when he was removed from office, and the assistant, Henry Brown, was appointed to fill the office vacated by Carr.

Henry Brown had an assistant appointed by the name of B. F. Wheeler, formerly from Texas. Wheeler was a man above the average height of men, was well built and proportioned, a perfect blonde, and appeared more to the desperado style than that of a cultured gentleman, although he was gentlemanly in deportment and dress, yet he bore the rougher marks of humanity, by expression and carriage of form.

These men kept law and order in the city, hence were efficacious in filling the office. They were looked upon as gentlemen of good habits and moral character. Neither of the marshals were men who frequent the saloon, nor enjoy the festivities of the dancing hall, similar to the one located in the "Red Light" building.

Henry Brown married one of Caldwell's brightest young ladies, who had long been one of the leaders in society, and a favorite of her associates and acquaintances. They lived happily together for some time, when her heart was almost broken by the startling intelligence of her husband's tragical death.

The marshals were reappointed to fill the office, and filled it satisfactorily for several years. But, alas! their sad and mournful ending.

CHAPTER XXXV.

The Marshals of Caldwell Attempt to Rob the Medicine Valley Bank—Brown Shoots the president—Wheeler and Wesley Shoot the Cashier—A Ride for Life—Robbers driven in a pit of water—surrender—"Boys I am into it with you, I'll go out and Die with You."

In the early part of May 1884, Marshal Henry Brown and his assistant B. F. Wheeler left Caldwell for the purpose, claimed by the marshals, of searching for horse thieves for whom a large reward had been offered. The marshals intended to be gone for several days hence it would be necessary to appoint a marshal to fill the vacancy until Brown and Wheeler returned from their hunt. A few days after their departure the people of Caldwell were shocked with the intelligence of an awful crime committed at Medicine Lodge, a town located in Barber County, about sixty miles west of Caldwell. In this crime the two trusty and respected marshals of Caldwell were involved. The citizens were particularly interested in the affair and the facts of the awful tragedy were told by our citizens Ben. S. Miller, Harvey Homer, Lee Weller, and John A. Blair, who went to the scene of the crime to ascertain a true statement of the sickening affair. When the terrible news

reached Caldwell, these gentlemen left on an early train for Medicine Lodge, and arrived there about ten o'clock in the night. The town was all excitement, the citizens were nervous about the arrival of strangers in their city, but luckily for our citizens they were met at the train by two friends, Mayor Eldred and Dr. Moore, formerly from this place, who soon put them on good terms with the men of Medicine Lodge.

The facts reported to us are as follows: The marshals left Caldwell and were joined by two pals Smith and Wesley by name, and they immediately went in the vicinity of Medicine Lodge, not for the purpose of hunting horse thieves, however, but on a terrible mission in which a foul crime was commited.

They camped west of Medicine Lodge in a grove on the Medicine River. The next morning was shrouded in mist and about ten o'clock a slight rain was falling making the roads slippery and filling the ravines with water. No one seemed to notice the four horse men as they approached, and rode into town from the west. They stopped in the rear of the Medicine Valley Bank building; two of the horses were hitched by ropes, and Smith holding the third, was sitting on the remaining horse. Wheeler went in the building at the front door while Brown and Wesley went to a side door and entered the bank.

It is presumed, the men did not anticipate a meeting with obstacles and failure in the attempt made by them to rob the bank, but supposing the officers in the bank would yield readily to their command of throw up, whereupon they would take the money, and, depart with their treasures riding rapidly to a place of saftey. The old adage "The best laid plans of mice and men, gang aft aglee" may be applied appropriately to the schemes of the robbers.

The bank president and cashier had been notified that an attempt would be made to rob the bank, and these two gentlemen talked over the matter and concluded to make no preparations to guard the bank. The note received by these men was written by "I. bar." Johnson, and stated that an attempt would be made to rob the bank and in order to save their lives the warning said, they must not resist the commands of the robbers, hence, it was agreed by the officers, to throw up conformably, and take the chances on recapturing the money in case of a robbery.

Wheeler entered the building and pressented his revolver at Mr. Geppert, the cashier, and told him to "throw up his hands." At the same time Brown covered Mr. Payne, the president, with the same order. Wesley said nothing. It is believed that his part of the terrible business was to cover and kill, if necessary, the clerk Mr——but luckily for him he had gone to the post office with the Harper mail and was not at that time in the bank.

Cashier Geppert threw up his obedience to Wheeler's command, and after a moment of pause, he turned to see what Mr. Payne was doing, then Wheeler fired, shooting the cashier through the body. When Brown heard the shot fired by Wheeler he immediately after shot president Payne.

Mr. Gepperts expiring effort was directed toward throwing on the combination of the safe and gave conclusive evidence of the fact that they had received a notice of the intended robbery, for had he had no previous knowledge of the attack, it would be hard to believe that a man having received two fatal shots, one supposed to have been fired by **Wesley**, would turn directly to the safe, and, with the last motion of his nerveless arm turn a lock on the property of which he was guardian. The dead body of the cashier was founded, and near the combination of the safe, sitting in the vault with his lifes blood streaming and crimsoning every thing about him. Faithful to the last, his expiring thought was of the property in his charge, and, with the shadow of death hovering over him he staggered to the vault, threw on the combination and sank into eternity.

Payne received but one wound at the hands of Marshal Brown. The shot staggered him, he fell from the shock and was found on the floor of the bank, writhing and groaning in the terrible agonies of death. He lived long enough to make a statement, saying Brown was his murderer and that Wheeler and Wesley killed Geppert.

While the shooting was going on, Smith was in the rear of the bank in charge of the horses. When the firing was heard in the bank, the marshal of the town observing Smith, and, thinking all was not right in the bank, he opened fire upon Smith with a six shooter. When Brown heard the shots fired by the marshal, he became uneasy and ran to the door of the bank, took in the situation at once, and opened fire on the marshal with his winchester, firing three shots. Smith began shooting at the marshal and everybody else he could see.

Brown, Wheeler and Wesley failing in their attempt to gain possession of the money, and, realizing they were murderers in the sight of the law and outlaws upon the face of the earth, and, to escape the justice and fate which awaited them, realized the only chance for them was to flee from the town of excited people, and, if possible find refuge in the canyons which wonld serve as a place of concealment until the excitement was over.

The robbers ran for their horses, which they had great difficulty in loosening, the ropes having become taut in the rain. Their horses once loose, they mounted them and rode as fastly as their horses could run. Wheeler had purchased a fast horse before he left Caldwell and it ran with good speed for a short distance, but after running several miles it began to show signs of fatigue and was completely wearied out, so the horse was abandoned; in order to escape two men must ride one horse, all going in a southwest direction.

The country southwest of Medicine Lodge is very rough and broken with deep canyons and ravines. The robbers were so closely pursued by the excited citizens of Medicine Lodge, that they left their horses and ran into a canyon, which was immediately surrounded by the men who crowded the robbers deeper into the recesses of the canyon until they were driven into a hole —— a pit in fact, filled with water. The robbers were defending themselves from the shots fired by the inflamed citizens, by shooting at them with their Winchesters and revolvers. At last, they are standing in water waist deep, and have become benumbed and cold and a surrender is necessary. Some of the posse have returned to the town for the necessary articles to bring about an immediate surrender.

Only nine men are guarding the canyon in which the robbers had retreated.

Brown was the first man to give up. He called out to the attacking party and proposed to surrender in case they would protect him from violence. The promise was made, and Henry Brown, the man whom our people have always thought so brave, walked out of the hole, into which he had been driven, and laid down his gun. The assistant marshal, Wheeler, came out second, Wesley third, and finally Smith the only game man in the band of robbers, the only man that seemed to realize the frailty of a promise of protection after their awful deed, walked out of the pit, saying "Boys I came into it with you, and I'll go out and die with you." Ah! if they only could have realized the terrible fate which awaited them, of the awful doom and death which was to be theirs, how differently would have been their intentions, and how they would have fought to the bitter end, resolving to die game. Their role as actors in the drama of life is not yet over; would that we could draw the curtain closing the scene in all its horror from the gaze and minds of the public; would could spare the facts of the heart sickening affair from the young wife of Marshal Brown.

It will be our business in the next chapter to give the account of the sorrowful death of these men upon whom the Medicine Lodge people had vowed to seek vengeance for the death of their honored citizens.

CHAPTER XXXVI.

The robbers taken to Medicine Lodge—Photograps taken—Letter written by Brown to his wife—The mob attack the jail—Brown shot—Wheeler wounded—Three robbers hung—Sentiments of the people.

The robbery was attempted about ten o'clock in the morning. The robbers were brought into town by the nine men to whom they surrendered, at about one o'clock in the afternoon. About three hours after the terrible crime was committed at the bank, the robbers were shackled and put into the calaboose, the only jail in which the prisoners could be confined. The prisoners were furnished with dry clothing and properly cared for by the citizens. During the day, a photograph was taken of the four prisoners, and a good picture was obtained of all except Wheeler; his features were so drawn that they looked unnatural. It is stated that when the time arrived for the prisoners to stand, so that the photograph could be taken, our former brave city marshal got down on his knees and implored for mercy. Is it possible that this is the man who held Caldwell in terror so long.

The men were furnished with paper with which they might write any word to friends or relatives they wished. Brown wrote an affectionate letter to his young

wife, telling her of his incarceration, crime, and his doubts as to the probability of not meeting with her again. Wheeler tried to write, but failed in the attempt; the facts were plainly shown that he had'nt the nerve to put his thoughts on paper.

About midnight the calaboose was surrounded by a crowd of men numbering about three hundred; they disarmed the sheriff, and opened the jail, intending to take the prisoners and lynch them to the nearest tree.

When the door was opened, Brown rushed out, having got free from his shackles; he only ran a few yards however, when the night air was filled with the sound of the guns fired at the fleeing man, who fell, with a pound of lead distributed through his body. Wheeler too, was free from his shackles, and also started on the run; he proved to be the fleetest runner of the two men and ran farther than Brown, perhaps one hundred yards, when he too, fell. He had been shot in the right arm, which was badly shattered; two fingers of his left hand were shot away, and his body was pierced by three Winchester balls. He made a confession, but it was never revealed to the inquisitive public. Wheeler implored for mercy, and it is said, his cries were so loud that they were heard half a mile away. The doomed man begged piteously to be spared until ten o'clock the following day, and said he would give away many things, that would interest the community at large. The excited mob could not wait, and Wheeler was not spared an hour, but was swung up with Smith and Wesley. Smith showed more nerve than either of the other men, and seemed unconcerned in reference to the awful death he was to die. He died without a murmer and was game to the last. Wheeler was hung with a lariat rope. Brown by his attempted escape, met a more preferable death than by hanging; probably he anticipated what his end would be and preferred to die by being pierced with bullets, than a death by the hangmans noose.

At the request of the gentlemen from Caldwell, the bodies of Brown and Wheeler were exhumed, and the boys reported that the features of the dead men were as natural as if they were merely asleep. The bodies were shrouded and buried in pine coffins. Their last resting place is just over the line of the Medicine Lodge cemetery.

I. bar. Johnson came into Medicine Lodge and made a sworn statement, to the general effect, that about five weeks before the terrible tragedy, Wheeler and the others came to him and urged him to enter into the plot to rob the bank. He refused to do so, and they told him that their intentions were to rob the bank anyhow, and that if he squealed they would kill him. He said that he notified Geppert and Payne that an attempt at robbery would be made, and that the robbers would order them to throw up their hands, and that if they complied, they would not be hurt.

At this time, and in this connection, it might be proper to state the council of Caldwell took notice of the affair by drafting and adopting the following resolutions, which were found in the city clerk's book, and are as follows:

"Mr. Mayor and gentleman of the council: Your committee to whom was referred the matter of drafting resolutions, expressive of the sentiments of the people of Caldwell in regard to the Medicine Lodge tragedy, have had the matter under consideration and submit the following report:

WHEREAS, Two men in whom the Government and people of Caldwell have heretofore reposed great trust and confidence, have to the unutterable amazement and mortification of our citizens, proved themselves murderers, robbers, cowards and villains of the worst type, by their criminal attack on the Medicine Valley bank, of Medicine Lodge, Kansas; and the wanton murder of Mr. Payne and Mr. Geppert, President and Cashier of said bank, and

WHEREAS, We recognize in the untimely death of Mr. Payne and Mr. Geppert not only an irreparable loss to the city of Medicine Lodge and Barber county, but by loss to Kansas of two of the best citizens of which our State could boast; and

WHEREAS, We recognize the fact that the two men who were the murderers of Mr. Payne and Mr. Geppert had received a large degree of credit, by reason of their employment by this city as peace officers, we deem it due to the citizens of Medicine Lodge that we should take some official notice of the terrible crime that has so shocked their community in regard to the terrible deed. Therefore be it

Resolved, by the Mayor and councilmen of the city of Caldwell that the people of Caldwell are horrified by the awful deed which so tragically ended the lives of Mr. Payne and Mr. Geppert, and that they extend to the citizens of Medicine Lodge, and especially to the families and intimate friends of the gentlemen, their deepest and best sympathies in their unconsolable loss, that the people of Caldwell keenly feel the disgrace which her former officers, by their desperately criminal conduct, have brought upon our community. That in no manner whatever, do our citizens entertain any semblance of sympathy for the depraved creatures who have proved themselves the worst enemies of civilized society. And while our people deplore the necessity for lynch law in any case, they do most heartily approve of the summary manner in which the sturdy men of Medicine Lodge administered justice to the scoundrels who so rudely brought death and sorrow to their door."

It seems the resolutions are unsigned and they show quite plainly that the committee was not very well experienced in drafting resolutions, but the sentiments shown seems plainly to be "an eye for an eye and a tooth for a tooth."

CHAPTER XXXVII.

A man borrows a shot gun and leaves the country—A warrant for his arrest—I search for the offender—The trip to Arkansas City—We spy the thief—A chew of tobacco—I make the arrest of the man—The return to Caldwell.

In the year 1880, a man living near Caldwell, borrowed a shot gun from a friend of his, and after obtaining possession of it he left the country taking the gun with him. After waiting a certain length of time for the man who had borrowed the gun to return it, the owner of it swore out a warrant for the arrest of the guilty party.

As I was an officer it became my duty to find the offender, arrest him and obtain possession of the much coveted article, and return it to the owner.

I left Caldwell in the early morning and started East, and my intentions were to proceed to the town of Arkansas City, located in Cowley County, Kansas. After I had traveled about two miles East of Caldwell, I met Dr. Black of that town, and I requested his company in making my journey to Arkansas City.

Dr. Black readily consented to go with me, so he got in the buggy and we started on our journey. We traveled all day and about sundown in the evening we arrived in Arkansas City. I looked around thinking perhaps the man was in the city, but my effort to find him proved futile, so we concluded to remain in the city until morning, when we would again resume our search for the man and the gun.

We had our team taken care of for the night, and we took in the sights which were to be seen in the small town of Arkansas City. That was before the days of the western booms, and Arkansas City had not been boomed as she has since, hence it was not difficult to view the sights, and in a very few minutes we had seen everything of any note and were ready to retire for the night.

On the following morning we were in readiness to look for the man who had stolen the gun. We drove our team to the state line, a few miles South of the town, but failed to receive any information concerning the object of our search. As we were returning to Arkansas City we met a man traveling on the road and made inquiry of him and described the team and men whom we were hunting to him. He said he had seen two men with a team corresponding with the description I gave, traveling on the road East of Arkansas City, and they were perhaps one mile East of the town when he saw them. He gave us information concerning the crossing on the Walnut River, and told us if we would drive rapidly we would probably reach the men at the river crossing.

We started in hot pursuit in the direction given us by the man, and when we came to the river to our surprise we saw the party for whom we were searching. When we arrived on the river bank, they were about midway across the stream, and had stopped the team which were drinking of the cool water.

We waited until the opposite bank was reached by both parties, when I drove my team alongside of the wagon and asked the men for a chew of tobacco. The man that was driving stopped his team, and the man, with the gun, handed me the requested "chew."

After taking the desired amount, I gave him his tobacco and asked if he wished to sell his gun, and at the same time, held my hand for it asking him for the privilege of examining it. Not thinking what my object was, in getting possession of the "deadly weepen," he handed it over to me. When I had gained possession of the gun, I felt confident that I would have no trouble in arresting the man. Without suspecting my intentions, the man asked me if I wanted to buy or trade for the gun.

I replied that I did not think I did, as I had gained the possession of it and that I had a warrant for his arrest, charged with stealing the gun. He was taken completely by surprise, and when the facts began to dawn upon him, he began to laugh and he said it was the "slickest arrest he ever heard of."

He asked me if I had a gun, I replied that I had "neither a gun, revolvers, pocket-knife or a chew of tobacco. He thought it was a strange thing on my part to go in pursuit of a thief, and carry no weapons to use in making the arrest, or in self-defence. I told him that was not my manner of securing an arrest, and I had always found it advisable and it was more satisfactory to me, to deal gently with a law breaker, and endeavor to secure his arrest without demanding a "throw up" before I was ready, to have him "throw up" probably, with a six shooter leveled at my head and within a few inches of my face. I have found this, that in order to accomplish a successful arrest you must be a correct reader of human nature, consequently it will be necessary to "know your man" and deal with him as his case of human nature may demand.

It is foolish for an officer to risk his life, when attempting to arrest a drunken cowboy or desperado. Nine times out of ten when a demand is made by the officer commanding a "throw up" the command is met with a volley of shots fired from the hands of the offender, the shot sometimes taking effect in the head or breast of the officer, and he dies while at his post of duty, and while endeavoring to quell disturbances and in attempting to make the arrest of a desperate and lawless citizen of the United States.

The man whom I had arrested got in the buggy and we drove back to Caldwell and was greeted with much warmth by the owner of the gun. The difficulty was settled satisfactorily, by the interested parties, without calling the case before a court.

Years after this occurrence, when I was in Arkansas City, I met the man who had stolen the gun, and he asked me for a chew of tobacco, and as he did so, he referred to the time when I asked the same favor of him and secured his arrest in such a quiet manner. He said he had never heard of such a case, and concluded if all officers would adopt my method of arresting a criminal, there would be less bloodshed and murders commited, and a less number of murderers and assasins at large.

CHAPTER XXXVIII.

The Indian's Custom when Traveling among White Settlers—Women Terrorized when Alone by Hearing, "How, John?"—Young Lady Refused to Give the Indian Food—Wild Horse plays with her golden Locks—Her Father comes to the Rescue—The Marshal undertakes to Make him "Throw Up"—Fires over his Head—"Hold on John, Me getting my Gun—Death of the Indian and his Burial.

After the advent of the railroad to Caldwell, all government supplies for the Indians was shipped to that place. Heretofore Wichita had supplied the freighter with his load of provision, for transportation into the Indian Territory, and to be delivered at the several Indian agencies.

The white man for many years had hauled the freight to the Indian reservations, and in doing so, he had endured the storms of winter and the heat of the summer, while lo, the poor Indian lived a life of idleness and laziness, and I might add, a life of ease and luxury, all at the expense of the government. The Indian passed the hours in hunting, lounging around in the tepee, apparently enjoying a life filled with satisfaction and comfort. The agent gives them their allowances of provision every month; each Indian, little and big, receive a certain proportion of the provisions which the white man had hauled for hundreds of miles.

The idea was conceived, finally, and put into execution by the leaders of our government, in which the Indian could haul their own freight. They had large herds of ponies, and the government furnished wagons and harness, and provided the Indians would haul the freight, and thus save the expense of hiring the white man. The Indians were pleased to visit the state, and the numerous towns along their route. An interpeter was sent with each band, to secure their freight for them, and to keep them from troubling the white people with whom they would come in contact in their travels.

As they traveled to and from Wichita, they would usually stop at the dwelling houses situated along the road, and beg provisions from the settlers. One of the strong characteristics of the Indian, is an inclination to beg articles of food or wearing appeal. Many times they steal articles of clothing, conceal them under their blankets, and afterwards either trade it, sell it, or adapt to their own use. They seldom wore a protection on their heads, but occasionally, one might be seen wearing, a hat many sizes too large for him, and a squaw with a parasol of some bright color held above and as a shield from the rays of the hot sun, long,

long after the day star had hidden himself below the horizon.

The Indian has a peculiar manner of walking, their feet are encased in a pair of beaded moccasins, which give no sound of their approaching footsteps. Their tread is so light, that upon their approach, you are usually taken by surprise to find their presence so near; you are greeted with their manner of salutation, "How, John." The friendly Indian extends his hand and grasps yours with vise grip, and assures you that he is a good Indian, then he wants corn for "ponce, chuckaway" for pappoose, and continues begging until he is either driven away, or the door closed and locked.

Many times when these pests are passing through the country, the husband and father of the house are from home, either in the field at work, or away from home on business. The Indian approaches with such quietness that the women folks are surprised and terrorized at the sight of their dusky faces. The fact dawns to the minds of the women that they are alone with the savage. They are so frightened by the presence of the Indian, that they lose self control, and probably, their common sense. The Indian, as usual, offers his hand saying, "How John?" and the trembling woman takes the offered hand saying, "How?" The small amount of the English language possessed by many of the Indians, leads them to think that, "How John?" is a proper greeting to a white person, whether male or female.

The terror which seizes the wife when alone, when receiving the greeting, "How John?" causes her many times to donate any article of the household that the Indian may chance to demand. A few cases have occurred in which the house-wife has given all of the flour, coffee, sugar and other eatables which her home possessed. This was done simply to get rid of poor Lo in a friendly way.

The Indian, like other animals, plainly recognizes the fact, that while women when alone, are suddenly seized with fear when he is seen at the door. Sometimes, however, when neighbors are near, or in towns, women are courageous enough to refuse the demands made for grub by the Indians.

On one of these occasions a case like this occurred in the town of Caldwell. Indians had come to Caldwell for government freight, or freight for themselves, but the freight not having arrived, they were compelled to wait in camp near the town for its arrival. While there, they concluded, begging would be in first class order. One of the Indians, Wild Horse by name, went to the house of Ephriam Beals, on one of these begging expeditions, not seeing any man in the house, and thinking Mr. Beals was away from home, and that the women are alone, he demanded that the young lady, daughter of the household, should get him something to eat. She refused pointedly. Whereupon he seized her by the hair, and attempted to force her to grant his request. At this time, Mr. Beals being in an adjoining room, came out and pushed the Indian out of the door, and followed him out, and seizing a spade which lay in the yard, and was about to strike him with it, when someone passing by, went into the yard and caught the uplifted spade, as the Indian was unwrapping his revolver from the blanket which he carried. The Indians by this time concluded it was best to leave, and go down into town.

Whereupon Mr. Beals reported to marshal Henry Brown what had happened and that the Indian was carrying a revolver, which was contrary to city ordinance. Marshal Brown went to hunt for Mr. Indian, and finally found him in Mr. Wm. Morris' grocery store. After leaving the house of Mr. Beals, from some source, the Indian had received a drink or two of "fire water" and was "Big Injun and Bad Injun." The marshal approached the Indian with revolver in hand, and pointing it toward him, demanded him to "throw up." The Indian, either not understanding what the marshal meant, or not being willing to submit, he refused to accede to his demand. The marshal thinking to frighten him, fired his revolver twice just above the Indian's head, which only tended to irate him and cause his desperate courage to raise. He saw there was a chance for a fight. The whiskey had aroused his savage disposition, and all the passions and vices of his savage nature. The novelist in his books of beautiful and pleasing romance, may picture the Indian to the minds of the reader, as an innocent, simple-minded character, and adopt for him the " noble red man " in place of the name of a savage.

Those who have lived on the frontier for years, do not address the Indian as the "noble red man;" their character and cruel disposition is too well known, and they are designated by the people simply as the Indian.

When the marshal fired at the Indian, instead of surrendering to the officer, he began unwrapping his revolver and said, "Hold on John, wait, me get my gun," at this statement the marshal saw the Indian was ready for a deadly contest, so he fired at the Indian before he had time to shoot his revolver. The shot took effect, and tore the top of the Indian's head off.

When the shooting occurred there were several Indians near the store; they hastily mounted their ponies and rode to the camp about one and a half miles from town. There were probably one hundred Indians at the camp, and great excitement prevailed throughout the camp. Some of the citizens of the town feared an outbreak among the savages, and the marshal was greatly censured by the timid people for creating a disturbance by killing the Indian. Those who were inclined to fear the cunning savages, were very uneasy and filled with anxiety, when they realized the character and disposition possessed by the Indian.

In a short time some of the Indians came into town, accompanied by the dead Indian's squaw. They did not manifest any spirit of revenge, and said, "Wild Horse was a bad Cheyenne." Their expressions lead the citizens to believe that Wild Horse's death was not greatly mourned by the tribe to which he belonged.

The citizens of Caldwell gave the body of Wild Horse proper burial at the city's expense. Several of the Indians attended the burial services, and expressed themselves as satisfied with the actions of the city marshal, and of the burial of Wild Horse.

While the Indians seemed satisfied with the burial given Wild Horse, his immediate relatives expressed a desire to kill his pony and place it on his grave in order that the animal might accompany him when he reached the "happy hunting ground." This custom

WILD HORSE.

was contrary to the rules of modern civilization ; the request was refused.

They remained several days in camp south of town, and according to their custom, held their pow-wow's, or times of lamentation, but manifested no disposition of revenge toward the people of Caldwell. All seemed satisfied that Wild Horse was dead, as none of them considered him very much credit to the tribe.

CHAPTER XXXIX.

Court in session before a Justice in Caldwell—Steaming up the lawyers—Bent's ludicrous plea to the court—The Justice furnishes money to treat the crowd—A second trial—A novel way of giving in a verdict—A third case before the Justice court.—The Justice gets drunk —The case settled by paying ten dollars—The editor of the Sumner County Evening Post publishes an article on the drunken Justice—A challenge to fight a duel—The editor declines to accept it.

The bell rings, the curtain rises, showing scenes which are not based upon fiction, but actual facts; which actually occurred in Caldwell during the years of 1872 and 1873. Caldwell, not like the novel hero, born of poor but respectable parents, was not born at all. It was like Topsy, "just growed," and while its population was waiting for a speedy realization of their most cherished hopes, and seemingly visionary prophesies, they are in the midst of jocund merriment. The adage for children, "Satan finds some mischief still, for idle hands to do," may be applied to men, whose life is complicated with entire idleness and the love of strong drink.

Life becomes monotonous to the idler, the cowboy and the Texas steer; for him no longer has it the charms it once possessed. His loneliness is increased when he looks at the immensity of the unpeopled prairie; the infinite sketching of the plains, unbroken by tree or shrub, by fence or house; and he gathers together all of his ideas, in which he may plant something new, and present it before the minds of the people. It has been said, "Idleness is the work-shop of satan," but whether his royal highness ever condescended to enlighten his clients, by giving them an opinion, remains a mystery.

I have briefly recorded the dark, gloomy days of Caldwell's early history. This history embraces many scenes of riot and discord, and many unfortunate victims are sleeping beneath the green surf, whose death can be attributed to the free use of the six-shooter, or hung by unknown parties; and whiskey, indirectly, may be said to have been the cause of much disorder, bloodshed and many deaths.

In this chapter I will give the reader an idea how court was held in the early days of Caldwell's history. The incident that I am going to relate, was probably instigated by some one belonging to that class of idlers to whom I have referred, and was gotten up as a scheme in which the participants could play a good joke on the justice of the town.

This mans name —— Fox; and he was the first justice elected after the township had been organized. Fox was a doctor and kept a drug store in Caldwell.

The trial of which I am going to relate was held in the drug store. Fox was a man of an excellent reputation, and filled the office of justice of the peace very satisfactory.

There had been no trials for a few days and people concluded it was getting pretty dull in court matters, and the lawyers were getting out of the practice of quoting Blackstone; so a little plot was laid, in which they were to have some fun, over a sham trial. The instigators of the plan did not let either of the lawyers into the secret. One of the men swore out a warrant before the justice, for the arrest of one of the parties, who was into the secret, and brought it to me to serve. I knew of the joke perpetrated, so I arrested the man and subpoenaed ten or twelve witnesses for the trial, all of whom were into the secret. While I was serving the subpoena, the leaders of the joke were getting the lawyers ready for action, by treating them freely to whiskey, or in words, to use their expression, they were "steaming them up." When they were "steamed up" about as high as they could be under control of the men, I called the court to order. The witnesses were sworn to "tell the truth." Good order prevailed while the witnesses were giving their evidence, and after all the testimonies were given to the court, a few minutes were needed in which the lawyers could add a little more "steam." Court was adjourned for this purpose and the crowd entered the saloon. It was expected the lawyers would make a lengthy plea for their client and a high guage of "steam" would be necessary, in order to have a fine time.

In about thirty minutes court was again called to order, and every one in the court room became silent. The lawyer on the defense was a very small man, and usually went by the name "Yank;" he had a large share of self conceit and placed great stress on his ability as a lawyer. He could make a good speech when he was well "steamed up."

The lawyer for the state having waived the opening speech, "Yank" took the floor and made a lengthy plea in defense of his client, but as soon as his "steam" began to be exhausted he weakened and took his seat. All the while "Yank" was speaking, the other lawyer was indulging in drinking whiskey every few minutes, and the consequences were that he was "steamed up" to the highest notch in the guage and yet had some to spare.

He was a large man weighing perhaps, two hundred and fifty pounds; was well known throughout the west; he served the office of deputy sheriff of Cowley county before he came to Caldwell, and was elected several times to act as an officer of Sumner county. By his intimate friends he was known by no other appendage, but simply "Bent," and in referring to him in this chapter, we will use the name which is familiar to his many friends. He was a man of good reputation, and had many excellent qualities as a citizen.

As "Bent" arose to take the floor vacated by his opponent, I saw the crowd was about to burst out into a laugh; I requested order and they were soon quieted; "Bent" had on such a powerful guage of "steam" that his locomotion was badly interfered with, and he took hold of the counter and tried to steady himself while making his plea. After speaking a few minutes, he turned to the justice and looking at him steadily in the face, raised himself to his entire height by standing on his tiptoes, and said; "Now Mr. Court, as the people say bind him over, you must say bind him over, and God says bind him over, and I say, By G—d, bind him over."

While "Bent" was finding a seat, the audience were yelling, and applauding the speech made by him. The justice began to look at the lawyers, then at the witnesses, meanwhile the crowd were hurrahing and shouting to the extent allowed them by their vocal organs.

The justice hesitated a few minutes, then the secret

began to dawn, and he saw through the whole plans, and knew the easiest and quickest manner to settle it. He saw it was a joke on him, for he had used all the dignity he could muster and looked very wise throughout the trail. He put his hand into his pocket and drew out a couple of dollars, and said, "Gentlemen you all know I do not drink, but you can take this and do as you wish with it, and I hope it will pay all costs which have accrued relative to this trial."

No dismissal of court was necessary, and the crowd went to a saloon and drank to the health of justice Fox, each one feeling it was good to be there. The reader will readily draw his own conclusions, concerning the object of the trial. Whiskey was the ruling element, and the man who, very often treated his friends and companions to a "social glass" was the most admired, and looked upon as the champion of the crowd, and in the community at large. The man who drinks, and carries a fat pocket book, and contributes largely towards treating his companions, is always favored among that class of people so long as his money and generosity lasts; but let the dark hours of adversity come to his abiding place, and share a large proportion of his life, then these friends flee from him, leaving him to share his hours of misfortune and disappointments alone. They "want full measure for all their pleasure" but do not want his woe.

How many men in after years, when taking a retrospective view of their life, wish when he started to spend the evening with wild companions, either at the saloon or club, they had heeded to the advice of mother, sister, or the wife: and how often, thoughts similar to these words come rushing to his mind : "the fondest hopes I cherished" "all have faded one by one."

I will now relate the facts concerning a trial held before the second justice of Caldwell

The evidence as shown in the suit, was that W. B. King and John Turner went on a buffalo hunt together, and while they were out hunting a horse was found, and each man claimed the right of possession. Turner was the successful man however, and got possession and took the horse home with him. King replevined the horse and the result was a trial before the justice court. Turner and King wanted a trial by jury to determine who would have the right of possession of the horse.

After the jury were selected the trial proceeded; and peace reigned throughout the trial, until the jury were ready to give their verdict to the court. The jury demanded their fees before they would proceed to give in their decision. The plaintiff and defendant, both refused to pay the jury fees. The jury stood firm in their resolution, and as the hour was getting late, court was adjourned until the following morning at ten o'clock.

I was constable and was ordered to take the jury and keep them from having any conversation with any one until their verdict was rendered to the court. I engaged a comfortable room and got their suppers for them. Everything was passing pleasantly along until about nine o'clock in the night.

One of the jurors was a clerk in C. H. Stone's store and he wanted the clerk to go to Wichita early the next morning, to haul a load of supplies from that place to Caldwell. Mr. Stone came to me and wanted me to dismiss the clerk, who was acting as juror. I told Mr. Stone I could not dismiss him until the jury gave their decision to the court. This did not satisfy the merchant, so he went to see the justice about it.

In a short time Mr. Stone and the justice came to me and the justice said the clerk could tell him what his decision was, and he was not to give in the decision until the jurors received their fees. This was satisfactory to the remaining jurors and the clerk went with Mr. Stone, and early the next morning he started on the road to Wichita.

The following morning I took the jurors into the court room, where the parties concerned paid them their fees and waited for their verdict. The justice and the five jurors gave in their verdict, giving the plaintiff possession of the horse. The defendant appealed the case to a higher court.

The reader will conclude that we were badly in need of a little knowledge relating to the profession of law. Caldwell like all the towns on the frontier, had to "live and learn;" in the learning, her officers would often afford a great deal of mirth and amusement, for those who were inclined to be merry.

In the year of 1872, a man by the name of McClain brought suit against me for the sum of sixty-eight dollars. This man McClain, was the proprietor of the Last Chance Ranch. He was in debt to me for the sum of eight dollars, and before the time of the suit he said he had the advantage of me, as the justice was a particular friend of his.

McClain sued me on Monday and the suit was to be tried on the following Saturday. I sent to Wellington and employed J. Wade McDonald, of Wellington, as my lawyer in the trial. On Saturday morning the justice began to indulge pretty freely in drinking whiskey, and about ten o'clock he was pretty well "steamed up." I went to his office and told him I wanted a change of venue. He said (hic) (hic) why can't the suit (hic) be tried before me. I told him he was too drunk to attend to the case. He said, "(hic) you may write up the nec

essary papers for a change of venue, and I'll sign it."
My lawyer had not arrived yet and I wrote the business
papers and took them to get the justice's signature; he
gave a couple of faint hic's and said he was not able to
sign the article, but if any one would sign his name for
him he would be very much pleased. No sooner had he
finished speaking then he fell off his chair and lay in a
drunken stupor.

I knew our suit could not be tried that day, and that
it would be proper and right that we should pay due respects to the court. We considered over the matter,
and finally decided the best way to pay our respects
would be to take proper care of the justice; so we took
him to a livery barn and tucked him away in the feed
room, and left him lying on the floor of the oat bin.

As I was leaving the barn, I met Mr. McDonald
and John T. Showalter at the door; they alighted and
had their team taken care of by the employe of the
livery stable. Judge McDonald asked me how I was
getting along with my trial. I replied that I presumed
my chances were pretty good, and that the prospects
were not favorable concerning the time for trial, for
the justice had entered a trance, and in all probability,
he would not recover from its effects for several days.
The lawyer went to the feed room and looked at the
justice, and returned to me, and shaking his head, said,

sadly, "There is no chance for a trial to-day, that poor fellow has taken an overdose of 'red eye,' consequently he must sleep off the effects."

While I was engaged in conversation with Judge McDonald, Mr. McClain approached us, and asked me how much I would give him to settle our suit without bringing it for trial. I replied that I would not give him anything. A fellow townsman who was standing near, turned to McClain and asked him how much he would take to settle it. Mr. McClain replied that he would settle it for ten dollars in cash; whereupon the man gave him ten dollars and took a receipt for the money received, also a written statement giving dates of the first acquaintance I had with Mr. McClain, and certifying the payments of all debts up to the present date.

McClain took the ten dollars and went to a saloon, and inviting the bystanders to come on and have something to drink. Before McClain left the bar, he had squandered all of the ten dollars, excepting fifty cents, which he said must be paid to the justice for the trouble and care he had experienced since the case had been brought before that honorable personage.

This justice was the lawyer I have mentioned who took part in the joke played on Justice Fox. This was lawyer "Yank," who took the case in behalf of the defense, and plead his mightiest plea, and after court adjourned, he, in company with others, drank to the health of Justice Cox.

The day was a dull one in court business; there being only five law suits brought before the other justice. Mr. McDonald was employed as lawyer on all the cases, and at night I went to him and asked what his charges were against me. He replied that it had been a poor day for law suits, as one of the justices was drunk. He also said, that his time had been well improved during the day, and he would not ask anything from me, as my case had not been called for trial, consequently I paid nothing, excepting the ten dollars, which I afterwards paid to the man who had settled with McClain.

Thus ended a day in which the lawyers were the victors; they having received the good will of their client, who treated them to an extra glass of whiskey, and they were also the fortunate ones, as I presume their pocket books were well filled with bright sheckels of silver, or a sufficient amount of currency to pay a board bill at a fifteen cent restaurant.

A few days after Judge McDonald's return to Wellington, the "Sumner County Press," published at Wellington, contained an article supposed to have been written by the editor, J. H. Folks. The article was something similar to the following, if not quite the same language: "While we were in the town of Caldwell, we met our friend and fellow townsman, John T. Showalter, who was quietly waiting for the justice to sober up so he could have a lawsuit."

This article insulted Justice "Yank," and he immediately sent a written challenge to the editor of the press, requesting him to meet him in the Indian Territory, and fight a duel to the death of one or both parties concerned.

The editor made mention of the challenge he had received in language something like this : "This was the first time in all our life we had received a challenge to fight a duel, and not being of a chivalrous turn of mind, we refused to accept it." It will be observed by the reader, that the press has made no mention of "Yank" being drunk, and why "Yank" had been insulted, it would be difficult to conjecture.

I presume the challenge was not accepted, or at least, I am certain the duel was never fought.

CHAPTER XL.

Escape of a Horse Thief from the Sheriff of Cowley County Kansas—The Arrival of the Thief at the "Last Chance" Ranch—I go to Assist the Deputy Sheriff in Making the Arrest—Our Arrival with the Thief Causes Great Excitement in Caldwell—An Attempt to Lynch the Prisoner—a Scheme in which the Prisoner was taken from the Town—The Mob Demand the Prisoner from the Guards—Foiled in their Attempt

In the month of July 1872 the Deputy Sheriff of Cowley county, Kansas, came to Caldwell in search of a horse thief who had escaped from the hands of the sheriff. It seems there was no jail in Winfield in which to keep the prisoner, so it became necessary for the sheriff to guard him. The sheriff shackled one of the prisoners feet, and allowed him liberty, to a certain extent, and everything was all right until one evening the prisoner was sent by the sheriff to get his cows and drive them home. The prisoner went to the wood pile secured an ax and succeeded in cutting the shackles from his foot, and once loose, he made the best of his liberty, and instead of going for the cows, he went to the Indian Territory and traveling west, he arrived, in a short time, at the Ranch called the "Last Chance," which the reader will remember as the place McCarty sought as a refuge after he had killed Fielder and Doc Anderson.

This Ranch has been brought very prominently before the minds of the reader, and what tales of dissipation, night revelry and bloodshed would be told could its old log foundation reveal to the minds of the inquisitive people of later years.

When the horse thief arrived at the "Last Chance" he remained there over night and on the morrow started for Pond Creek Ranch, which is located twenty-six miles south of Caldwell, and the ranch derives its name from the name of the Creek upon which it is located.

When the sheriff became aware of the prisoners escape, he sent the deputy sheriff, T. H. B. Ross by name to Caldwell in search of the horse thief. Mr Ross, or "Bent" as he was familiary called, came to me, and asked my assistance in making the arrest. It was then about six o'clock in the evening, and I told "Bent" that I would go to the "Last Chance" and see if the man was there. The Ranch was kept by McClain, and when I arrived there I asked McClain if the man had been there, giving a description of the thief. McClain said there had been no one there answering that description. I imagined I could see a change of countenance in Mr. McClain, and I was satisfied in my own mind that the thief had been at the Ranch, and had probably received assistance from McClain.

I turned my horse and started toward Caldwell and when I had rode about fifty yards, I met a young man who motioned for me to stop. I did so, and he said if I would give him one dollar and not tell any person about it, he would tell me where the man was I wanted. I gave him the money and he said a man came to the Ranch the night before, arriving there about twelve o'clock. The man was given something to eat, and he left a couple of hours before daylight, and had told the proprietor of the ranch, that he was going to Pond Creek, and remain at the Ranch until he could get into company with some cattlemen, and travel with them until he reached Texas.

I went to the town and reported the information I had received to the Deputy Sheriff. "Bent" did not care to arrest the man alone and asked me to accompany him to Pond Creek. I declined doing so, unless he would give me half of the reward which had been offered for the arrest of the escaped thief. "Bent" readily agreed to share the reward with me, and also said, he would furnish the team and buggy to take us to the Pond Creek Ranch.

We made preparations to start for the Ranch; we took along some provisions, and a large quantity of beer. "Bent" was a lover of beer hence he laid in a good supply of that article. When we were ready to start, a man by the name of Colonel Connoble offered to help us make the arrest, so we three "lit out" and reached Pond creek about noon. We drove up near the door and I jumped out of the buggy and entered the ranch. The Deputy and Colonel Connoble followed me, and as I entered the door, I noticed a man, answering the description of the thief, as it was given me by "Bent."

I stepped near the man, and waited for the other two men to come in the house. When "Bent" came in he gave me an introduction to the man; I held out my hand to shake hands, and I seized his with a good grip, and at the same time, reached into my pocket with my left hand and produced a pair of hand-cuffs; I put one of them on one of his wrists and requested him to hold his other hand while I made the cuffs secure; thus I acquainted him of my purpose and mission into the Indian Territory. The prisoner was very much frightened and shook as though he was sitting astraddle of an electric wire, with the full force of the electricity applied to that particular place in the wire.

We ate dinner at the ranch, and had the ranchman feed our horses, and that afternoon we started toward Caldwell. Our prisoner gave us no trouble, but became very submissive to our wishes and requests.

Upon our arrival in Caldwell, we were met with some difficulty which nearly proved the fate of the prisoner. When we stopped the team, the spring wagon was surrounded with a crowd containing twenty-five or thirty men. I got out of the wagon on the left side of it; the prisoner and the deputy got out on the right side of the wagon, and the men began to crowd around the prisoner, shutting him from our view; then he was seized by several men, and their intentions were, I suppose, to deal with him according to the justice they deemed best. I saw the condition of affairs, and realized the perilous situation the prisoner was in, so I ran around the wagon, and was followed by three men who came to my assistance, and by immediate action, we succeeded in getting the prisoner from their power, where upon, we took him to a house and put a strong guard of men around it, to protect the prisoner, in case of an attempt to get him by force. The crowd assembled themselves near the house and made a demand for the prisoner. I was very anxious that the prisoner should reach the adjoining county, and have his trail, which would undoubtedly prove his guilt or innocence, as the jury might decide; but here the case looked very doubtful whether the prisoner would ever see Cowley county again. I feared the men would take him from us by force and lynch him by hanging him to the nearest tree. I went to the group of men and talked with them concerning the crime for which the prisoner was arrested. I told them the horse had been stolen in Cowley county and I did not think it was of any interest to them as the crime was not committed in our county. I informed them that I would accompany the deputy in taking the prisoner to Cowley county. This seemed to quiet the men and after much talking and hesitancy on their part, they said, if I would see that the prisoner reached Winfield as soon as possible, they would not make any more trouble. This satisfied me, and I supposed I would not experince any more trouble. But not so; in less than half an hour a friend came to me and informed me that the party had assembles themselves together in a barn and were making arrangemtt to take the prisoner from me at about two o'clock that night.

Upon receiving this startling intelligence, I began to ponder and wonder how I could get the prisoner out of town. I thought if I could get him out of town I could rush to Wellington with him, and thereby escape falling into the hands of the mob. I was aware of this fact, that I would be unable to take the prisoner from Caldwell, unless it was under concealment, and I began to make the necessary preparations to start immediately with the prisoner, and take him to a place of safety. I took four men into my confidence and we laid a scheme, which if properly carried out without exciting the suspicions of the mob, we would be sure of a successful operation, and would reach Wellington in safety.

In order to successfully carry out our desired plan, we resorted to a little game of stratagem, in which the prisoner was to get into the buggy, or spring wagon, and lie down, placing himself in a doubled up positon and the buffalo robe was thrown over him carelessly, but in such a manner as to conceal him from observation. The harness was, also, thrown into the wagon and one of my assistants took hold of the wagon tongue while another, lead the horses, walking behind the wagon, and giving some assistance by pushing the wagon along, thus making the load much easier to pull. I designated a place, at which they were to take the wagon, and I would put in an appearance as soon as I possibly could, without exciting the suspicions of the mob. As the men, with the horses and wagon, passed a group of men, the man leading the horses asked if any of them knew of a good place to lariat the horses? And likewise in hearing if the crowd, the men who were guarding the house in which the prisoner was supposed to be kept, were cautioned to attend strictly to their business, and endeavor to keep the prisoner at all hazards, and that they would return as quickly as they could lariat the horses, and go home and eat their suppers.

Of course the guards knew the prisoner was into the wagon, but in order to carry out our scheme they were to remain at the house, on guard until two o'clock, when we supposed the mob would congregate at the house, and demand possession.

I borrowed a horse from a friend and when started home, I went to the barn, where a large crowd of men had assembled, and informed them that I was going home, and in all probabiltiy would not be back to town until the following morning. I assumed a very indifferent manner concerning the fate of the prisoner, which had the desired effect on the men. I turned and rode toward home and on my way I chuckled with delight at the success I had had so far. When I reached my pasture I turned the horse loose which I was riding, and bridled and saddled my own pony; I knew the speed of my horse was hard to beat and in the case at hand, I needed a good horse, consequently I took my horse. I rode up to my house, informed my wife where I was going, and hastened on my way to overtake the parties who had the horses and wagons.

I did not enter the town but started north-east, and rode across the prairie and soon found the men, whom were waiting, very anxiously, for my arrival.

Quickly we put on the harness and hitched to the spring wagon, and started for Wellington. We did not know, how soon the mob would learn of our trick, and start in pursuit of us, so we drove as rapidly as we could under the circumstances. I rode the horse, and the deputy drove the team, and about two o'clock we arrived at Wellington with the prisoner. We stopped in Wellington long enough to feed and rest our horses. Our party went to a hotel and ordered a lunch, and after we had finished eating it, we started for Winfield, Cowley County. About eight o'clock in the morning we arrived in Oxford, where we stopped and fed our horses and went to a restaurant and ordered breakfast.

When we left Oxford I found that "Bent" the deputy, had indulged freely in drinking Oxford "fire water," and its effects were betrayed by various symptoms; the most prevalent was a desire to run the horses. His rapid driving landed us in Winfield about two o'clock in the afternoon. As we entered the town we met the sheriff, who took charge of the prisoner.

The prisoner was tried, convicted, and sent to serve a term of two years in the state penitentiary. When I arrived in Caldwell, I was informed of the proceedings which occurred on the evening I left there. It seems the mob did not "catch on" to our plans, and about two o'clock in the morning a posse of armed men came to the house in which they supposed the prisoner was guarded, and demanded of the men who were guarding the house, that they should give them possession of the prisoner; one of the guards told them that I had taken the prisoner about eleven o'clock, and started to Win-field and he presumed we were at Wellington. This caused great excitement, and they said they would settle with me when I returned to Caldwell. But I have never heard from them concerning the "settlement," from that day, to this.

CHAPTER XLI.

Jim Talbot and his gang of desperadoes arrive in Caldwell—They remain several days—Arrest of one of the desperadoes—His fine payed by a comrade—The bloody battle between Talbot's men and the citizens—Jim Talbot stands boldly to the front—Balls flying in all directions — Frightened women and children—Jim Talbot shoots the City Mayor—George Spears is killed in the battle — The desperadoes leave town—A posse of citizens in hot pursuit.

The winter has come, and the autumn months have gone. December, the month most cherished by the children, because Christmas is coming, has at last arrived. This month is celebrated by much merry making, both by the younger people and the aged ones. The opera house is opened for the theater; "Uncle Tom's Cabin" has been attended by the lovers of the dramatic stage. The month is to be a festival one, and filled with all descriptions of mirth and gayety which compose a season of festivities.

Some time during the forepart of December, 1881, a man by the name of Jim Talbot, formerly from Texas, arrived in the town of Caldwell; he had in company with him a woman who was represented as his wife. Talbot rented a dwelling house in the eastern part of the town, and moved there with his wife. He was joined by six confederates, men who had formerly lived either in Texas or in the southern part of the Indian Territory.

These men were desperadoes, and were constantly giving the marshal trouble by their daring feats, and the free use they made of their sixshooters. They visited the numerous places of amusement accompanied by the prostitutes of the "Red Light" dancing hall, and made disturbances by using loud obscene language in the presence of ladies, or by their braggadocia, which they displayed while they were under the influence of whiskey.

W. N. Hubble was the city mayor, and six or eight men were detailed to act as policemen, and to assist the marshal in suppressing riots, and in preventing disturbances. Talbot's men were frequent visitors of the "Red Light," and several of the men were arrested and fined for creating a disturbance. His confederates paid his fine, and he was set at liberty. His arrest was censured by Talbot and his men, they resolved to take the town in true desperado style. The citizens had prepared themselves, and the marshal with his assistants were on the alert.

Jim Talbot has never been equaled by the bravery

and daring which he portrayed in the city of Caldwell. On the morning of December 17th, 1881, he, in company with his men, had been drinking and firing off their revolvers promiscously. The citizens together with the marshals resolved to rid the town of the blood-thirsty men, or make them submit to the rules and regulations of the city laws. Talbot and his party has made several threats, prophesying what would be the fate of ex-mayor and city marshals.

Talbot acted as the captain of his men, and about nine o'clock in the morning of December 17th, 1881, a disturbance was raised by Talbot, purposely it was presumed, thus affording him the advantage he wanted. He was standing on Main Street, when he began firing his revolver, his voice sounded in the air, "Hide out little ones." A number of citizens armed themselves to assist the marshals. Each man armed with a gun or revolver were in hiding behind the stores, outhouses and any place that would serve as a fortification, or would shield them from the shots fired by the desperate Jim Talbot and his gang.

The bold and fearless form of Jim Talbot was the center of the firing. He stood bravely to the front, with revolver in each hand firing at the men he had premeditated to kill. Shots fired by the citizens were striking the buildings and tearing up the ground in all directions near the fearless leader who stood undaunted by shot or bullet, watching for the men who were to be his victims.

The sharp cracks of the deadly revolver rang out in the cool morning air. Women were running to and fro, looking for a loved husband or a son whom they adored. The white, blanched faces of the women foretold the fright, anxiety and suspense they were laboring under.

Those who were unfortunate enough to be in the city shopping, hurried themselves to a place of safety; some taking refuge behind dry goods boxes, while others in their fright, rushed hither and thither looking for a better place to hide and escape the stray bullets, which were crashing through the glass front windows of the stores, and tearing through doors and windows of the dwelling houses, damaging pictures, breaking mirrors and defacing the walls of the buildings.

The bullets flew thick and fast, and still the daring Talbot stood as a target for the guns of the many citizens.

Was his a charmed life? Had fate decreed that his escape should be a fortunate one? I was standing in the door of the blacksmith shop, and had a good view of the battle which was raging, and I expected every moment to see the form of Talbot reel and fall to the ground, shot by the fatal bullet fired at the hands of a law-abiding citizen. But not so. When Talbot had emptied his two sixshooters, he called to his men and said, "Boys, let's get our Winchesters," and started on the run for his house followed by his gang of outlaws.

The men appeared again; this time armed with Winchester rifles, which fact showed very plainly that the affair was plotted, and under the management of the desperate Jim Talbot.

The firing was again resumed by the outlaws, and the firing was returned by the citizens. The marshals were reinforced by a number of citizens who were among the unfortunate ones that had had no gun, they borrowed one, however, from the hardware and supply stores. The battle was kept up, and, when the leader saw the form of Mike Meagher sway, and fall to the ground, he then told the boys to run for their horses. The citizens were closing in on the desperadoes, but from the fact that their guns were Winchester rifles, the citizens were very cautious about endangering their lives by approaching within full view of the desperadoes.

The citizens were informed of the killing of Mike Meagher, (an ex-city mayor,) by Jim Talbot, who had manifested the determination to kill Meagher. Meagher had become aware of the intentions of the fearless leader, and was all the while shooting at Talbot, but his aim had not been true, or his destiny had been sealed by the arrival of Jim Talbot in the city of Caldwell.

While the desperadoes were running for the livery stables, the bullets fired by the citizens flew thick around them, but the stables were reached and the proprietor was ordered at the point of a Winchester, to saddle a sufficient number of horses on which the outlaws could make their escape. While the horses were being saddled, a strict watch was kept by the outlaws, who was prepared to shoot the first man that attempted to reach the livery barn, and in this manner the armed citizens were kept at bay by the long range Winchester rifles held in the hands of a desperate gang of desperadoes.

George Spears, a citizen of Caldwell, was shot and instantly killed, while he was in the act of getting a horse which was standing near the "Red Light."

Whether Spears was a sympathizer with the desperadoes and was getting the horse for them, thus aiding them in making their escape from the excited citizens, is not known, but the presumptions were that Spears was killed by a shot fired by a citizen of the town, who supposed that Spears was helping and encouraging the desperadoes in their murderous attack on the citizens of Caldwell.

When their horses were in readiness, five of the desperadoes started east on the run, and when they had gone but a short distance, one of their horses was shot and killed; as quickly as he could the rider jumped behind one of his comrades, and the two men rode away on the same horse. The excited citizens ran to their homes, secured a horse and started in hot pursuit of the desperate men. A telegram was sent to the sheriff at Wellington, and in a short time a special train was run down from Wellington, bringing the sheriff and a posse of the citizens from that place.

Upon the arrival of the sheriff, he went immediately to a livery stable and arrested the remaining two outlaws, who had failed to get horses, and thus escape with the desperadoes. When they failed to get horses, they threatened the life of the livery man if he informed the citizens of their whereabouts, and they secured themselves from the infuriated citizens by remaining in the barn.

Those who were inclined visited the spot where George Spears met his death. Among those who wished to view the scene of slaughter were the inmates of the "Red Light," who mingled their tears of sympathy with those shed by the grief-stricken relatives of the unfortunate man who had met an untimely death while he was yet in his early manhood.

The body of the murdered ex-mayor was tenderly carried to the home of the wife, who was prostrated with grief when she beheld the dead body of her husband, and the protector of her now fatherless children. When she looked upon the face of him who years before had promised to care for and protect her, she could not help but feel a ray of consolation, when she realized he had met death while he was defending his home and town from the desperate works of the desperadoes.

As quickly as possible a posse of men started from the city in pursuit of the Talbot gang. The posse was reinforced all along the route by the arrival of a new man armed with a gun or revolver. The citizens were infuriated at the work done by the gang of desperadoes, and they resolved to follow them, and, if possible, arrest and take them either dead or alive, and thus avenge the life of Mike Meagher.

The desperadoes were probably three miles in advance of the posse, but the gang had been followed by a number of citizens on horseback, and a firing was kept up by both parties. The citizens would not get within the range of the desperadoes' Winchesters, hence they waited for more help to arrive.

When the desperadoes were about a mile from town, they met a farmer going to Caldwell. He had a horse tied behind the wagon, and was leading it to town for his son's use. The desperadoes took this advantage of securing a horse, and replace the one that was shot by the citizens, so they halted the team driven by Mr. Mose Swaggart, commonly called "Uncle Mose," and with the muzzle of their guns drawn near his head, bade him to let them have the horse, which they appro‐ priated to their use, and, mounting it, they started south-east, riding their horses on a rapid run. "Uncle Mose" watched them until they were some distance away, then gave a cluck to his horses and drove on toward town, where he informed the people of his esca pade with the fleeing men.

Talbot and his men met a boy riding a horse, near Bovine Park, the stock ranch and beautiful home of W. E. Campbell, located one mile and a half south-east of Caldwell. The boy's saddle was demanded by the men, which was hastily put on the pony taken from "Uncle Mose." Now, the desperadoes were fully equipped with horses and saddles, and were making their way as fast as they could travel toward the Indian Territory.

As the different squads were leaving town in pur‐ suit of Talbot, I concluded to go and help round up the gang of outlaws. My son had just driven up to the shop with my team, so I unharnessed one of the horses and went to a livery barn, obtained a saddle and Winchester rifle. I started to the Bluff Creek Ford, intending to arrive there in the advance of the outlaws, and thus I could change their course. I started my horse on the run, but I arrived at the crossing a few seconds too late, for I could see the desperadoes ahead of me, probably two hundred yards, and they were riding as fast as their horses could run. When they were about four hundred yards ahead of me, the girth of one of the saddles broke, causing the saddle to fall to the ground; the desperadoes were so closely pursued by the people, that in order to make their escape, there was no time to be lost, so the saddle was left lying on the ground where it had fallen from the horse. I took the saddle and went back to town, intending to get a fresh horse, and a force of men to follow the fleeing fugitives.

I arrived at town about sundown, and quickly made the necessary arrangements to leave town in company with others wishing to partake in the pursuit of Talbot. At last we were ready to start, and in a few minutes we were galloping over the prairies, up hill and down on the supposed trail of the outlaws.

After traveling for some time, we met the county

sheriff and several men coming toward the town. They informed us that the desperadoes had been rounded in near a cattle ranch, then owned by Chas. H. Moore, of Caldwell. This ranch was located at the head of Deer Creek.

The sheriff said the fugitives were riding on the run, and when they had arrived about half way between a canyon and the ranch, which was located about one-half mile north of the canyon, their horses were so overcome with heat and fatigue, that they were unable to carry the outlaws any further, so they left their horses and run to the canyon and took refuge in an old dugout, which had once served as the home of the herders.

The sheriff wanted me to go to Deer Creek, and take charge of the horses, and see that the desperadoes did not get them. He said a posse of men had surrounded the canyon, and were waiting until daylight, when they would make a charge and get the desperadoes.

We started on our errand; it had now become so dark that we could no longer keep the road, and finally we concluded we were lost. We traveled around on the prairies and found a road which we supposed was the same we had left, but it proved to be a road leading to the L. X. Ranch, where we arrived, and found to our surprise, that were within five miles of our starting place. We had traveled too far east to find the trail leading to the Deer Creek Ranch.

We watered our horses and ate supper at the L. X. Ranch. We had not had anything to eat since noon ; our appetites were keen, and we relished the "good, square meal" set before us by the cook at the ranch.

We concluded, after much reasoning and the adding of many suggestions, that we would go back to the town and get a man that was acquainted with the route we were to travel, and in company with him, we would make another effort to reach the ranch on Deer Creek.

This time we had no adventure, and after traveling until three o'clock in the morning, we arrived at the ranch whereupon I went immediately to the place where the horses had been left by the fleeing men. I found the horses at the place designated by the sheriff, and a couple of men in company with myself remained near the horses, and quietly watched them, wishing for the appearance of the desperadoes.

We were prepared for their approach, and we fully intended to welcome them with a volley of shots. We had an idea that the outlaws had spent all their ammunition, consequently we could easily take them in. We waited in vain for their appearance, so our cherished hopes were blasted, and our wishes were not realized.

CHAPTER XLII.

Jim Talbot and party reach the canyons near Deer Creek—The citizens of Caldwell round them in—W. E. Campbell shot, and is taken to Caldwell—John C. Hall receives a bullet hole through his hat—At daylight the charge is made—"The birds have flown"—The reward offered for the capture of Talbot—The desperadoes take five horses from a freighter—Talbot's wife—Rumors giving reason for the killing of Mike Meagher—Talbot said to be a brother of George Flat.

I will endeavor to give the reader facts concerning the early operations which took place before my arrival at the Deer Creek Ranch. The different squads of men had arrived at the ranch in a very few minutes after the desperadoes had reached that point. The horses were completely exhausted by the constant speed in which they had been compelled to travel since leaving Caldwell. Had the desperadoes had the use of good running horses, they could have evaded the posse, but their horses were large ones, such as are usually found drawing heavy loads, or hitched to the plow of a farmer; consequently after they had traveled a certain distance, and being unaccustomed to traveling at such a rapid gait, they were soon overcome with heat and fatigue, and the desperadoes must trust to their agility and active use they have of their legs to carry them to a place of safety. The fleeing men were so closely pursued by those in pursuit, that in order to escape from being taken by them, a run must be made to reach the canyon, about one-half mile south of the ranch.

When the desperadoes gained their retreat, the men were deployed and surrounded the canyon. The men were located in close proximity to each other, and they secreted themselves by lying down in the tall grass, and quietly awaited and watched the movements of the desperate men whom they had followed and surrounded.

Two of the posse came near losing their lives. W. E. Campbell received a shot fired by one of the Talbot men. Campbell was approaching the old dugout; the roof had long since caved in, leaving the perpendicular sides of earth. This dugout had been dug in the side of the canyon, and the fugitives when last seen, were entering within its inclosure which afforded them as a fortification against the shots of the posse. While Campbell was nearing the place of refuge, crack went a shot fired by one of the desperadoes.

When the men nearest him heard the assertion made by Mr. Campbell, "I am shot;" they went to him and found he had been shot, the charge taking effect in his arm. Some of the posse started to the city with Mr. Campbell, while the remaining men secreted themselves as best they could from the view of blood-thirsty Jim Talbot and his men.

The desperadoes were on the alert, and watched every movement of their enemies. They were ready for any emergency which might call their attention. Their watchfulness and caution was manifested by the shots fired by them, when one of the enemy was getting too near their place of retreat.

John H. Hall, a young man living near Caldwell, in company with a friend, had joined the pursuing party of citizens, and, arriving at the scene, they too, took a position near the dugout with the intention of remaining as watchers, and they were to allow no man to escape by running through the rank. The young man, Hall, and his companion, when they entered upon the chase, remarked, that this is "simply fun;" and indeed, it was so long as there was no danger connected with the sport of riding at "tip-top" speed over the broad prairie lands, closely pursuing a squad of fleeing desperadoes. Youth is not presumed to be filled with thoughts of caution, propriety or consideration. These young men did not consider the probable danger, nor give due exercise to their reasoning faculties; but, concluding there would be some sport, attended with the attempt at capturing the desperadoes, they resolved to try "their luck" at becoming a "Young America" with the crew of older men.

John Hall was lying in the grass, which was probably three feet high, and after creeping towards the place of retreat held by the desperadoes, he raised his head with the intention of looking over into the canyon, when the sharp crack of a Winchester sounded in the still night air, and Hall felt his hat raise from his head as the bullet passed on without accomplishing its bloody errand. Hall dropped to the ground, and upon examining his hat, he found a bullet passed through it, leaving an awful hole which had a tendency to warn the young man of his dangerous position. Had the ball struck the hat one inch lower in the crown, the top of the young man's head would have been blown off.

When the light of the stars began to wane by the approaching daylight in the east, all men were in readiness to advance upon the hiding place of the desperadoes. When it was sufficiently light the charge was made, and it was soon found that the birds had flown.

A man by the name of Rhodes, in company with myself, entered the hiding place, and found a pair of gloves and a coat belonging to one of the desperadoes. We discovered where they got out of the canyon; from the height of its bank, we concluded, one of the party was helped to the top of the canyon, and he lent his aid in pulling up his comrades ; and they probably made their escape by creeping out of the rank which easily could have been accomplished, as the night was dark, the twinkling stars gave the only light ; and then again, the grass was of a rank growth, and probably two or three feet in height and would afford a hiding for the creeping men.

They arrived at a freighters' camp, and of them demanded five horses, promising to return them. After they had secured horses of their own, or when reached their destination which was Texas. The freighters came to Caldwell and reported their bad luck, for they concluded the desperadoes would never return their horses to them. But in this they were mistaken, for in about three weeks a man came into the city of Caldwell, bringing with him the five horses that had been taken by Talbot and his band of desperadoes.

The Indian Territory was scoured by different posses hoping they might possibly be successful in arresting Talbot or his men, and thus secure the large reward that was offered for the arrest of Talbot or his accomplices. But all efforts to capture Talbot proved futile. Several of the county officers went to Texas at the requests of parties, and searched for the outlaws, but no trace of them could be found. Several letters were received by the officers from parties in Texas and Colorado, stating a man was there under arrest who answered to the descriptions of the notorious Jim Talbot. The officer would obey the requests, and go to the place where the supposed outlaw was held in bondage, but upon his arrival the prisoner was set at liberty, as the officer failed to identify him as the man who for several days had held the citizens of Caldwell in fear and terror. Reports reached Caldwell that Talbot had been killed in Texas, but whether the report was a true one remains a mystery.

His wife remained in Caldwell a short time. Talbot had left her in destitute circumstances, and the citizens gave her support by furnishing the necessaries of life. She afterwards left town, whether she went to Talbot, I am unable to say, as her whereabouts were never heard of after she left Caldwell.

There were many rumors advanced concerning the murder of Mike Meagher; one of them was that in the early history of Wichita, Mike Meagher was an officer in that city, and it was reported he killed a cousin of Jim Talbot; and to avenge the death of his cousin, Talbot had come to Caldwell for the purpose of killing Meagher. Meagher was keeping a saloon in Caldwell at the time of his death. Another rumor advanced and reported was that Jim Talbot and George Flat were half brothers, and Talbot came to Caldwell to avenge his death. The reader will remember the manner in which Flat met his death, and that the suspicions had rested upon the police force for this sudden ending.

In order to kill the policemen, Talbot was compelled to have help; so he organized a band of desperadoes of which he was leader. His coming to Caldwell to reside, it was presumed was for the purpose of learning the facts concerning the death of his half brother, George Flat. It was presumed by some at the time of the battle, that Talbot intended to murder the entire corps of officers, thinking in this manner he would get the assassinator of Flat.

Jim Talbot had the characteristics of a bold and fearless man, and a desperado who recognized cowardice as a crime. He loved to be feared. He had an indomitable will, and, once entering the ring as a contestant in a race, he was sure to come out victorious. He spilled the blood of his fellowmen, freely and without reluctance or care. In the bloody affray he asked no quarter, he would give none. His heart was filled with bitterness and hatred against an offender, and lurking within his bosom was the brooding of revenge. Such was the character of the courageous and fearless Jim Talbot.

CHAPTER XLIII.

The Citizens are Struck with Horror with the Information that a man was Found Hanging, Within the City Limits—The Body Proves to be that of Frank Noyes—Enos Blair's House Burned by an Incendiary—Theories concerning the Burning of the Building—Rumors concerning the Hanging of Frank Noyes—His Father comes to Caldwell.

On the morning of Dec. 8th, 1885, the citizens of Caldwell and vicinity, were filled with horror when they received the startling intelligence that a man had been found hanging to a beam over the gate of the shipping pens, located near the A. T. Santa Fe Depot.

Words would be indeed poor vehicles with which to convey to the minds of the readers, the amazement and excitement which this news caused in tne minds of the citizens. They were astonished with wonder, that in this late date of civilization, that such a deed should be committed in the midst of a civilized and christianized community.

The residents of a later date than 1872, '73 and '74, and who had not been eye witnesses of the thrilling and blood-curdling events that took place during the early part of Caldwells history. These recent settlers were filled with astonishment at this unexpected event, while those that had had a knowledge of the extent to which the daring deeds of desperadoism and lawlessness were indulged in by the frontier desperado, were struck with awe and surprise, when they remembered that the years were advancing toward civilization, and now in the year of 1885, scenes like this were placed before the gaze of the people and deeds of lawlessness was still carried on in the midst of a christianized people.

Early on the morning of Dec. 8th a man went to the stock pens of the "Santa Fe" R. R. for the purpose of loading stock to send on the railroad to an eastern market. It was scarcely daylight, and in visiting the various pens the stock shipper was suddenly confronted by the body of a man, hanging in the gateway of one of the pens. The news was quickly circulated through the community and at an early hour the scene was surrounded by a crowd of excited citizens.

The residents recognized the features of the dead man, and it was at once reported, that the victim was none other than Frank Noyes, a gambler who had been residing in the city of Caldwell.

What he was hung for remains a mystery to the many citizens; the only reason for the hanging, was founded upon the knowledge given to the public by the finding of a note in the pocket of the dead gambler. This note was written and placed in his pocket and contained the information that Noyes was hung for house burning.

There had been a house burned in Caldwell, some time previous to the hanging of Noyes, belonging to Enos Blair, editor of the Free Press, and evidence showed it had been burned by an incendiary; the walls had been saturated with kerosene and about one o'clock the fatal match was struck, and in a short time the house was enveloped in flames and was entirely consumed by the fire. Mr. Blair barely escaped with his life, and had it not been for the immediate actions of friends in rescuing him from the building, he would in all probablity, perished by the heat and flames of the fire. There were many theories advanced concerning the reasons for the incendiary's work. One of the floating rumors was, the house had been burned by enemies of Mr. Blair, caused by the active part he took on the side of law and order, and the publishing of articles in the Free Press, relative to the acts of lawlessness and bloodshed committed within the borders of the city. Mr. Blair was a strong advocate of prohibition, and published many articles against the influence of intemperance. This together with his encouraging the enforcement of the city laws, and against drinkig gambing and carousing in hours of dissipation until the " wee sma hours" of the morning, caused the rougher element of society to become bitterly opposed to Mr. Blair; consequently by some the burning of Mr. Blair's house was attributed to the roughs of Caldwell.

The evidence given by a woman with whom Frank Noyes was living until the time of his death, covered the whole affair with a mystery. She testified that at a late hour in the night a rap on the door was heard by Noyes; he went to the door and was notified that he was wanted by an officer to go with him to Wellington. Upon looking towards the door, she discovered the forms of three or four men. Noyes hastily dressed himself and went with the men, whom the woman said, drove rapidly away. Noyes had been gambling and had won several hundred dollars, and some advanced the theory that Noyes had been taken by some of his former associates and robbed, hanged, and to throw off suspicion, a note was placed in his pocket saying he was hanged for house burning.

Whether or not either of the theories advanced, was a correct version of the hanging, we are unable to say, but of this we are certain: Frank Noyes met his death in a terrible manner, and the jury gave in a verdict that he was hanged by unknown parties.

The aged father of Noyes came to Caldwell, but left without the necessary evidence to convict any party of the death of his son. Mr. Noyes Sr., seemed to be greatly affected over the shameful manner in which his son met his death.

Frank Noyes was highly connected with respected and honored relatives. He was formerly from Illinois, his relatives on the paternal side of the family were highly respected officially, by the residents of his native state.

As Frank Noyes drifted West with the tide of im migration, he also drifted into the habits of dissipation and ruin. He is said to have been finely educated and an intelligent young man. He was quiet and unassuming, but his evil habit of drinking whiskey, gambling and passing his hours in idleness and dissapation, were the influences which undoubtedly caused his sorrowful and untimely death, at the hands of the men who pre meditated his hanging and death.

Thus is added another victim, killed by unknown parties.

CHAPTER XLIV.

Caldwell's development — The "Queen of the Border" — A friendly game of cards—Douglass Riggs attacks Robert Sharp—Stabs him eleven times—Effort to stanch the blood proves futile—"Bob" Sharp enters the sleep that knows no waking—Arrest of Dug Riggs—Convicted of murder—His sentence—Conclusion of the chapter.

Years roll on. The scene changes. The summer has gone. The bright, sunny days of the autumn are here.

Caldwell's record during the past ten years is simply wonderful. Her population has increased with her years. She is no longer the favorite resort of the desperado and the cowboy, who years ago reigned supreme in her borders.

The medicine tepee of the savage tribes has been a thing of the past, and in its place is the church and school; savagery has given way to civilization. The long-horned Texas cow has disappeared from the grazing lands, and now in their place may be seen large herds of thoroughbred hereford and shorthorn cattle.

Caldwell has assumed the name of the proud "Queen of the Border," and she sits on her throne of peace and prosperity.

The immigrant of later years do not have to suffer

CALDWELL AND AN INDIAN CAMP.

the privations they did ten years ago in the new countries, and the early pioneer settler, who commenced the battle of pioneer life without a penny in his pocket, who has endured the many privations and suffering caused by the grasshopper raid and Indian scare of 1874, and entered upon the long, weary chase in pursuit of horse thieves, has by honest labor and toil become the owner of a lovely spot, where men love to go, on this once wild tract of land, which he calls home he has gathered about this little spot, his cows, pigs, horses and chickens. He writes to his eastern relatives and friends: "There is no place like home," especially if it is located in Sumner County, Kansas.

A new Kansas has been developed. The youth of 1874 has grown to the full stature on strength of confident and intelligent manhood. The people have forgotten to talk of droughts, which are no more incident to Kansas than to Indiana or Iowa. The newspapers no longer chronicle rains as if they were uncommon visitations. A great many things besides the saloons have gone, and gone to stay. The bone hunter and the buffalo hunter of the plains, the Indian and his reservations, the jay hawker and the Wild Bills, the Texas' steer and the cowboy, the buffalo grass and the dugouts, the loneliness and the immensity of the unpeopled prairies, the infinite stretching of the plains unbroken by tree or shrub, by fence or house—all these have vanished, or are rapidly vanishing. In their stead has come, and come to stay, an aggressive, energetic, cultured, sober, law-respecting civilization.

No matter whether in the far east, or in the wild, wild west, there are characters of men portrayed to the minds of the people by the courageous and offensive characteristics, or the reckless daring and remorseless cruelty which mark their daily transactions in life.

The reader will go with me to the city of Caldwell; it is the year of 1888, and the 29th day of the month of October. The leaves are clothing themselves in the yellow of autumn, and making ready for the appearance of the cold, grim winter.

The afternoon hours have faded into evening dusk, and thence into the silver radiance of the moon's warm beams. A small party of men had assembled in the office of Thos. Snow's livery barn. A game of cards was indulged in by several of the party, including a couple of men by name, Robert Sharp and Douglass Riggs.

But little attention was given to the game by the proprietor of the barn, and as it progressed, several bystanders were watching the game with much eagerness. It seems a bet was made, and after the game was finished, Bob Sharp and Dug Riggs got into a dispute over the sum of twenty-five cents. This caused a quarrel between the two men, in which Riggs called Sharp a liar. Young Sharp retorted such treatment as he had received from Riggs, and ended by saying: "Who is a liar?" Riggs replied, "You are." Sharp quieted and said he would not have any further trouble over the twenty-five cents, which Riggs claimed was due him from Sharp.

Riggs went down the stairs, but soon returned however. Sharp had not anticipated any more trouble over the money, and when Riggs returned, he was conversing with a friend of his. As Riggs gained the second floor of the barn, one of the party noticed he held an open knife in his hand, but he did not imagine that Riggs had come back with a spirit of malicious resentment, and intended to use the knife as his weapon of vengeance. As Riggs approached Sharp, he noticed the glistening blade of the upheld knife. He took in the situation at once, and having no way of protecting himself from the murderous fiend, and knowing his means of escape was impossible, for the only way to reach the ground was the rude stairs, up which the enemy had come, and in order to reach them, he muts pass the hostile form of Riggs.

As Sharp caught sight of the murderous knife, he said, quickly, "He has got a knife," and started for the stairs, only to be shut off from that means of escape by his dexterous foe. Riggs rushed at Sharp with the knife. His character assumed the remorseless cruelty of a wild tiger; the countenance which a short time before bore a calm and placid expression, was now the picture of a fierce and angry human fiend. Sometimes the morning breaks in calm loveliness; the sun shining in splendor, and the heavens are azure blue with nothing to mar its beauty; but before the evening shades draw near the thunder sounds can be heard in the distance, and the sky is black with the raging storm. And you wonder that a day that had dawned so fair could hold concealed in its shining bosom so fierce a tempest. It would have been hard to have prophesied correctly the ferocious disposition which was hidden beneath the bosom of Douglass Riggs.

He plunged the knife into the body of his antagonist, withdrew it reeking with blood, only to plunge it deeper and fatally into the body of the struggling man. Again and again is the knife thrust into the body until the fiendish murderer turns and leaves the scene. Sharp weak and exhausted falls from the loss of his life's blood. Messengers are sent hither and thither. Friends and relatives of the injured man arrive at the scene of the bloody conflict.

Riggs becomes conscience stricken, or is awakened

from his terrible state of mind, when the remembrance of the awfulness of the crime comes to his reason, he rushes to the office of a doctor, and sends him immediately to the scene of the slaughter.

Riggs then left Caldwell, going a short distance from the city. Dr. C. H. Hume arrives at the barn, and endeavors to stop the flowing of the blood. Upon examination the Doctor found eleven wounds made by the knife. A deep stab was found under the right arm and another in the small of the back. Dr. Hume did all he could to save the young man, but the flowing of blood could not be stopped by human aid or power, and the end was drawing near.

Kind friends and sorrowing relatives drew near and tenderly cared for the young man until death should claim him.

When he was almost too weak to stand, he mentioned the twenty-five cents and offered it to Riggs, who declined to accept it.

Mournfully and attentively the friends watched the dying man. Shorter and shorter came each breath. Fainter and fainter came the sounds of his breathing. A gasp, a struggle, and all was over. Death had ended his suffering and sorrows of this life.

The scene was a sorrowful one to look upon. Everything near the dead man was crimson with his blood which had slowly ebbed from his body.

Robert Sharp, was about 22 years old. He was an intelligent young man, full of hope and promise of an honorable citizen. He was the youngest boy of his parents, and was tenderly nurtured and cherished by his immediate relatives. He had many young friends who mourned the loss of their friend "Bob."

"After life's fitful fever, he is at rest."

Douglass Riggs was arrested the following morning on the charge of murder, found guilty, and sent to the Wellington jail. When the district court convened, he was tried, convicted of murder, and received a sentence of ten years confinement in the state penitentiary.

This chapter closes with the last murder committed in Caldwell. Do I hear the question, "How many murders have been committed within the borders of the 'Queen of the Border,' or in her immediate vicinity?" I will refrain from answering the question; probably the reader can enumerate the number, count them and give a correct answer.

So ends the bloody tragedies which were enacted within the proud "Queen of the Border" and vicinity.

CHAPTER XLV.

Sketch of the lives of the remaining 71 'ers—J. M. Thomas, Ballard Dixon, W. B. King, J. A. Ryland, A. M. Colson, M. H. Bennett and J. A. Blair.

It would perhaps be unfair, and would treat the reader unjustly to conclude this book without giving a brief autobiography of the remaining few original settlers who are still to be found in and about Caldwell. The history of California would be no less complete without a sketch of the 49 'ers, than would the history of Sumner County, Caldwell and vicinity without a condensed sketch of the most prominent 71 'ers. The number has dwindled to less than a "baker's dozen." Yes, they can almost be numbered on the fingers of one hand. We hope not to weary the reader in this, our last chapter by a wordy introduction, but will proceed at once to our task of jotting the important events in the lives of those who are still left to tell the tale after almost a score of years on the frontier. The first of these about whom we will write, will be

J. M. Thomas came to Caldwell in March, 1871. His has indeed, been a varied and checkered career since he came and settled on the extreme border of civilization. Checkered not in the sense of having his name tarnished by the daring deeds of lawlessness that made os many names of young men on the frontier become so infamous on account of deeds of daring and of crime, but checkered by the different occupations in which he engaged at different times, and his life was varied by the many successes and financial failures in the business in which, for the time being, he seemed willing to engage.

J. M. Thomas was a native of Ohio, but after the war he emigrated to the state of Missouri. While in the latter state, he received a fair education, and was thus qualified to be one of the leaders in the settlement of a new country. Soon after his arrival in Caldwell, he hewed the logs and erected a building; in size about 24 by 30 feet, and a story and a half in height. This building he rented to Cox and Epperson of Kansas City Mo., to be used as a drovers supply store. Mr. Thomas now became the employee of this company, sometimes acting as clerk; and as the firm owned a bunch of cattle, he acted in the capacity of herder.

The firm of Cox and Epperson did a thriving business during the summer of 1871, but after the drive was over, the stock of goods in the store ran low, and Mr. Thomas bought what remained. Now we find him a merchant. In the following spring, as the reader will remember, while negotiating for goods to replenish his stock, Anderson was killed by McCarty. Thomas was an eye witness to this tragedy. While he was never courting a chance to see deeds of desperadoism, being a permanent fixture in Caldwell he beheld many a revolting scene.

In 1876 Thomas was elected justice of the peace and by re-election held the office four years. He was elected trustee in 1880 and served one term. In 1885 he was again elected justice of the peace, and by continued re-elections, he still holds that office; he is also a dealer in real estate.

Financially, Mr. Thomas has made several fortunes; but as the old saying is "easy come, easy go" he barely maintains his own. The boom of 1886 in the West, left many an enterprising man with less funds than it found him. Probably Mr. Thomas made thousands of dollars at this time, but possibly the relapse had caught him. In conclusion I will say he is the oldest settler still living in Caldwell; having settled in March, 1871.

Ballard Dixon was also quite an early pioneer of this vicinity, having settled on a claim six miles northwest of Caldwell, in March, 1871. He came to stay, and was willing to endure for the sake of a home in the "Far West." Fortunately or unfortunately, as the reader may be pleased to term it, Mr. Dixon seems to never have found his affinity in a female form, and claimed it as his own. All these years he has remained in single blessedness; having no gentle one at his "shanty on the claim" to molest or make him afraid. When coming to Kansas, he looked out for the evil day when hunger might appear; bringing with him about eight hundred dollars in cash.

While Mr. Dixon is unpretentious and unassuming, he commands the respect of all who know him. He was elected to the office of trustee of Caldwell township, and filled the office with great credit to the township and honor to himself. It has been truthfully said, that " every man however perfect, has defections in life." To this rule Mr. Dixon was no exception. The only thing however, of which he will have to plead guilty is: that he never took unto himself a wife and thereby help to build up society and the future generations. For almost a score of years he had been the cook of his shanty, and the farmer of his farm. This however is a matter of his own.

It will be remembered by the reader that on several occasions, that Ballard Dixon has been identified with those who were hastily formed into a band, to make a long and weary chase after thieves. It will therefore easily be conjectured that the name of Ballard Dixon, in future history, will stand second to none in upholding the laws of the land. Financially he is now rated some ways up in the thousands of dollars. Enough I have no doubt, to support himself in ease and luxury the balance of his days is at his command.

W. B. King, or as he was usually called, Buffalo King came to Caldwell, as the reader will remember, in company with me, in May, 1871. It is often said "it takes all kinds of people to make a world." This adage in truth is quite applicable in the case of our friend King. His was one of those peculiar temperaments which can endure pain, hardships and privations, without the least sign of a murmur. Always ready to take the world as it came, if in his efforts it failed to conform to his wishes. He made his settlement seven miles southwest of Caldwell. During the early part of his western life, he, like quite a number of the early settlers, had'nt the least faith in Kansas as a farming country. For this reason he did not open his farm at once, but touched the farming business rather lightly at first; spending much of his time on the plains hunting the buffalo and poisioning wolves, in order to secure the hide and meat of the former, and the furs of the latter. It is said that as a buffalo hunter Mr. King had no superior and very few equals. He seemed almost unerring in his markmanship. While he was not inspired, yet it seemed for him to point his gun toward a buffalo, meant sure death to the animal. In this manner he lived and supported his family for the first few years with what little land he saw fit to cultivate, raising a few vegetables and some grain. Time rolled on, however, and farming was no longer an experiment, and the buffalo were fast receding toward the setting sun. Mr. King could now plainly see that there was a good living on his farm for himself and family, and so gradually gave up his hunting and turned his attention to cultivating and improving his farm.

In 1872 he was elected constable, but failed to qualify; but, as the reader will remember, on a number of occasions he was found as one of the sheriff's or constable's posse to help chase and capture thieves.

Mr. King came and settled in the vicinity of Caldwell and made it his home until 1886, when he emigrated to Washington Territory. We write his history as one of the 71'ers that is still here, as he left so recently and that his name has been so frequently mentioned in these pages.

Financially he came here poor and bare-headed; when leaving he had property to the amount of six thousand dollars, with respectable clothes.

J. A. Ryland, as, perhaps, the reader may remember, came to Caldwell from Slate Creek, with myself and others, on May 25. 1871. Soon after his arrival he formed a partnership with A. M. Colson to engage in the stock business. The company thus formed located on a claim on the Chicaskia River, six miles northeast of Caldwell. Here the boys erected a hewn log house, in which to live and call "home" while they followed the business mentioned above. They bought from different herds, at a low price, sore-footed cattle that from the effects of the long drive on the trail had become so disabled that they could not be driven any farther toward the shipping point. Buying these cattle at so low a price, with limited means the boys got together a herd of 125 head. Most of the cattle, after resting awhile, became well; but the uncommonly severe winter of 1871 and 1872 caused a large number of the brutes to succumb to the severity of the wintry storms, and in the spring of 1872 the original number of cattle was found to have decreased by about half. The firm now dissolved, Mr. Ryland retaining the claim, which, by the way, was a very desirable one and susceptible of being made into a fine home and a grand farm. It is still owned by the original settler and by him has been well improved, and is known by the name of "Riverside."

In the fall of 1873 Mr. Ryland — in Indiana, his native state, having received a fair academic education — concluded to engage in his former occupation, that of a teacher. On October 6, he took charge of the public school of Wellington, the county seat of Sumner County. After six months teaching, he again returned to his farm and endeavored to raise a crop, but the drouth of 1874 nipped the crop in the bud, and in July the grass-hoppers closed the deal, leaving the farmer naught for his labor.

In September, 1874, Mr. Ryland was appointed examiner of applicants for teachers' certificates, which position he held for two years, and finally resigned to go east and make a lengthy visit with friends. In the winter of 1874 and 1875, and also in 1875 and 1876, we find the subject of this sketch engaged in teaching the school at Alton, Kan. He has also taught school at other places at different times since then, but his chief occupation has been that of a farmer and stock-raiser. He has always seemed to be willing to "labor and to wait," having great faith in the future of Southern Kansas. He has accumulated quite a considerable of this world's goods, so that now, I am told, he owns property to the amount of from fifteen to twenty thousand dollars, having his original farm as a home, and sufficient "filthy lucre" to keep the "wolf from the door."

A. M. Colson came to Kansas, May 19, 1870, and to Caldwell, May 25, 1871. The first year after his

coming was spent six miles northeast of Caldwell, in partnership with J. B. Ryland, handling cattle. In the spring of 1872, the partnership was dissolved, he continuing in the cattle business ever since that time. Quite a portion of the time he has been engaged in the business alone, but of late years has been running it in partnership with Judge McAtee, of Caldwell.

Mr. Colson is a native of New York State, and in youth received fair educational advantages. When settling in Sumner County, the county being unorganized, he took an active part in its organization; and was elected the first county superintendent of schools, but, finding that to fill the office properly, would materially interfere with his private business affairs, he failed to qualify, and hence let the office go by default.

Mr. Colson now considered himself of proper age to take unto himself a wife, and in the year 1875 he was married, Miss Mary Goldy becoming his wife. In 1879 his wife died leaving an only child—a daughter who was named Fawny, and was undoubtedly the first white child born in the land known as the Cherokee Strip.

In 1880 Mr. Colson's widowhood was brought to a sudden close by his contracting a second marriage, with Mrs. Mary J. Garretson; she likewise having an only child, named Katie. He has been engaged in the banking business for several years past, and at present holds the position of president of the Citizens Bank of Caldwell; and has also held the office of mayor and president of the council of Caldwell continuously for five years. Upon the opening of Oklahoma he, like thousands of others, became affected by the Oklahoma craze and took an active part in the grand horse race made by President Harrison's proclamation opening that country to settlement. Being one of the first to enter, he, by rapid riding, secured a choice claim adjoining the townsite of Kingfisher, where his home now is.

Financially Mr. Colson has been a success; having brought with him when he came to Caldwell less than $1,000, and now he is estimated to be worth from $30,000 to $40,000.

M. H. Bennett also came to Caldwell in the fall of 1871. He worked for three years for A. Drumm and at the expiration of that time went into the cattle business on his own account and has succeeded remarkably well. Mr. Bennett, however, seems to have been of that disposition that to risk much will gain much. I presume that in different ventures he has probably made several fortunes. But, perhaps he, like all others who take great risks, will in time meet reverses. When coming to Kansas he brought no money, but he brought that which always succeeds — perseverence and industry. I should not like to form a guesss as to how much he is worth, but one thing I do know, he is in charming circumstances and ranks high, as a citizen, in Caldwell.

Mr. Bennett, in disposition, has never thirsted for notoriety, but has rather courted obscurity, and, I think has never accepted any official position of any importance. Being a lover of home and family ties, he was slow to accept positions requiring him to be absent from home and to assume responsibilities. He is a native of Ohio, but came to Kansas in an early day and may well be termed a pioneer.

John A. Blair is the last, but by no means the least, of the 71'ers whose biography we will attempt to sketch. It would seem strange that so few are able to "hold the fort" for a score of years, but such is the fact. Some of the original settlers have long since been claimed by that grim monster, Death, while others have gone east and are now safe in the home of "wife's people."

Johnnie Blair, as he was usually called, came to Caldwell in May, 1871. For the first year he clerked in the store of Cox & Epperson; while at this occupation he was gaining an experience in the mercantile business which proved to be the golden stepping stone to success in future life. In 1872, Johnnie became a herder of Texas cattle. Here, likewise, he gained knowledge which proved to be of great benefit. He seems to have had a well balanced temperament which enabled him to engage in any kind of business with equal success; whether a clerk, a merchant, a herder, or a cattle owner, his efforts were always crowned with success.

In 1874 we find Mr. Blair clerking in the store belonging to C. H. Stone, of Caldwell; but before the year closes we find him the owner, he having bought the store from Mr. Stone. It seems that Johnnie was now in his element and at home in the business. He soon became the popular merchant, and, in fact, a very popular man. It is doubtful if any one who ever lived in Caldwell can lay claim to surpassing Johnnie in popularity.

He continued in the mercantile business until 1881, when he sold his store and engaged in the cattle business. His success in his last venture has been almost phenomenal. When coming to Caldwell he was a comparative youth, with very limited means; but having a disposition that will always make friends and a determination to succeed, he now finds himself rated high up in the thousands of dollars. He now lives in Caldwell in a fine home of his own, where he and his family live in luxury and ease, holding the confidence and esteem of all who know him.

We, the undersigned pioneers of Caldwell, Kansas, and vicinity, have read "MIDNIGHT AND NOONDAY" by G. D. Freeman, and pronounce the facts therein recorded to be correct, as near as present research can make them. The reader therefore can safely conclude that when reading the book, he is reading correct history.

Names of pioneers:

J. A. Ryland, A. M. Colson, Representative at large, Oklahoma, W. J. Lingenfelter, C. B. Dixon, J. T. Richmond, H. J. Devore, J. M. Thomas, J. P.

I desire to state that I am acquainted with the above-named signers, and know them to be men of truth and veracity. R. T. SIMONS,

Editor *Caldwell News*.

www.ingramcontent.com/pod-product-compliance
Lightning Source LLC
Chambersburg PA
CBHW051725300426
44115CB00007B/473